PIPE FITTINGS

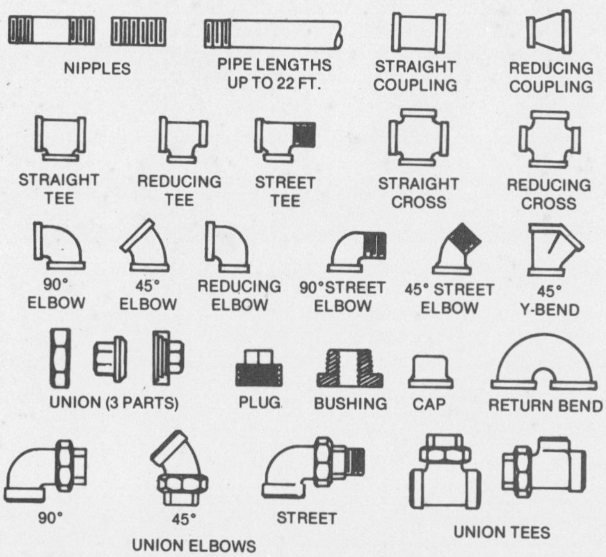

Here are the common steel pipe fittings. Nipples are simply short lengths of pipe threaded on both ends. Reducing fittings join two different sizes of pipe.

Compression fittings of the flared-tube type are the easiest for the novice to handle when working with copper tubing.

STANDARD STEEL PIPE
(All Dimensions in Inches)

Nominal Size	Outside Diameter	Inside Diameter	Nominal Size	Outside Diameter	Inside Diameter
1/8	0.405	0.269	1	1.315	1.049
1/4	0.540	0.364	1 1/4	1.660	1.380
3/8	0.675	0.493	1 1/2	1.900	1.610
1/2	0.840	0.622	2	2.375	2.067
3/4	1.050	0.824	2 1/2	2.875	2.469

SQUARE MEASURE

144 sq in = 1 sq ft
9 sq ft = 1 sq yd
272.25 sq ft = 1 sq rod
160 sq rods = 1 acre

VOLUME MEASURE

1728 cu in = 1 cu ft
27 cu ft = 1 cu yd

MEASURES OF CAPACITY

1 cup = 8 fl oz
2 cups = 1 pint
2 pints = 1 quart
4 quarts = 1 gallon
2 gallons = 1 peck
4 pecks = 1 bushel

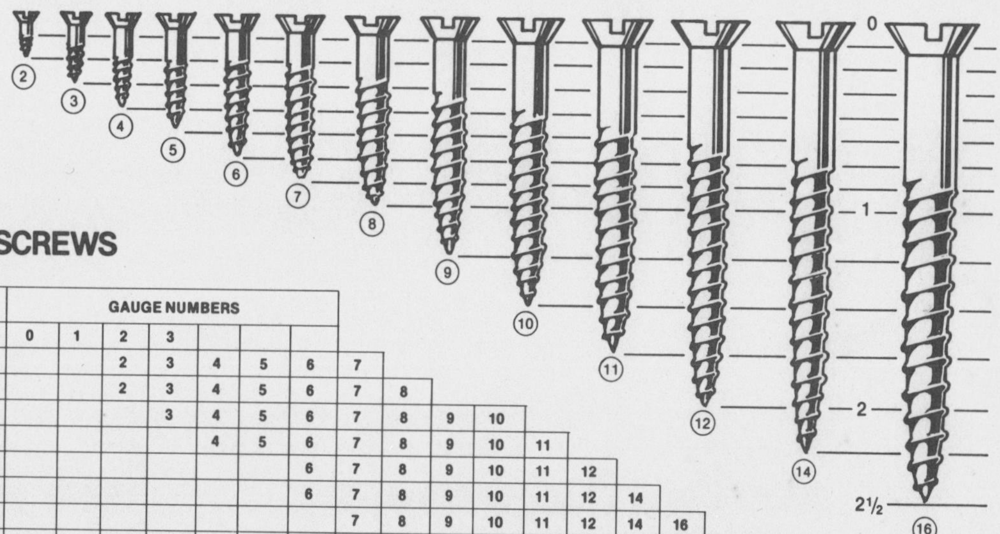

WOOD SCREWS

LENGTH	GAUGE NUMBERS																
1/4 INCH	0	1	2	3													
3/8 INCH			2	3	4	5	6	7									
1/2 INCH			2	3	4	5	6	7	8								
5/8 INCH				3	4	5	6	7	8	9	10						
3/4 INCH					4	5	6	7	8	9	10	11					
7/8 INCH							6	7	8	9	10	11	12				
1 INCH							6	7	8	9	10	11	12	14			
1 1/4 INCH								7	8	9	10	11	12	14	16		
1 1/2 INCH							6	7	8	9	10	11	12	14	16	18	
1 3/4 INCH									8	9	10	11	12	14	16	18	20
2 INCH									8	9	10	11	12	14	16	18	20
2 1/4 INCH										9	10	11	12	14	16	18	20
2 1/2 INCH													12	14	16	18	20
2 3/4 INCH														14	16	18	20
3 INCH															16	18	20
3 1/2 INCH																18	20	24
4 INCH																18	20	24

WHEN YOU BUY SCREWS, SPECIFY (1) LENGTH, (2) GAUGE NUMBER, (3) TYPE OF HEAD—FLAT, ROUND, OR OVAL, (4) MATERIAL—STEEL, BRASS, BRONZE, ETC., (5) FINISH—BRIGHT, STEEL BLUED, CADMIUM, NICKEL, OR CHROMIUM PLATED.

TURNED FROM CHERRY, this early American candlestand lamp will add warm elegance to any hearth, and its richly tinted table will add convenience right at chairside. If you're tired of hammer and saw projects, here's a new challenge. See plans on page 1664.

In this volume . . .

WHAT COULD BE HANDIER—or handsomer—than this lazy Susan centered on your dining table? Surprisingly, you don't need a lathe to build it; the little spindles are available commercially. It makes a fine setting for a small flower arrangement. See page 1704.

MAKE YOUR KITCHEN a thing of utility as well as beauty by covering cabinets and countertops with gleaming plastic laminate. Learn how to use laminate on page 1658.

WHAT GRADE OF LUMBER should you use—and where—in your home or vacation home? Learn the basics of lumber sizes and grading on page 1747.

IN MODERNIZING A KITCHEN, the first step is usually the installation of new cabinets. You'll find complete instructions for installing cabinets on page 1616.

WANT TO HAVE THE BEST LAWN in your neighborhood? Then you should know about grass seed, fertilizer and chemical treatments. See page 1688.

LEARN THE FINE ART of layering wood. You simply laminate two or more types of wood, then use the resulting block as the basis for your project. See page 1652.

THIS CHARMING table lamp is made in the form of a miniature cobbler's bench. And it's more than just a lamp. There's a rack for letters, a drawer for stamps, and a place for a live or artificial plant. The plans are on page 1668.

Popular Mechanics

do-it-yourself encyclopedia

in 20 volumes

a complete how-to guide for the homeowner, the hobbyist—
and anyone who enjoys working with mind and hands!

All about:

home maintenance
home-improvement projects
wall paneling
burglary and fire protection
furniture projects
finishing and refinishing furniture
outdoor living
home remodeling
solutions to home problems
challenging woodworking projects
hobbies and handicrafts
model making
weekend projects
workshop shortcuts and techniques
hand-tool skills
power-tool know-how
shop-made tools
car repairs
car maintenance
appliance repair
boating
hunting
fishing
camping
photography projects
radio, TV and electronics know-how
clever hints and tips
projects just for fun

volume 11

ISBN 0-87851-076-1
Library of Congress Catalog Number 77 84920

MANUFACTURED IN THE UNITED STATES OF AMERICA

contents

VOLUME 11

Build this kitchen island

By HARRY WICKS

Its chopping-block top, king-size storage area and walk-around convenience make this work center the handiest counter in the kitchen. And it's an attractive piece of furniture

■ IF YOU HAVE THE NEED—but not the wall space—for additional countertop work area in your kitchen, why not consider the advantages of this attractive island work center? Besides its generous work top (more than 13 sq. ft.), the elegant cabinet below will permit your wife to store almost all her kitchen utensils out of sight. And, from a practical standpoint, she'll have the advantage of being able to work from all four sides of a food preparation table—a luxury chefs have enjoyed for years.

Designed by Marsh Wall Products Co., Dover, Ohio, the cabinet has a laminated chopping-block top that offers:

- A surface where foods can be chopped, pounded, cut and scraped—with cleanup afterward a snap.
- A top that can be quickly and easily dressed

THE EMBOSSED-LEAF PATTERN gives this island work center its elegant look. Hardboard panels are available in two colors: ivory-white (shown below) and a dark-stained, walnut look.

to almost-like-new with a belt sander in the event tool marks, cuts or scratches start to make it unsightly.

- Embossed sides of textured hardboard that are easy to clean and make this handy kitchen center fit into any modern decor.

Building the center. Since the cabinet rests on a base nailed to the finished floor, a mock-up—left in place for a while—is a good idea. Simply lay the 2 x 4s in the chosen location and leave them there. Then, after a couple of days of walking about the planned center, you'll know whether you have picked the best site. If you find that a mobile island would be more desirable, you can fit the base with lockable casters instead of nailing it down, but be sure to adjust the vertical dimensions accordingly.

The cabinet. Constructed of ¾-in. plywood and 1 x 3 pine, the cabinet is kept simple by using butt joints rather than grooving and letting in the members. (For example, shelves rest on one-by cleats.) For maximum strength, use plenty of wood screws and waterproof glue.

Chopping-block top. Birch or maple should be

TEXTURED HARDBOARD comes in 16 x 96-in. panels and requires no finishing. You'll find it available at many lumberyards.

SEE ALSO
Butcher blocks . . . Cabinet furniture . . . Cabinets, kitchen . . . Cupboards, china

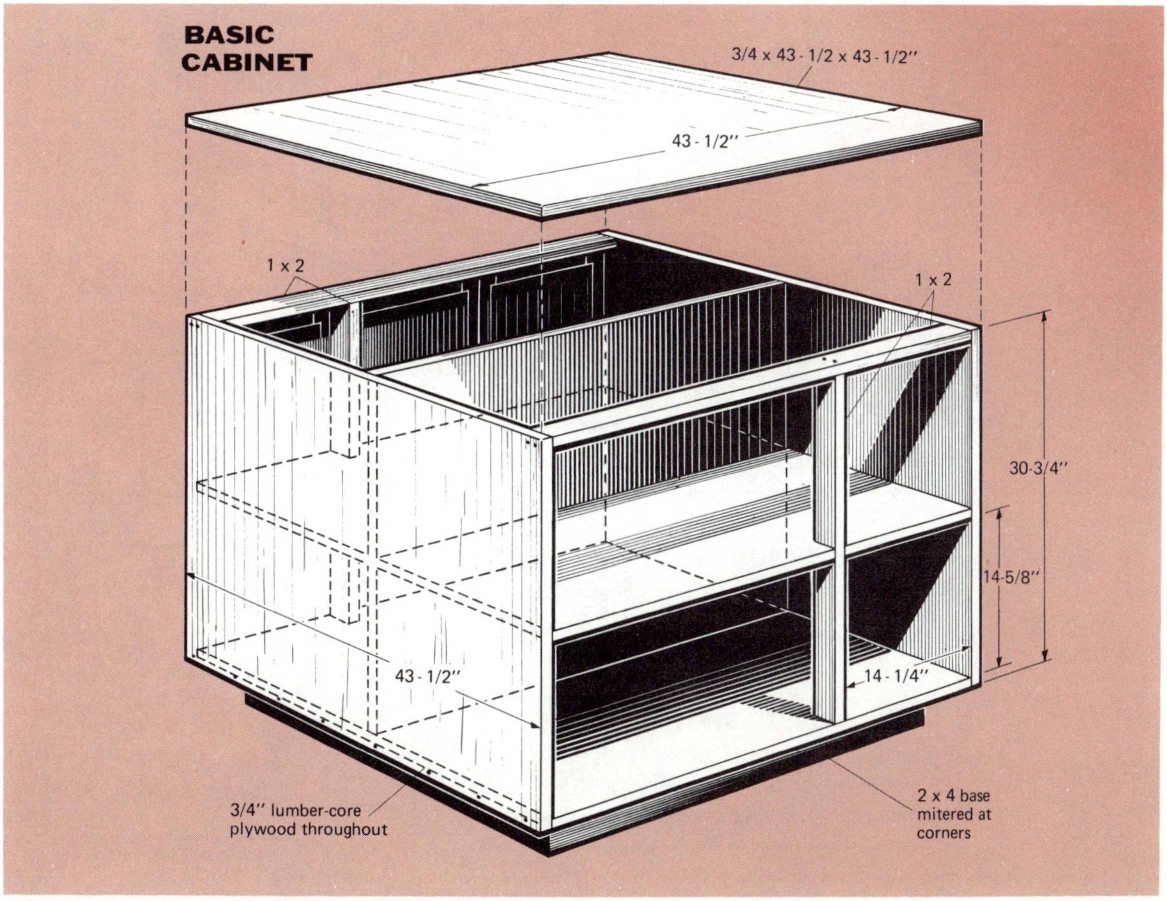

your choice for the laminated top. Both hardwoods have handsome grain characteristics, are long-lasting and are extremely resistant to scratches and mars. To insure lineup for the holes in the 47 pieces that receive the threaded rods, take time to set up a jig. A simple way is to cut a 47-in. length of inexpensive material, mark off and bore the three required holes. Then use this pattern as a drilling guide. Since the holes may vary slightly from edges or ends, mark each piece as it's drilled with an arrow for up and an X at one end to keep holes matched.

With all boards cut and drilled, slip the rods through. Next, apply waterproof glue liberally to all meeting surfaces and draw the boards tight with bar clamps. (If you have good, warp-free stock, the joints should be mere hairlines with glue oozing out evenly.) Wipe off all excess glue with a damp cloth, and set the top aside to dry overnight. Next day, counterbore the holes, cut rods to exact length, slip on the washers and run the nuts tight. Do not remove the clamps until all six nuts are fully tightened.

The embossed-leaf pattern inserts (Marlite) in the 12 panels are let into rabbets on the inside back edges of the stiles and rails. These can be cut and rabbeted assembly-line fashion at one time. Assemble the frames and cut the hardboard to fit. Again make match-marks in case of variations. With inserts removed, paint or stain the frames and then reassemble them. The top, of course, should not be painted.

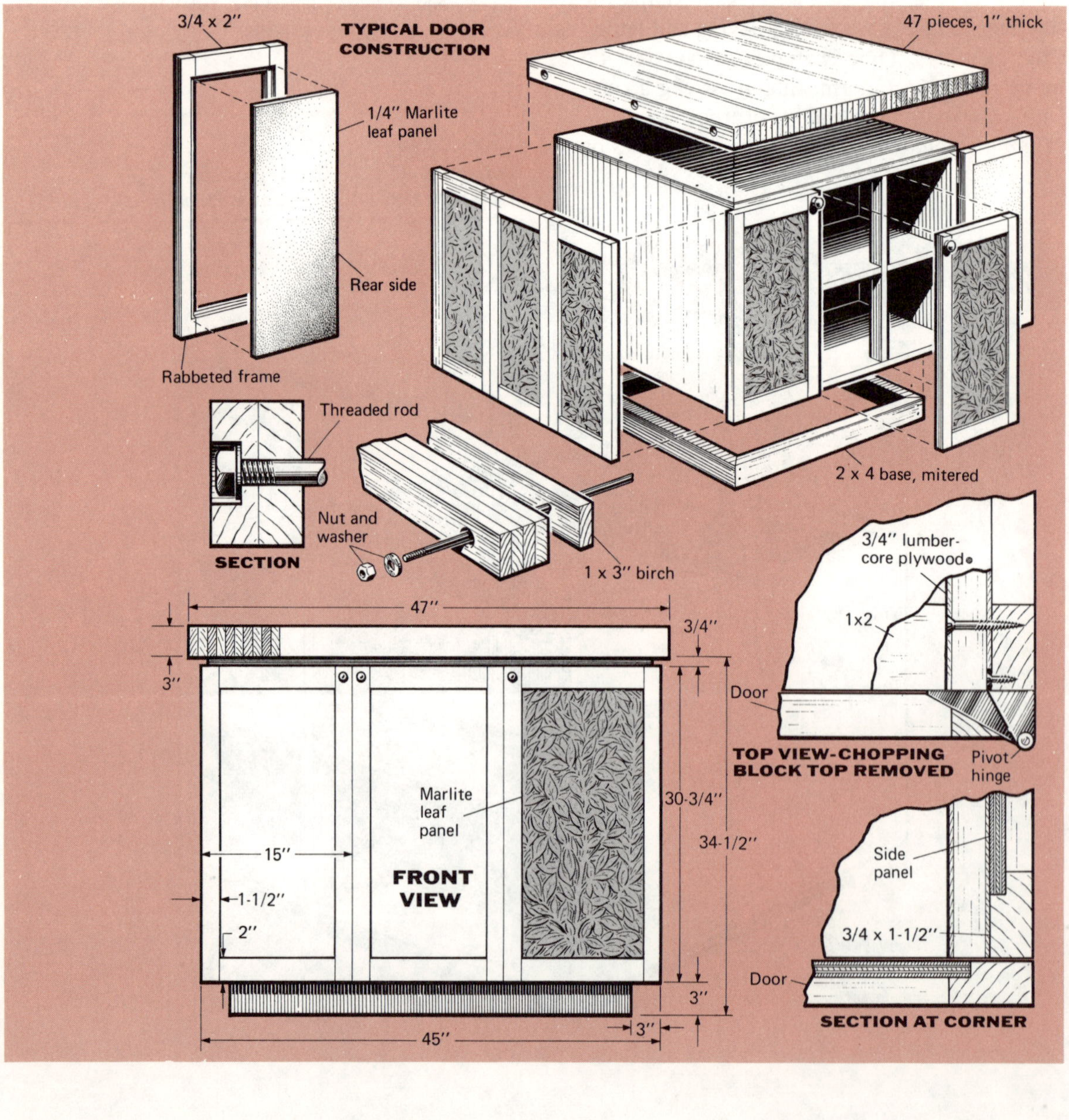

TIP-OUT BIN fully open. The front compartment stores long kitchen tools. A hole provides access to rags.

HALF-OPEN POSITION. Bin sides are hardboard painted with epoxy enamel. The front is faced with sheet metal.

Kitchen space saver

By E. B. SILSBY

WHAT DO YOU DO when a new stove turns out to be 6 in. narrower than the old one and leaves a gap too small for drawer or cabinet? One solution is to fill the space with a tip-out bin and add a longer counter-top. I did this and wound up with such a neat job it looked like an original installation. This was partly because I was able to use a section of an old dishwasher to face the front and make a perfect match with white metal cabinets alongside.

We use the extra space to store kitchen tools which are too long to fit in conventional drawers. There is also a hole in the side for easy access to a hidden compartment.

As you see in the drawing, the bin was made pie-shape for balance. The shifting center of gravity will hold the bin fully open as shown above left, halfway open as shown above right, and fully closed. The dotted lines show where I formed hidden storage compartments in the bin, with front space being accessible from one side. The back compartment makes a dandy place to keep rags which can be grabbed through the hand hole in the side. The bin itself is hinged to a 2x4 toeboard that is painted black to match that on adjoining cabinets.

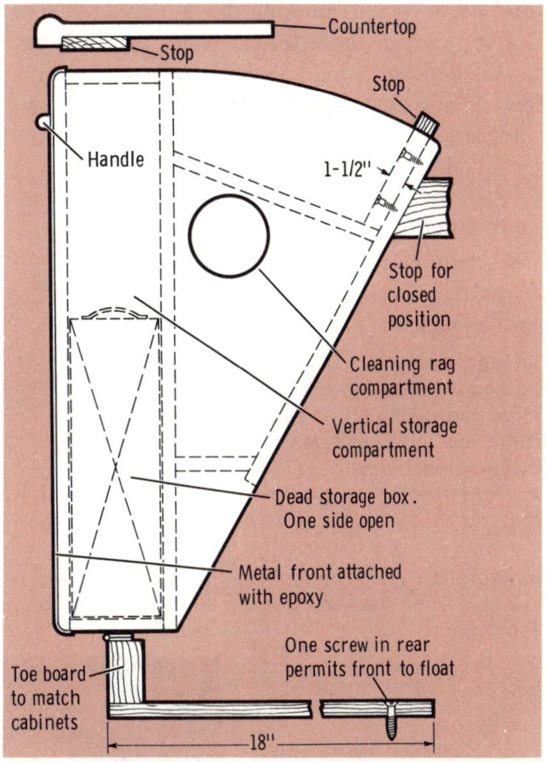

SEE ALSO

Cupboards, china . . . Drawers . . .
Home improvement . . . Kitchen accessories

An efficient kitchen in one weekend

By MIKE MCCLINTOCK

■ A LOT OF THE chores done on a daily basis in your home center around the kitchen. So it's a good place to start making things more efficient to give yourself more leisure time. You can cut the kitchen work load in half by building in a new dishwasher under a new countertop that holds a new sink and a new garbage disposer. It's a weekend job. Here's how to do it.

a new counter

Modern laminate surfaces look good, install easily, clean quickly and last a long time. We picked a buff-finish white Formica. It looks bright, but the textured surface won't glare with reflected light. First, make sure the cutoff faucets are closed and then detach the sink fittings. Remove your old counter by prying along the edges of the cabinet, a little at a time.

Now check the instructions that come with your new dishwasher for minimum width and counterheight allowances. The GE Potscrubber we used called for a 34½ in. height, so we had to add 1x2 strips along the edges of the cabinets to build them up. Make your counter from ¾ in. A-C exterior-grade plywood, with 2-in.-wide strips on the flat to reinforce the perimeter. Glue the panels down with laminate adhesive (watch the vapors—keep the area well ventilated) and cover the 1½-in.-thick edges as well. Make all your cuts

SEE ALSO
Cabinet furniture . . . Cabinets, kitchen . . . Clothes dryers . . . Dishwashers . . . Home improvement . . . Kitchen accessories . . . Mudrooms . . . Remodeling . . . Storage walls . . . Washing machines

1. New counter rails. We screwed new predrilled 2x2 rails along the back wall to support the counter.

2. Extra support. A 2x2 block added to the cross brace makes the counter stronger. Predrill it for 2-in. screws.

3. Reinforcing. 2-in.-wide plywood strips screwed to the ¾-in. counter provide backing for the laminate edge.

4. The opening. Leave ¼-in. clearance on each side of the dishwasher. The plywood side panels are ⅜-in. thick.

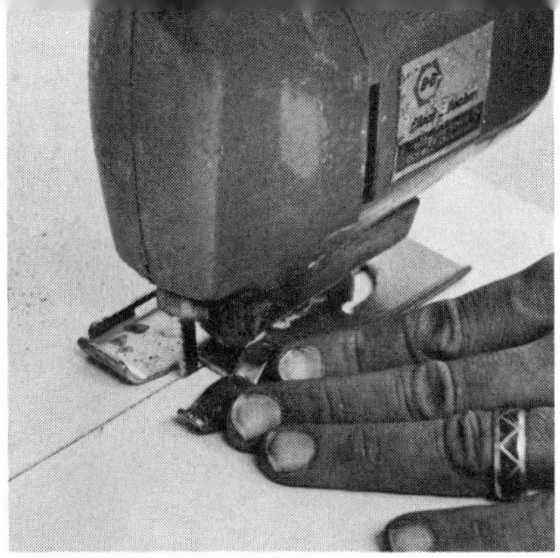

5. The cutout. Turn the sink over and mark perimeter outline on counter. Cut ⅜ in. inside this line.

6. Watertight. Use a clear silicon or white butyl bead along the flange. They won't dry or crack.

7. Fit the sink. L-shaped clips come with the sink. Extra caulk is forced out as you tighten them.

8. Water supply. Install a cutoff in each sink line. Use a tee fitting to run hot pipe to dishwasher.

9. Soldering. Clean the surfaces with steel wool, then wipe on a layer of flux. Heat joint and apply solder.

10. Compression fittings. These joints don't need solder. They can also reduce between different pipe sizes.

11. The control box. GE box mounts on floor. Attach the pipe, turn on the water and test for leaks.

12. Drainage. This 1½-in. drain line has a presoldered tee for clamping on the end of the dishwasher hose.

13. Leveling. Slide unit into opening over control box. Unload (lift up) to adjust leg height.

14. Counter tabs. After all lines are attached and the unit is leveled, screw tabs up into counter.

15. Checkups. Read the instructions for the unit you buy. Plan the job so you'll have the fittings you need.

THIS TWO-COMPARTMENT, stainless steel sink features a soap dispenser. It's made by Elkay.

THE THIN SILICON bead inside the flange on the drain basket will make a leakproof seal when the flange is tightened down from below.

USE TURPENTINE liberally on a clean cloth to wipe away any excess caulking compound which oozes out from the edges as the clips are tightened.

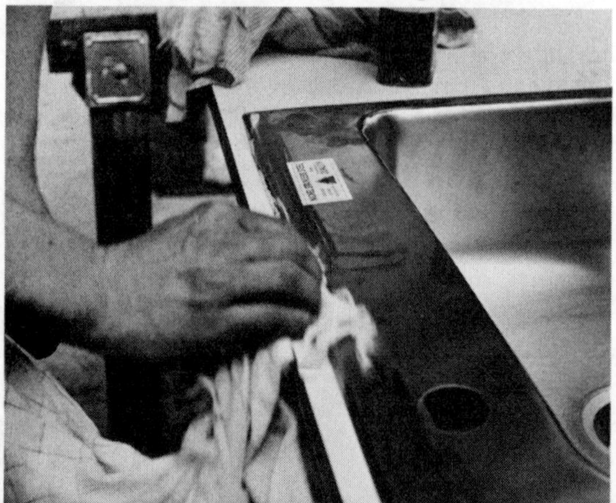

A FAUCET WRENCH is a specialized but inexpensive tool that fits neatly up into the small space behind the sink to tighten fittings leading to top.

slowly (with a carbide-tipped blade if possible) to avoid chipping the edges.

the dishwasher opening

You do have to give something up to gain all these conveniences. It's cabinet space. We left ¼-in. clearance on each side of the dishwasher, cut away the cabinet base to expose the floor and added ⅜ in. plywood partitions to box in the sides. Since most makers build kick-space into the base of their units and design the doors to cover the edges of the cabinet, this simple flush opening is all that's needed.

the supply lines

You'll need one BX cable (14-gauge 2-wire plus ground) to supply the electricity. Pick up the feed from the nearest junction box and make sure it's grounded. Don't forget to turn off the appropriate circuit breaker before you start working. Now check your instructions again. Most manufacturers specify an area toward the back of the opening where the utility lines must enter. About the best place to tap into your hot-water line is at the elbow where the line starts its vertical run to the sink fittings. Close off the supply to this line and replace the elbow with a tee fitting.

Although new copper fittings need only a quick steel-wooling to assure a good solder bond, old fittings must be carefully sanded and steel-wooled to remove all traces of dirt and corrosion. Extend a ½-in. copper line from the free end of the tee about 4 in. into the dishwasher opening, as shown in the photo. Now your utilities are roughed in—that is, ready for the fixture installations.

attaching the new sink

Photos 5, 6 and 7 tell the story. Make your sink cutout with a saber saw, cutting very slowly. This way, it will be easy to follow your pencil line and you won't chip the laminate edge. We used a two-compartment, stainless-steel sink made by Elkay. Run either a silicon or butyl caulking bead around the perimeter of the flange and set the sink in the cutout. L-shaped clips attach to a channel on the flange and lap over the plywood counter base. As you tighten them, the flange clamps down on the counter, forcing out the extra caulking to make a permanent, watertight seal. Now you can attach the counter (including the sink) to the cabinets. We first attached Formica-covered splash-boards to the back edges of the counter with screws. To anchor the counter in place, run 2-in. flathead screws up through the 2x2 (nominal) rail supports.

attaching sink fittings

We used Elkay's single-control faucet with a soap dispenser fitting on the left and a rinsing spray on the right. The key to an easy installation here is the faucet wrench. It's a vertical drive, cam-action pipe wrench that will save you a lot of time and a few scraped knuckles. It shouldn't cost more than $5.

The single-control faucet has two ⅜-in.-diameter copper pipes already attached to it. In photo 9 you can see the reducer fitting we used to make the connection between these pipes and the ½-in. copper supply lines. The light-colored material just above the fitting is called flux. It's a paste you should wipe onto the end of the pipe before assembling the fitting. As you heat the joint with a propane torch, concentrate the blue tip of the flame on the fitting. It will heat up and cause the flux to sizzle. At this point the fitting should be hot enough to melt the solder. The flux will make the solder flow into the joint and bond more evenly and securely.

the drainage system

The top of the garbage disposer is attached to the small-compartment sink drain and fitted through its outlet to the 1½-in. drainage pipe. The large compartment is fitted with a standard drain basket. Below it is a special section of pipe with a presoldered dishwasher tee, as shown in photo 12. The drain hose from the dishwasher is clamped over it.

the final steps

The GE unit has a control box (photo 11) that should be screwed to the floor. It holds a junction box for the wiring and inlet for the water supply. The electrical splice is made with wire nuts. The final plumbing connection can be made with compression fittings (photos 10 and 11) to avoid soldering.

Now carefully slide the dishwasher into place. Your unit will be equipped with a short hose that connects the water pump on the control box and the spray jets in the washer. Complete the drain system by clamping the hose that runs from the tee fitting under the sink onto the outlet under the dishwasher. Photo 13 shows the automatic leg levelers. Adjust them up or down until the unit is dead level. Lastly, screw the unit to the counter through the two tabs shown in photo 14.

I started the job Friday night and Sunday night's dinner dishes came out crystal clean.

Put all of that wasted space to work in your kitchen. Here are some simple projects that will make your kitchen more efficient and livable

CAREFUL SEARCH for hidden spaces usually will yield two or three areas that can be utilized for storage. Here a space was found for tablecloths wound on tubes.

More storage space in your kitchen

By D. SWANSON

SIMPLE DRAWERS and pull-out rods can be used effectively to store pots and pans within your reach.

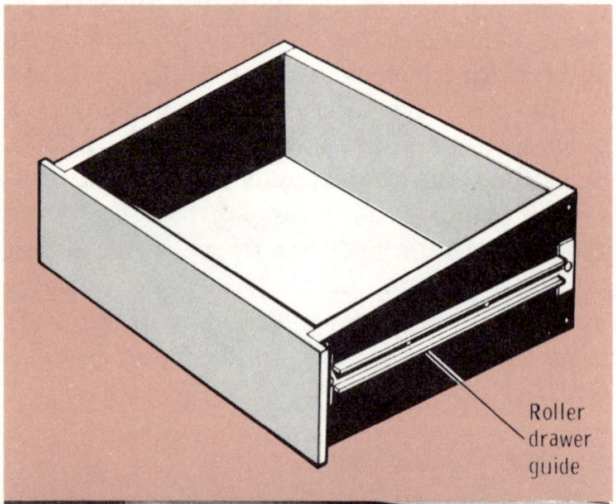

SEE ALSO
Cupboards, china . . . Drawers . . . Kitchen accessories . . . Storage ideas . . . Storage walls . . . Towel racks

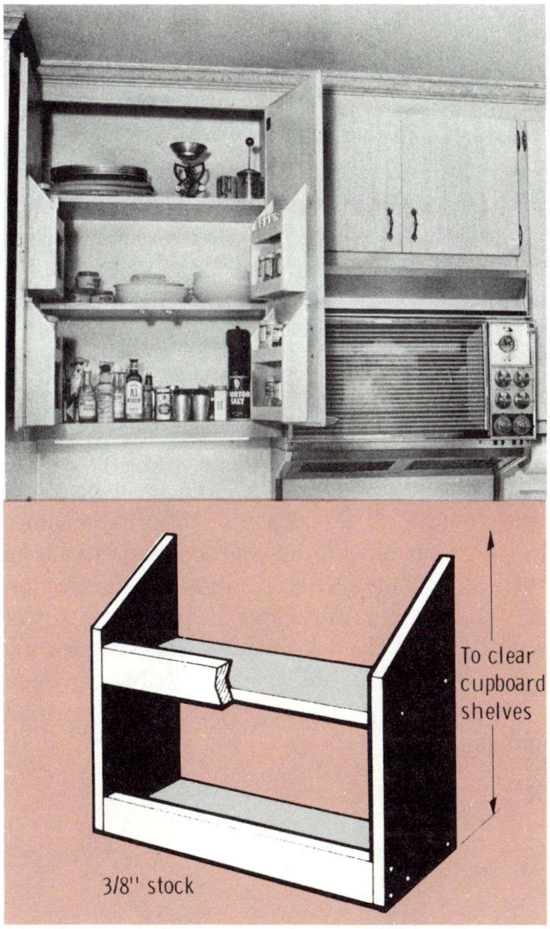

SMALL BOTTLES of spices can be neatly arranged in a simple rack fitted to the inside of a door.

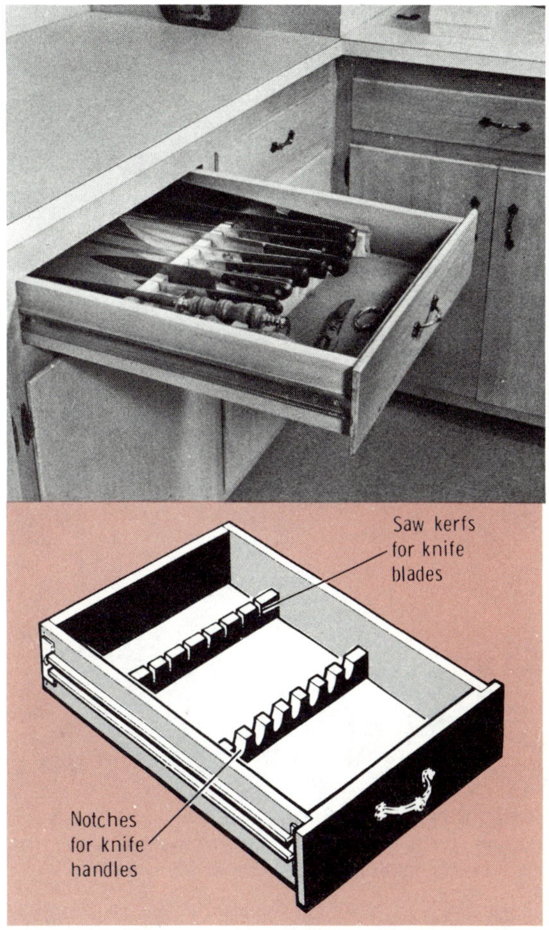

KNIFE DRAWER with two shaped cross members will stow knives out of sight and protect them from damage.

■ WANT TO BE the real hero of the family? Then turn the high-traffic room of your home, the kitchen, into a comfortable, livable and highly efficient area—simply by incorporating just a few of these storage ideas in it or by building in two or three of these worksavers.

What's more, they're all uncomplicated enough to be tackled one or two at a time each winter weekend so that by the time spring rolls around, the value of your home will have increased considerably—dollar-wise as well as convenience-wise.

One such convenience feature is the storage area for rolled tablecloths (shown at top of facing page) while another is a pair of simple drawers (left) used exclusively for pans and trays that are too awkward to store in a conventional fashion.

These and additional spacesavers (and spacemakers) were found originally in the home of Mr. and Mrs. Frank Myers of Winston-Salem, NC. The couple's specialty is finding simple solutions to big problems. Their island unit, for example, has a triple sink and stainless steel top; it could be installed easily in the wasted space in the center of an average kitchen. It also offers the bonus feature of providing enough under-the-sink space to hold trash cans and cleaning supplies. A pull-out Formica-topped shelf rests hidden in the island until needed, while a separate, but nevertheless handy, cutting board is similarily built-in next to the sink.

The cabinets around the perimeter of the 12 x 14-ft. kitchen also were designed with livability in mind. With careful planning, the Myers were able to transform a single 12-ft. wall into more than 300 ft. of shelving. To the right of their refrigerator, for example, four standard-size doors open to uncover a broom closet and shallow pantry type storage. Three of the doors are lined with shelves and three deep drawers at the bottom hold odd-sized containers, supplies and bottles.

HANDY CUTTING surface is easy to build and install. It's basically just a bottomless drawer fitted with a top that will hold up under a knife blade.

In fact, there are drawers and shelves neatly tucked away in nearly every cabinet. In one, a linen drawer replaces the bottom shelf; in another, two drawers hold large pans and pan covers; while in a third, pull-out racks hold pans with handles in a vertical, spacesaving position. Thus, the spacemakers are also backsavers since it's possible to reach any item without resorting to kneeling or bending over for more than a few seconds.

In most kitchens, it's usually possible to find hidden or otherwise wasted space that could be put to effective use as a storage area. The Myers, for example, discovered unused space above the airconditioning unit installed between the garage and their dining room. Since the space ended at the kitchen wall, it was a relatively simple chore to cut an opening in the wall and build in a long shaftlike cabinet to hold tablecloths rolled on cardboard tubes. A careful study of the plans of your home likely will reveal a similar space between the walls of additions, at the back of deep closets or around stairways and built-in appliances.

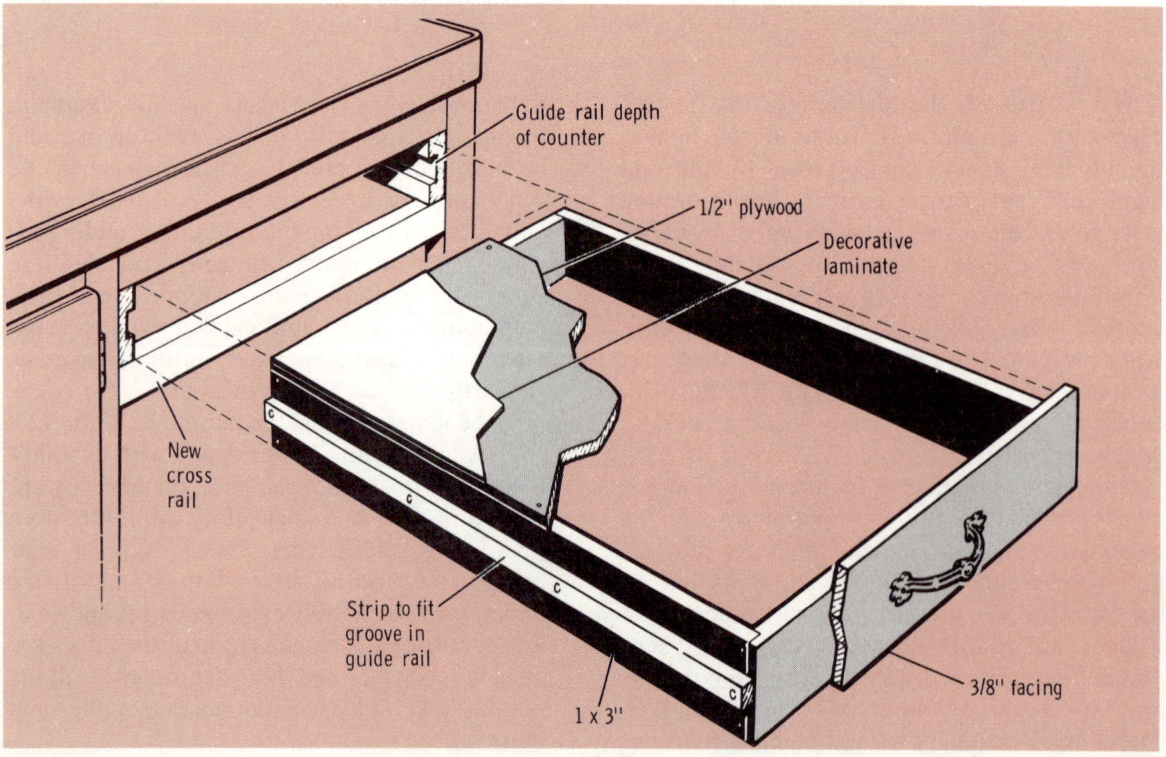

Other special-use spacesavers that you could easily build into your kitchen take the forms of spice racks, knife drawers, bread bins and multi-shelf units used strictly for canned or bottled goods. Here again, the trick is to search out unused space and put it to work—preferably using it to solve the problem of storing awkward, bulky, shelf-robbing items such as toasters, mixers and similar appliances.

Combine these simple kitchen aids and worksavers with such conveniences as lighting fixtures concealed under the cabinets and adequate electrical outlets, and you'll find that your once-congested kitchen will be transformed into a highly organized, highly livable center.

Yet, as previously pointed out, you can make these additions and changes gradually and without great expense since you likely have enough odd pieces of lumber left over from old projects to complete five or six of these weekend projects at your leisure. Also noteworthy is the fact that it's not necessary to tear up the kitchen and disrupt its use during this modernization program.

ROLL-OUT BINS placed in the bottom of cabinets are for storage of kitchen towels and cleaning supplies. They eliminate kneeling to remove item in back.

PANTRY SHELVES built on doors can provide storage space that's ideal for canned and bottled supplies.

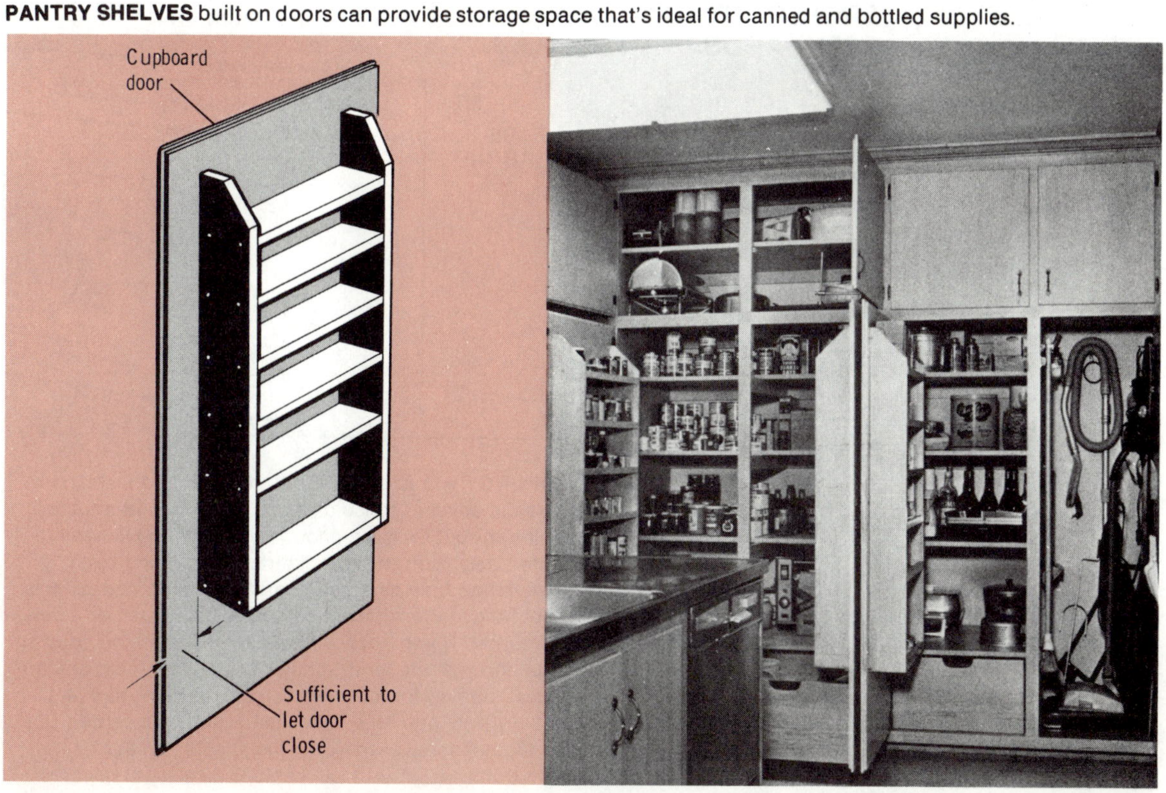

How to install kitchen cabinets

■ THERE ARE THREE basic points to keep in mind when you install kitchen cabinets: 1. Base cabinets must be set level, thus shims are usually required. 2. Cabinets must be securely fastened to wall studs. Although many contractors install cabinets using hefty (16d) common nails, proper-size wood screws are a better choice. 3. You must stick to the architectural kitchen standards shown in the drawing at left, below. These dimensions are important; any variance from standard working and reaching heights and depths will result in an uncomfortable-to-work-in kitchen. Also, keep in mind that kitchen cabinets are, in fact, pieces of fine furniture; handle with care to avoid scratching or marring the finish. And keep tools off the countertop.

SEE ALSO
Cabinet furniture . . . Laminates, plastic . . . Remodeling . . . Storage ideas

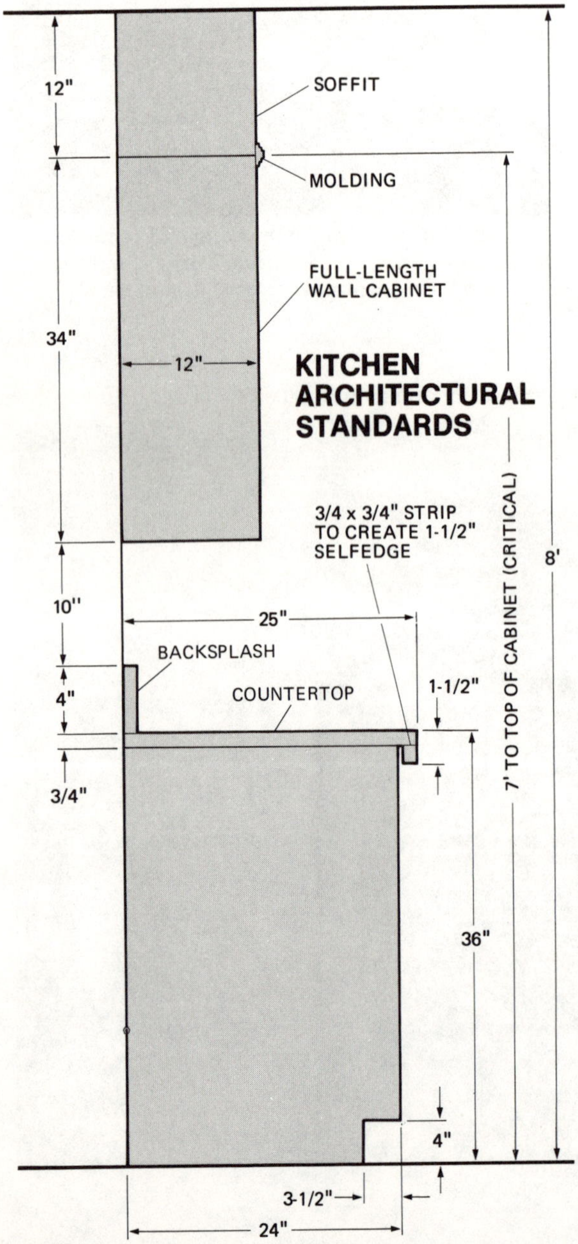

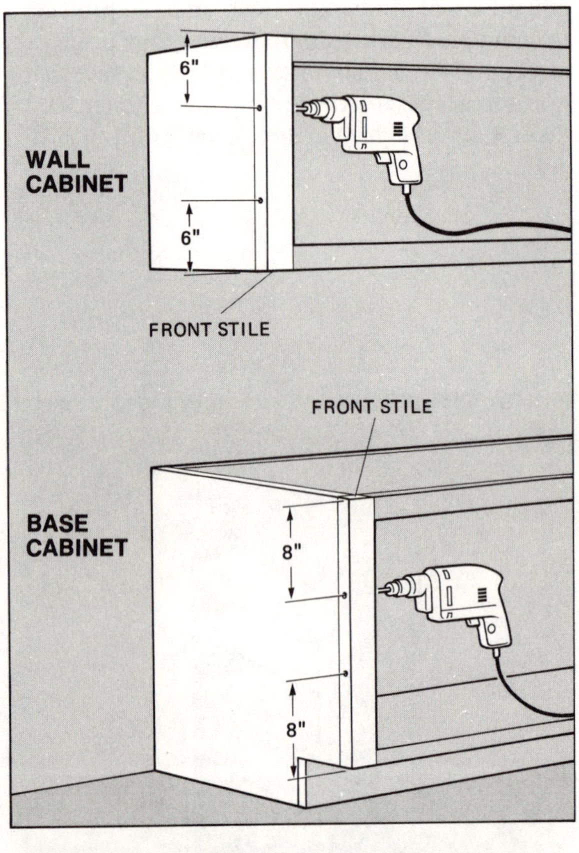

JOINING TWO CABINETS. Start by drilling installation holes in stiles of those cabinets that will butt another. Holes should be large enough for fastening screws to slide freely. Butt the two cabinets and, using each installation hole as a guide, drill a smaller, correct-size pilot hole in the adjacent cabinet's stile. Later, as screws are turned home, they will take their bite in the adjacent stile and pull the joint tightly closed. Hole locations are shown above; for less than full (34 in. high) hangers, usually only one hole is needed at the stile center. Use additional screws wherever the joint is not tight.

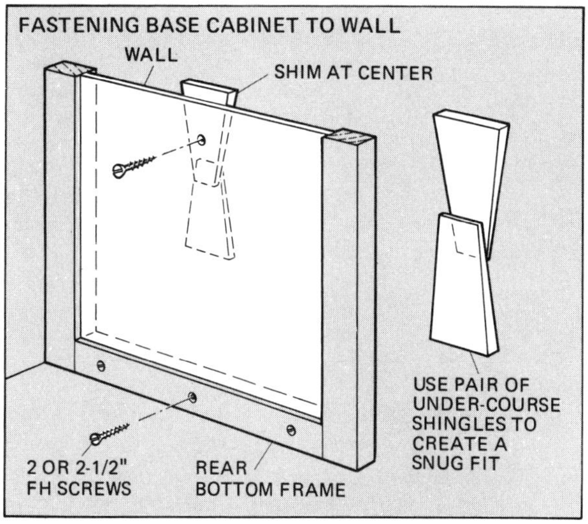

FASTENING CABINETS TO THE WALL. If it is necessary to drive screws through the back plywood panel to penetrate a wall stud when attaching a base cabinet (above), use shims—undercourse shingles—to assure a rigid installation and to prevent bowing the cabinet's back. Use this method on base cabinets only. For wall cabinets, install 2-in. No. 10 wood screws through the wood fastening rail at the inside top back of the cabinet.

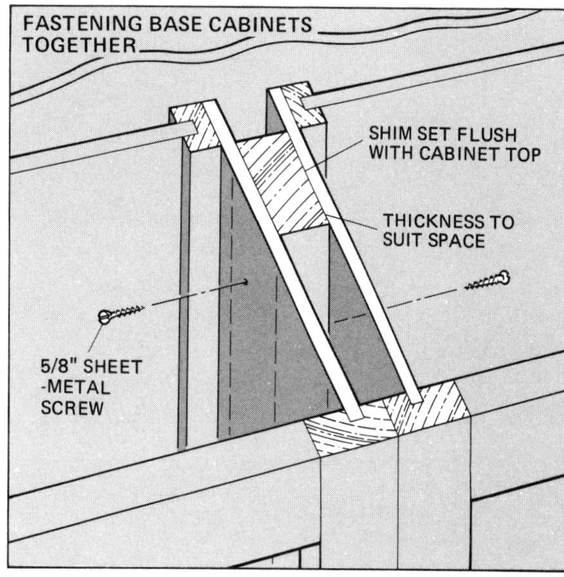

SHIMMING BETWEEN CABINETS. If stiles project beyond sides, use a shim between cabinets as shown. The shim can be of solid wood if the dimension matches stock lumber. For example, if the space between is ¾ in., simply use ¾-in. pine or plywood. For odd dimensions, use a pair of shingles (as shown above, left), to obtain a good snug fit.

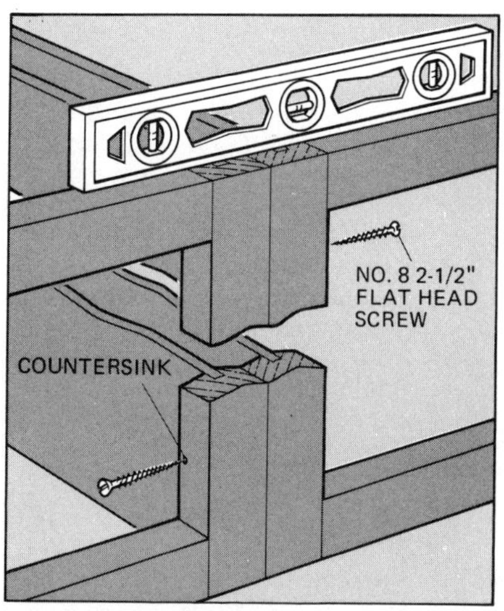

JOINING FRONT FRAMES. Use your spirit level (a 4-footer is best) to level cabinets. Where necessary, slip a shim under a low cabinet to bring it up into the same plane as the fastened first cabinet. When satisfied with alignment and plumb, join the cabinets by installing 2½-in. screws through the installation holes you drilled earlier. Use flathead screws and countersink them so operation of doors, drawers will be smooth.

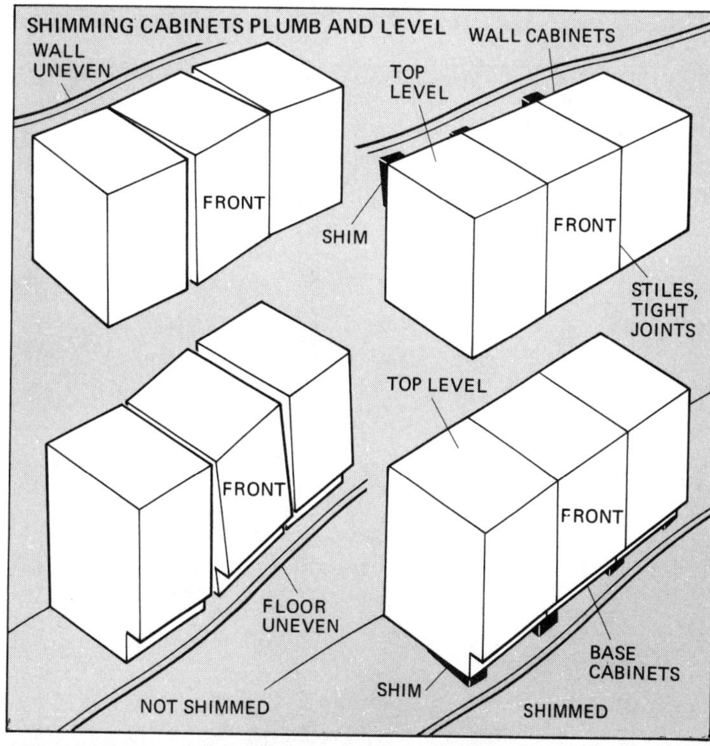

FLOOR AND WALL SHIMMING. If your floors and walls are not level and plumb, it is a must to shim behind the base and wall cabinets to the highest point as is shown above. Shimming assures proper alignment of horizontal cabinet rails for appearance and is necessary to assure that the doors and drawers will function properly after installation.

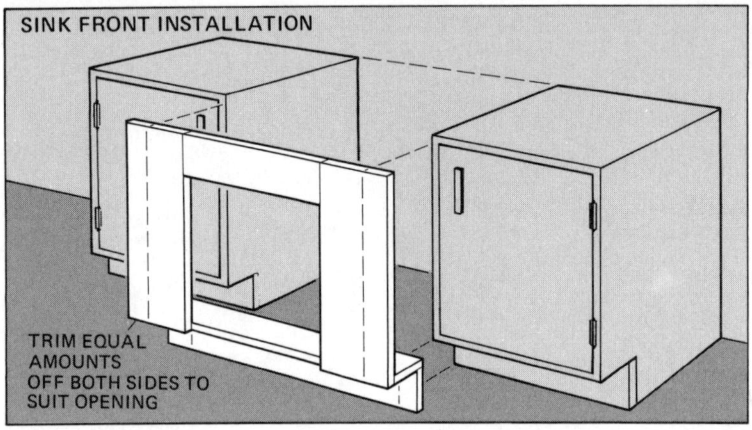

SINK-FRONT INSTALLATION. Generally a sink front (designated SF), not a cabinet, is used below a kitchen sink. Since the most widely used single sink is 24 in. wide and 21 in. deep, most sink fronts come in 24-in. widths. Larger widths for oversize and double sinks are also manufactured. Some makers put extra-wide stiles on the SF so that they can be trimmed to the required size (width) on the job. Sink fronts are secured by fastening through stiles to the side cabinets.

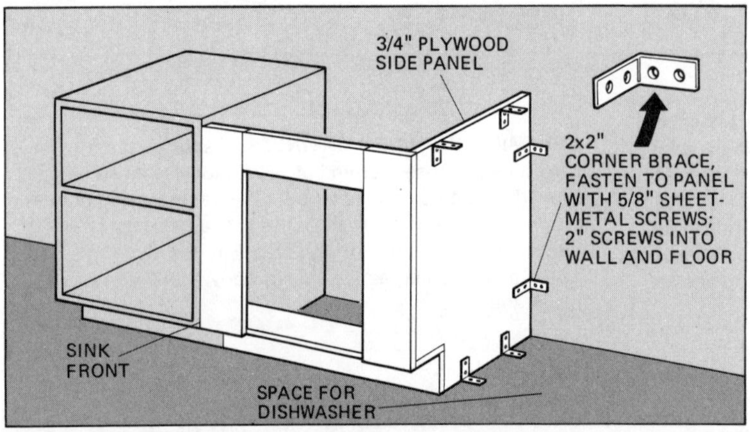

DISHWASHER NEXT TO SINK. If your layout calls for a dishwasher (DW) to be located next to the sink, an extra step will be necessary. Since there is no cabinet for fastening SF on DW side, it is necessary to cut a ¾-in. plywood panel to serve as a sidewall. For rigidity, fasten the plywood "side" to the floor and wall using 2x2-in. corner braces. After countertop is installed, add corner braces from plywood panel to underside of countertop; use ⅝-in. sheet-metal screws to top.

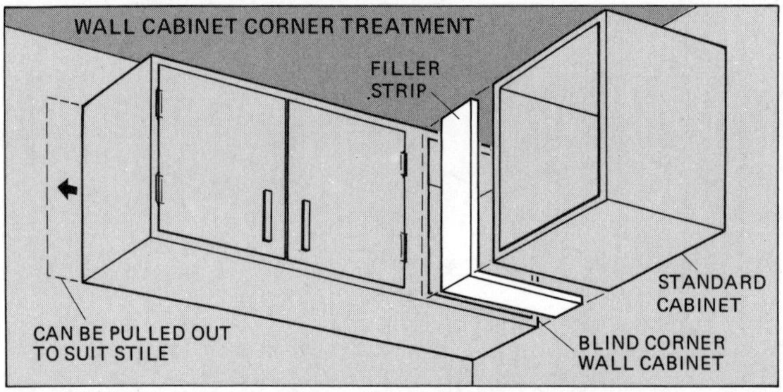

BLIND CORNER WALL CABINET. Installation is the same as for other wall-hung cabinets except that a 3-in. filler is used between the blind cabinet and the cabinet butting it at 90° (to assure clearance for door swing). The filler is attached by screws through the hanger cabinet, and from inside the blind corner hanger into the filler. Butting cabinets are hung conventionally using screws through the inside back top rail into the wall studs.

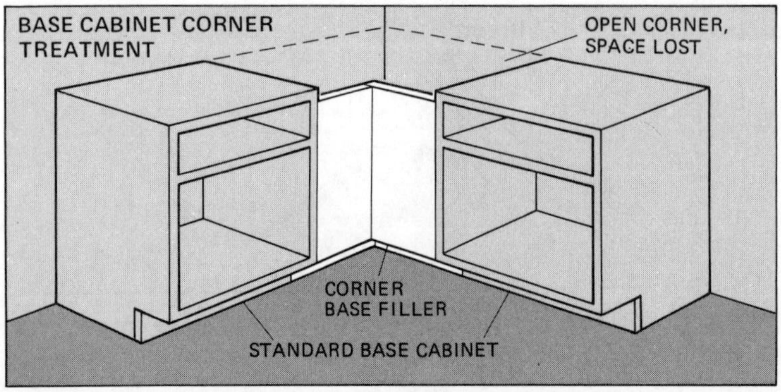

CORNER BASE FILLER. Base cabinets can be installed as shown at left by using a corner base filler. Though there is a cash saving initially when this type corner is used, it is recommended only for kitchens with ample space. Once closed in, that corner area is space lost for good. To utilize corner space, consider instead installing a blind corner cabinet (BCC). For a drawing of a BCC, see upper left drawing, page **1619**.

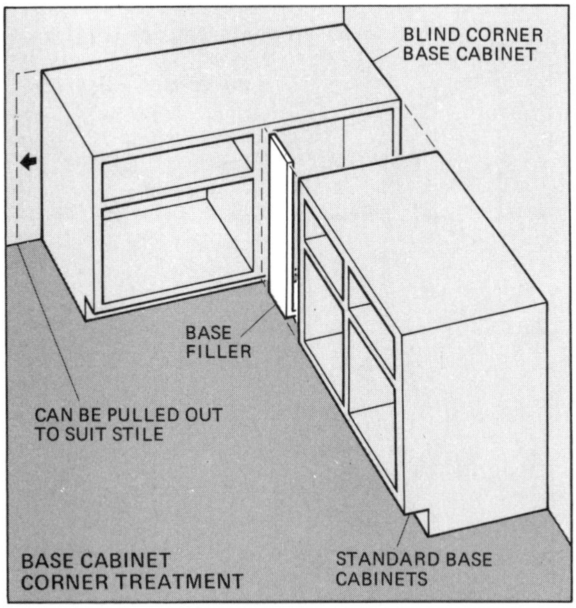

BLIND CORNER BASE CABINET. A standard cabinet is installed with filler between it and the blind corner base cabinet (BCC). Fasten the filler with screws through standard cabinet's stile and if possible, with screws through BCC center stile into opposite edge of the filler. Access to corner space is through the standard-cabinet door.

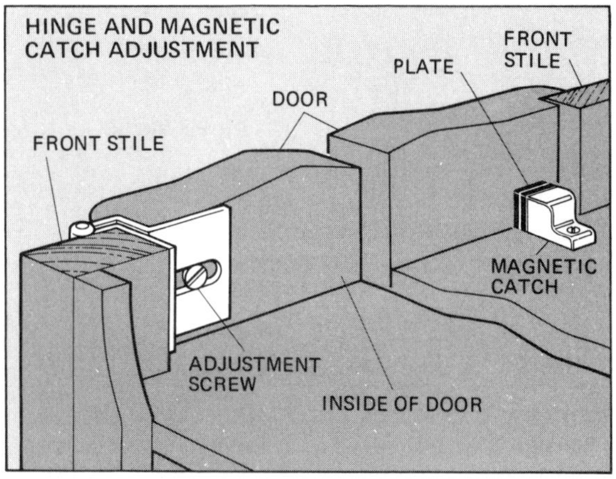

ADJUSTING DOORS. Since misalignment of doors and drawers can be caused by rough handling during shipment, most of the manufacturers pack door and drawer adjustment right in with the cabinets. Realignment of these parts generally consists of simply loosening the hinge screws slightly, squaring the doors and retightening the screws. It is also frequently necessary to adjust a magnetic catch; you simply loosen the screws and slide the magnet forward or backward in its slots until the desired contact action has been accomplished. Then retighten the screws.

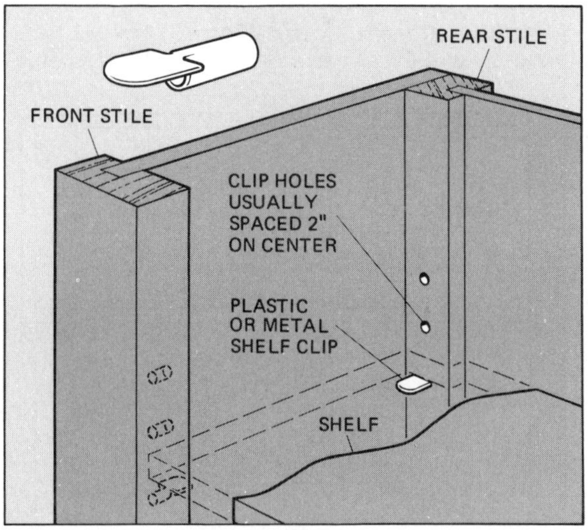

SHELF INSTALLATION. Most base cabinets come with a fixed shelf; full-height wall cabinets usually contain two adjustable shelves. Though there are several kinds of adjustable shelving systems, a commonly used type consists of plastic or metal supports pushed into predrilled holes in wall-cabinet stiles. Simply insert four supports for each shelf and lay it in place. If the shelf rocks, firmly "slap" it in the middle to true up supports and seat the shelf squarely.

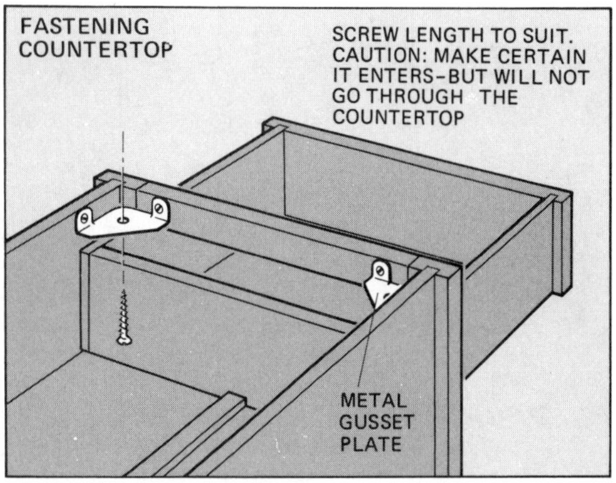

INSTALLING THE COUNTERTOP. Usually, base cabinets have metal gusset plates in each corner at the top. These serve a dual purpose: Adding strength to the cabinet and anchoring the countertop. With the countertop in position, carefully measure the length of screw required to obtain a purchase in top's underside without coming through the laminate finish. Not many screws are required here as their primary function is simply to keep the top from shifting laterally.

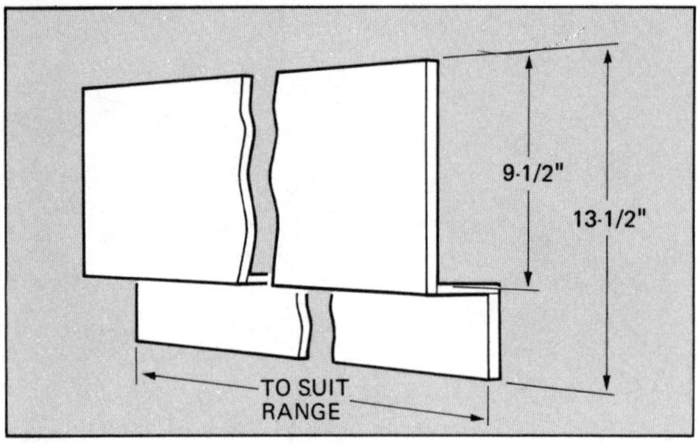

RANGE FRONT FILLER AND PANEL. The range front filler and panel are used when a drop-in range/oven is to be installed. Some ranges call for more elaborate filler pieces than others; thus the range should be picked before the cabinets are ordered and the maker's specifications checked to see if—and what type of—a wood front is needed. A specified size of ¼-in. paneling, finished to match the cabinets, may be all that's required. Bring these specs along when you order the cabinets.

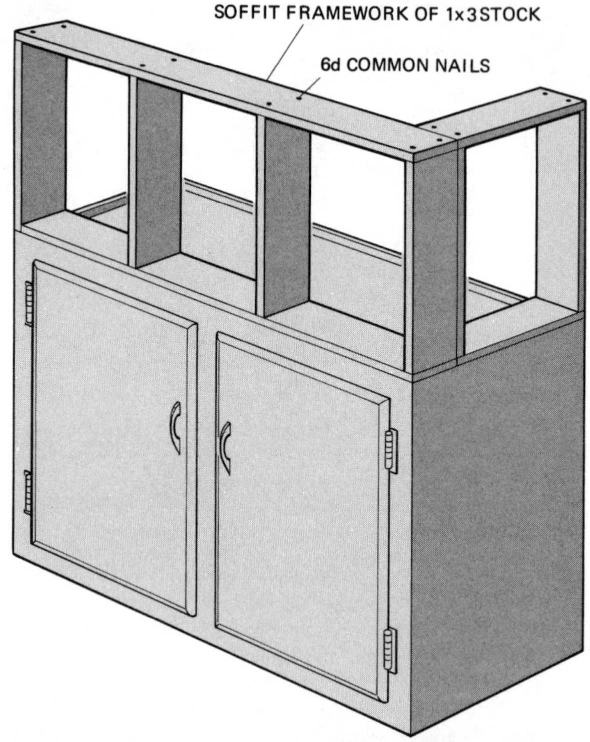

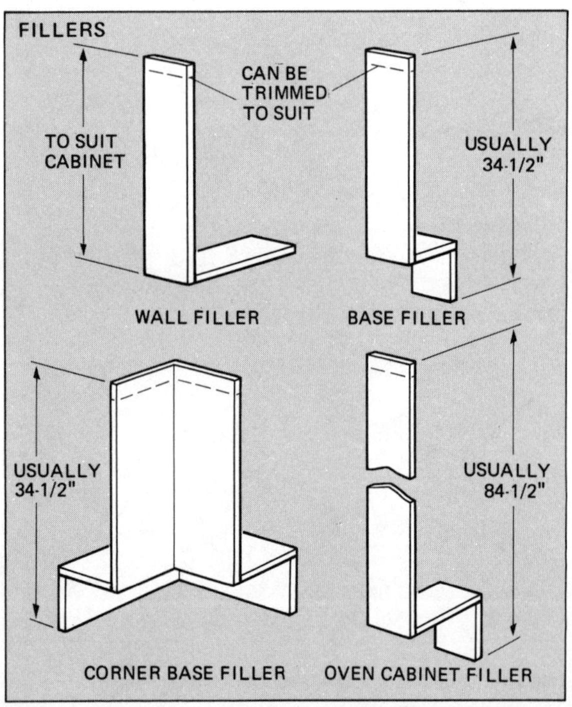

TYPICAL FILLERS. The most commonly used fillers are shown above. Besides serving for blind corner-cabinet installation, these are required when a cabinet run will butt a wall at 90°, and when a wall is so out of plumb or irregular that it will be necessary to scribe (custom-fit) the last cabinet to the wall.

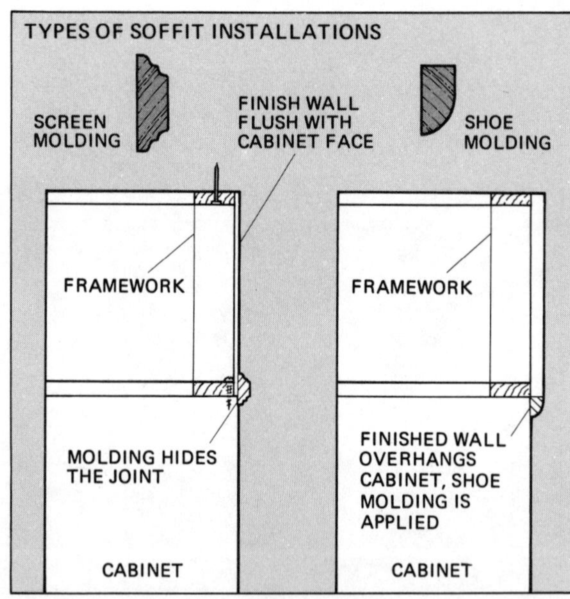

INSTALLING THE SOFFIT. The easiest-to-make soffit enclosure is a ladderlike structure made of 1x3 furring. Take accurate measurements between the cabinet and the ceiling at ends and middle of run and assemble sections on the floor. Then hoist the sections in place and fasten using shims as needed. Framework can be set back a distance equal to thickness of material covering it, or installed flush with the cabinet fronts.

Skylight leaks—or does it?

I've installed combination skylights and vents in my attic and last winter they leaked, wetting the attic floor directly underneath. I've examined them and can find no place where water gets in. Yet it does, somewhere. There are louvers in the gable ends, but apparently these are not large enough, as the attic gets very hot in summer. Have you any suggestions?—H.O., Tenn.

If these skylights are of the "bubble" type and have been properly installed, they shouldn't leak. The wetness you're getting on the attic floor is probably condensate that forms on the underside of the lights and drips onto the floor. The moisture is condensed from the air in the attic. It does not leak in from outside. I hesitate to suggest closing the skylights with a tight-fitting insert, but this would seem to be the only preventive step. The disadvantage of this is that you may get condensate forming on exposed nails or plumbing vents.

To be effective, the inserts, or covers, must fit tightly to prevent warm air from the attic reaching the inside surface of the bubbles. You might try frames paneled in either glass or sheet plastic; the former sealed with putty, the latter with a mastic. If there is a door to the attic, be sure it is closed tightly in winter and also see that louvers in gable ends are open and that the screening is not clogged with paint, leaves or other debris.

Wood "putty" beads

I have to reputty my window sashes every two years or so; the new putty loosens and falls out. I use a standard glazier's putty that can be painted immediately after application, or so it says on the label. Isn't there some substitute for putty that won't loosen and drop out, at least within a reasonable time?—D.A., Ala.

Do you clean the sash rabbets thoroughly—both wood and glass—before applying? Are you sure the wood and glass are thoroughly dry before knifing in the putty? Do you press the new putty firmly in place to force it under the edge of the pane as well as to fill the rabbet? Only affirmative answers to these questions indicate that you are carrying out the necessary steps to assure adhesion of new putty in what I assume are old sashes.

A substitute for putty? Well, yes, you can rip triangular strips of white pine to the size of the putty bead and brad these in place, mitering the strips at the corners to form a neat, tight joint. The strips should be painted on the unexposed faces before application, and must be painted immediately after application.

Spindle scraper

I often clean old finishes off chairs having spindles or turnings. A flat scraper is not good for this purpose as it leaves ridges. Even scrapers with curved edges don't work well. Isn't there a better way or trick I don't know about?—R.E., Tenn.

Do you have an old pocketknife with a large blade that will hold an edge? Then grind a half-moon, or quarter-moon shape on the edge and hone it sharp. This is the best tool I've ever found for scraping the old finish off chair turnings or any small turnings. You can, of course, do this with any cabinet scraper, but the knife scraper is easier to manipulate and gets into the tight places. However, don't use this method on a valuable antique. Here, it's better to use a wash-off-type varnish remover. This will preserve the natural patina of age.

Insulating plank patcher

A room in my basement is finished with what I suppose are insulating planks of a soft, fibrous material. There are several unsightly digs and gouges. The color is off-white. What can I use as a filler?—L.G., Kans.

You might use a wood filler in powder form that's mixed with water—proportions are given on the container—provided the openings are small or no larger than a thumbprint. Press any extruding fibers back into the recess to be filled and then knife the mixed filler back in place, topping out the filler just slightly above the plank surface. Let the patch dry thoroughly, then sand it lightly until flush and finish with an off-white flat paint. It might help to add a transparent white glue, such as Elmer's, to insure patch adhesion.

Condensate on floor

The floor in my basement recreation room is tiled and walls are paneled. The poured-concrete foundation forms two walls of the room. The floor is drawing water along these walls. How do I stop this leak without taking up the tiles along the baseboard?—Robert Ash, Cleveland.

"Drawing water" is an unfortunate term—it does not describe what is happening. Water you see along the baseboard is condensate that will form on any surface at a lower temperature than the room air. Usually, improved ventilation is the cheapest cure; screen the basement windows and open them on cool days to let cooler, dryer air circulate freely. If there are no windows, use an automatic dehumidifier to lower moisture level of the air.

Build a patio appliance center

By WAYNE C. LECKEY

With this handy appliance center you can take your kitchen outside for those summer cookouts

■ WISH YOU COULD USE your kitchen appliances out on the patio? You can with this rolling appliance center which offers a convenient plug-in counter for your electric griddle, casserole, bun warmer, fondue pot, coffeemaker and other appliances normally used indoors.

It's sure to make your cookouts a lot more fun and easier since you can serve such things as hamburgers, chicken and franks without the work of starting up a charcoal grill. You just plug in the appliance and you're in business.

The affair provides you with the convenience of a kitchen since the roomy cabinet and counter, plus cutting block, make "dishing it out" extra handy. Lift up the hinged cutting block and there's an ice-filled cooler under it full of chilled soda and beer. A shelf across the back provides a space for all your cooking spices and condiments, and the roomy cabinet offers cupboard space galore for storing all the gear that goes with outdoor entertaining. It rolls freely on ball casters, the counter is Formica-covered, and a retractable reel saves the bother of rolling up a plug-in cord. A striped-awning top adds a gay festive look to the party.

THE COUNTER features a lift-up, maple cutting block that is handy for preparing salads.

The whole idea was presented to us by the Aluminum Assn., and Bud Johnson, our cabinetmaker, built it. Materials ran about $100, but you can build it for less by using less expensive casters, forgetting the Formica on the counter and using softwood for the maple cutting board. Most of the cart is made from ¾-in. exterior plywood, the lumber being common ¾-in. (actual) white pine. The back panels are ⅜-in. plywood. The styrofoam cooler sells for about $2.50. The cover of the cooler is cemented to the underside of the cutting board. The fluorescent fixture is controlled by a separate switch and, along with the plug-in strip, is wired to the cord reel. The canopy can be removed to facilitate storage.

Construction details on the next two pages show how the cart is made.

SEE ALSO
**Barbecues . . . Benches, deck . . .
Carpeting, outdoor . . . Cookout bars . . .
Firepits . . . Garden shelters . . . Grills . . . Patios . . .
Picnic tables . . . Privacy screens**

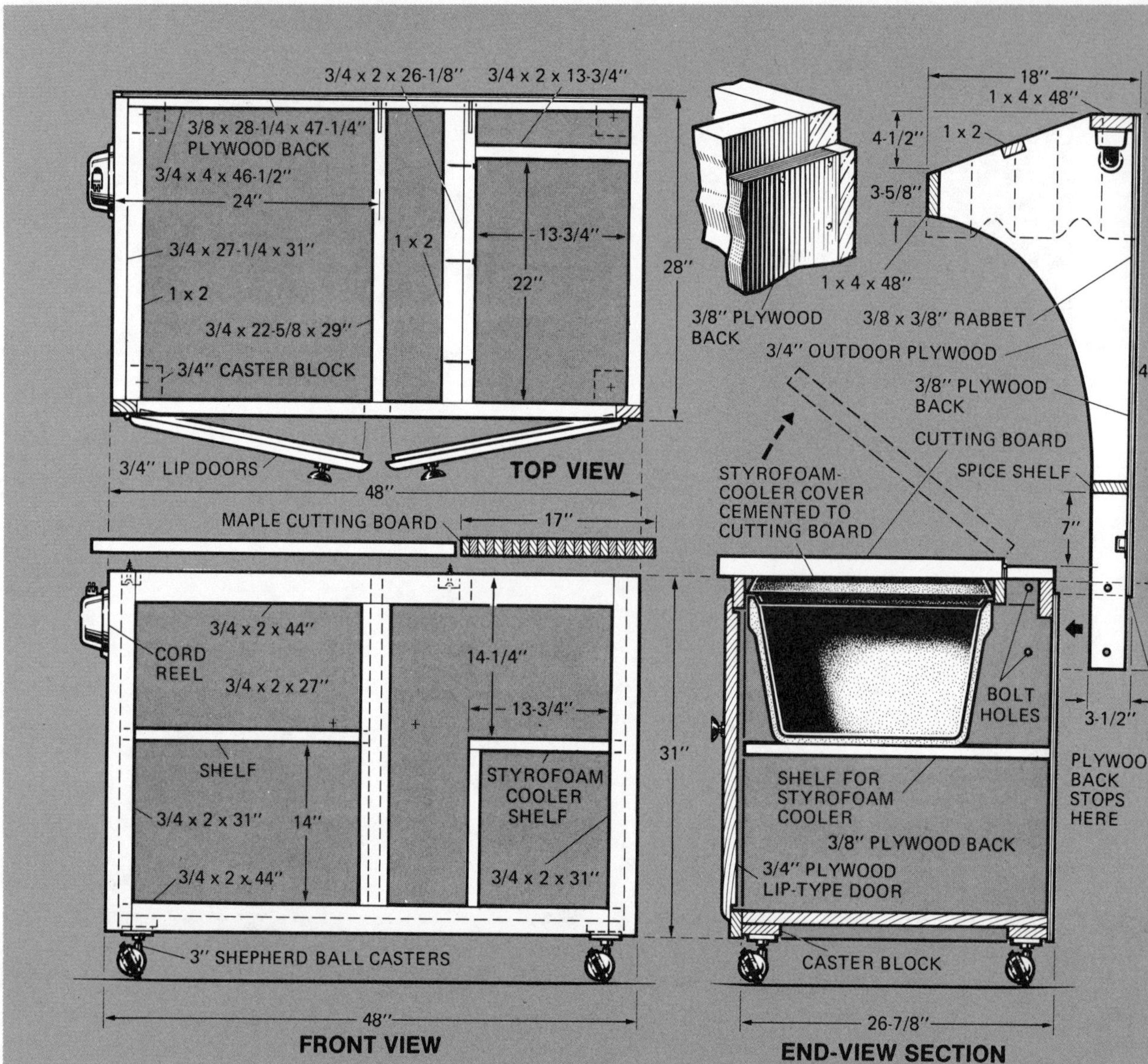

Retractable cord reel corrals 6-ft. plug-in cord. It sells for about $15; A. A. Peters, Inc., 404 Union Blvd., Allentown, Pa. 18103

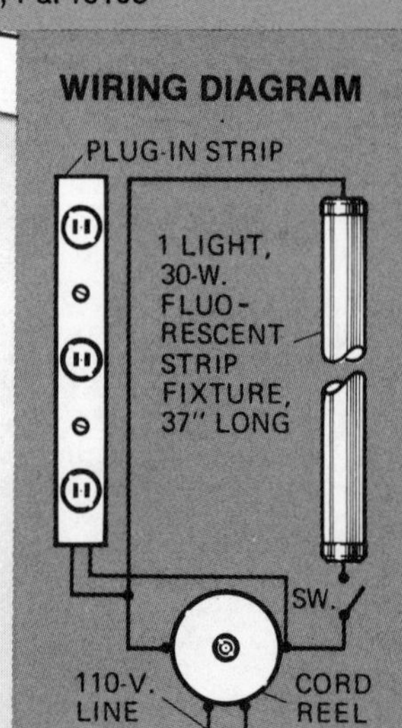

Plate-type ball casters, two with brakes, are screwed to the corners

PATIO APPLIANCE CENTER— CONSTRUCTION DETAILS

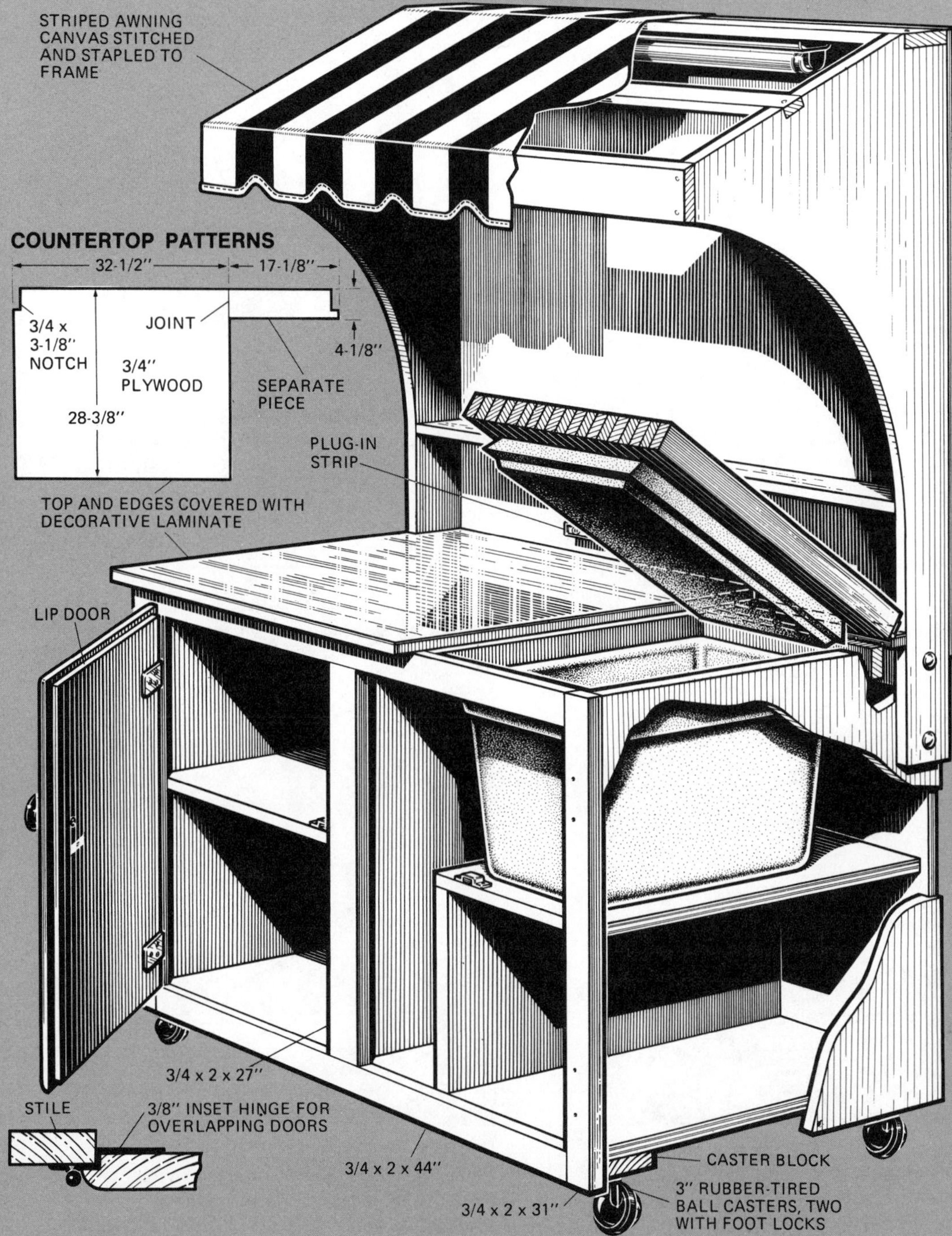

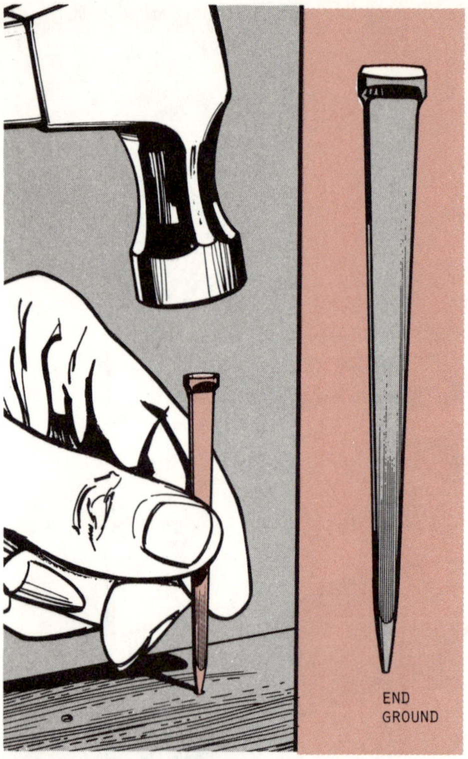

A QUICKIE NAILSET that can be used safely for setting brads and small finishing nails is made by rounding the tip of a masonry (cut) nail. Hardened-steel nails won't bend.—*Alan R. Haberton, Ogden, UT.*

A SCREEN-DOOR-CLOSER SPRING can also be used to correct any minor sagging. Simply fasten the outboard end at an angle until the frame is pulled into square.—*Dennis G. Richardson, Perkinsville, VT.*

DROOPY CLOTHESLINES can be pulled taut with a tightener stick and three nails. Hold the stick vertical with a piece of rope between two nails, take up the slack and secure with the third nail.—*W. H. McClay, Pasadena, CA.*

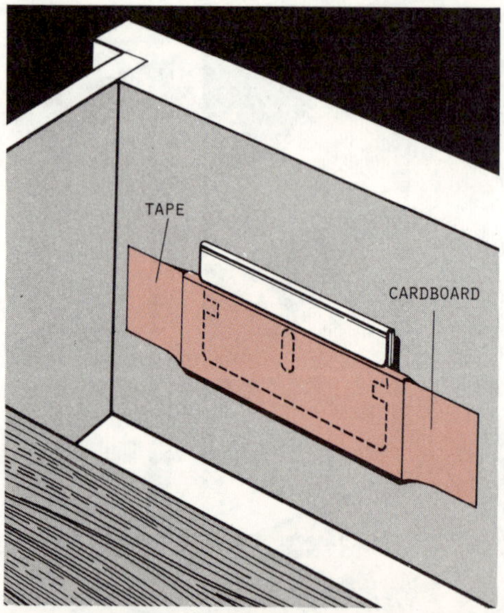

SINGLE-EDGED RAZOR BLADES can be stored safely inside a desk or bench drawer using this "holster." Simply tape a piece of cardboard so that the cutting edge will be covered.—*J. David Lambert., Prospect Park, PA.*

THE PLANS for this Scott sled kite are shown at the top of the following page. It has no horizontal struts and depends entirely on wind pressure to remain open in flight.

Go fly a kite

By LEN HILTS

When brisk breezes blow and the fragrance of spring is in the air, the time for kite flying has arrived. These soarers will put you in the fun

■ YOU HAVEN'T really flown a kite until you have graduated from the standard store-bought two-stick jobs and tried one of the more exotic fliers.

It is true that experts call the two-stick kite one of the best all-around fliers, but from an esthetic standpoint, it can't begin to compete with such marvelous oddities as the Japanese bird or delta wing kites. So if you want to become the center of attraction at your local park, or see your prestige zoom skyward in the eyes of your children, try one of the designs illustrated on the following pages.

You can now buy an amazing variety of kites at kite stores—places that specialize in kites from all over the world—but kite making is easy, so there is no need to buy one. The materials are readily available. Assembly takes only a couple of hours at most. And your personal design variations can produce a flier that may be better than anything you might buy.

Materials. Kite-making materials fall into three categories: sticks, coverings and glue. Sticks, of course, are used to make the frames, and small wood slats are the most common stick material. The best are of white pine or spruce. Yellow pine and fir are not too good for this purpose because they tend to snap too easily. Balsa wood is wonderfully light but is altogether too fragile for kite use. Many kite makers today use hardwood dowels, ranging in size from 1/8 to 3/8-in. in dia. Oriental kites are made of strips of rattan or bamboo. Any store which carries materials for caning chairs will have rattan, and you'll find bamboo at places which sell bamboo window shades.

SEE ALSO

**Airplane models . . . Dump trucks, toy . . .
Gifts, Christmas . . . Pull toys . . . Toys**

THIS WINGED box kite looks like a high-flying flag with its striped wings and starry box. Great for flying on the Fourth of July. Plans for it are at the right. Note that it is made of $^3/_{16}$-in. dia. hardwood dowels. The plans call for Bristol paper, but any covering can be used.

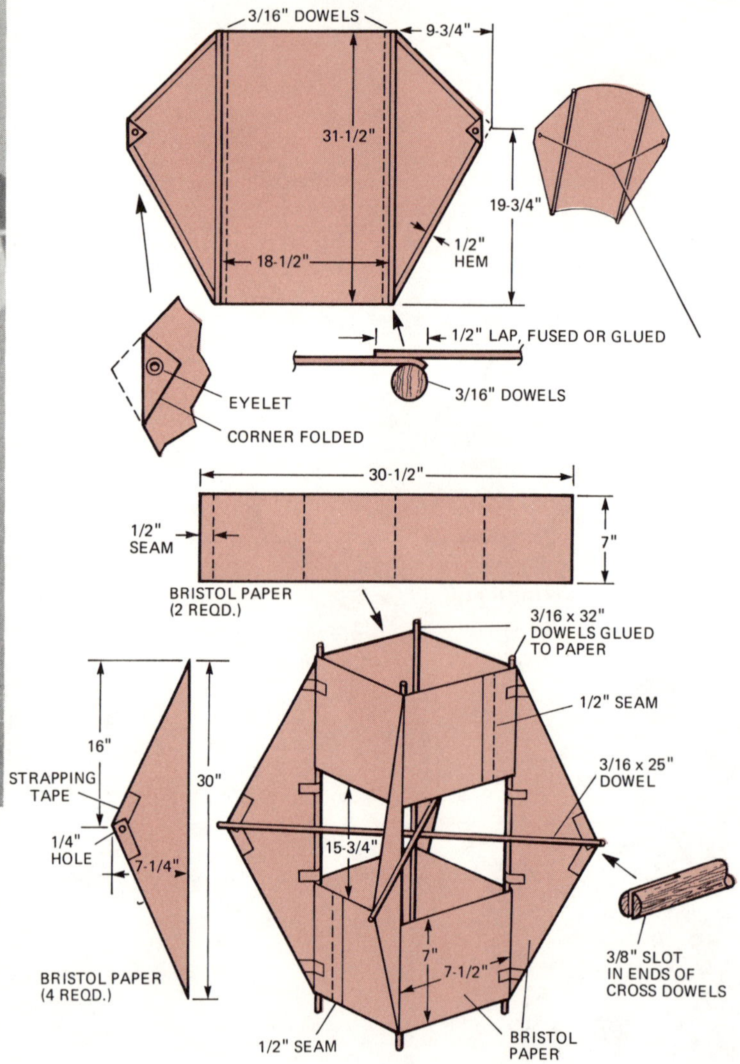

WINGED BOX KITE

Coverings for kites are of three types—paper, cloth and plastic. During the days of the Depression, I covered many a successful kite with last week's newspapers, though if you are shooting for durability, newspapers aren't the best route. Brown kraft wrapping paper is stronger. Japanese rice paper, available at art supply stores, is an old standby in the kite trade, but it is a little heavy. Probably the best compromise between strength and weight is Madras tissue, an oriental tissue paper likely to be found in stores which sell oriental goods.

Cloth coverings include ordinary muslin, cambric, silk and lightweight nylon spinnaker cloth. Think about using a cloth covering on high fliers such as box kites, which need the strength of cloth and can carry the weight. Plastic coverings include polyethylene—the stuff of which plastic garbage bags are made—and mylar polyester. You'll find the latter at most paint stores, sold in big sheets for use as dropcloths. It is light and very inexpensive.

You'll need adhesives to attach the coverings to the frame. Ordinary paper paste was the standby for years, still works on paper kites. Modern quick-drying white glues are probably better, and they work on cloth as well as paper. Rubber cement and its cousin, contact cement, are good. Just remember that to get a good bond with rubber cement you must coat both pieces, allow the cement to dry, and then press the surfaces together. When you coat just one surface, you get a weak bond. If you are working with plastic, you'll need a cement which works on the particular plastic you have. Check the glue counter at your hardware store.

You'll find use for adhesive tapes, too, in kite-making. Clear cellophane tape is fine for many jobs. If you need real strength, use one of the packaging tapes, which are reinforced with fibers. For cloth kites, iron-on tapes are good for making seams and joining pieces of cloth. For the lightest of all seam joiners, use Stitch-Witchery, a plastic ribbon which, when placed between two pieces of cloth and heated with an iron, bonds the pieces of cloth.

Once your kite is built, you need a line on which to fly it. The experts say that wrapping twine is too heavy and regular string is too fuzzy. (The wind catches the fuzz and creates too much drag.) They recommend, for very light kites, carpet thread of 12/4 size. For heavier kites, think about fish line. You can buy nylon monofilament line in a variety of thicknesses. Furthermore, fish lines are rated by the weight they can carry, which is convenient for kite fliers. A 28-lb. test line is fine for medium-sized kites, and for bigger models, the line can range upward to about an 80-lb. test.

When you really get into the spirit of kite making, you turn artistic and become concerned with the appearance of your creations as well as their flying ability. The winged box kite shown on page 1736, done in red, white and blue, for example, is great for patriotic occasions such as the Fourth of July. And the highly imaginative bird and face kites on pages 1632 and 1633, are typical of the artistry put into their kites by the Japanese, who probably have been flying kites longer than anyone else around.

Most of the drawings of kites on these pages are self-explanatory. Follow the dimensions shown for making the frame, and then cover it as shown, using the materials of your choice. About the only trick you need to know is that the best way to join two sticks in frame making is to wrap the joint with fairly heavy thread and then soak the thread with Elmer's glue. When the glue sets, you'll have a very strong joint. You can drive staples or brads through these joints, but when you do, you run the risk of splitting the stick.

I can remember that my biggest problem as a youthful kite flyer was in finding material to make the tail. Most kites need some kind of a tail, and the standard tail for years has been strips of sheeting tied together, but it costs money to tear up sheeting. Kite fliers who live near me have found a neat substitute: They buy rolls of crepe paper—the kind used to decorate gymnasiums for homecoming games—and make colorful kite tails from them.

DELTA WING KITE

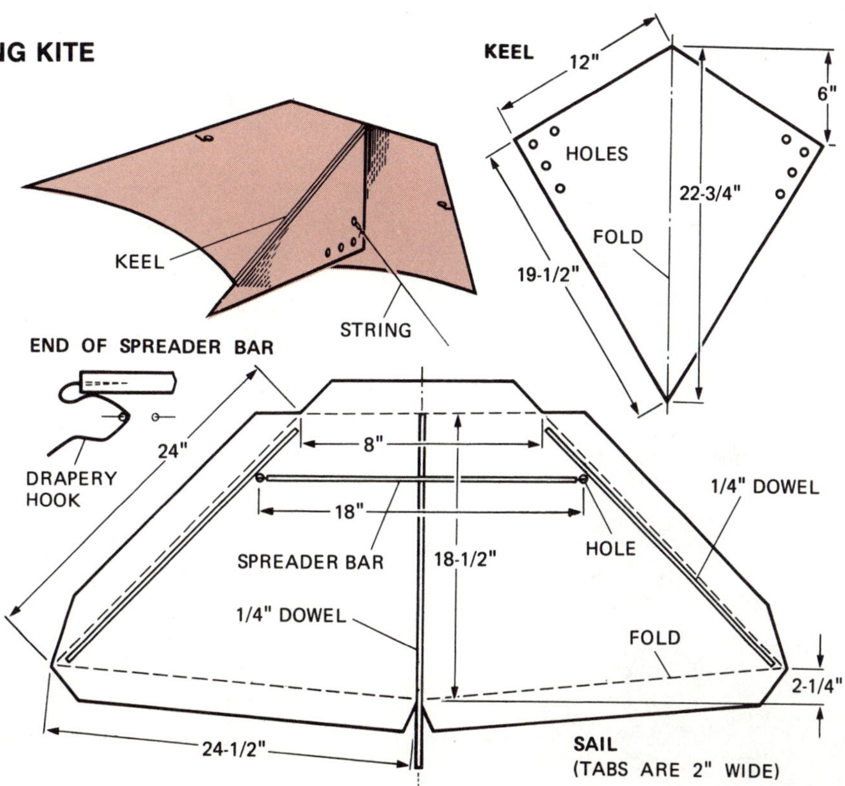

fly a kite, continued

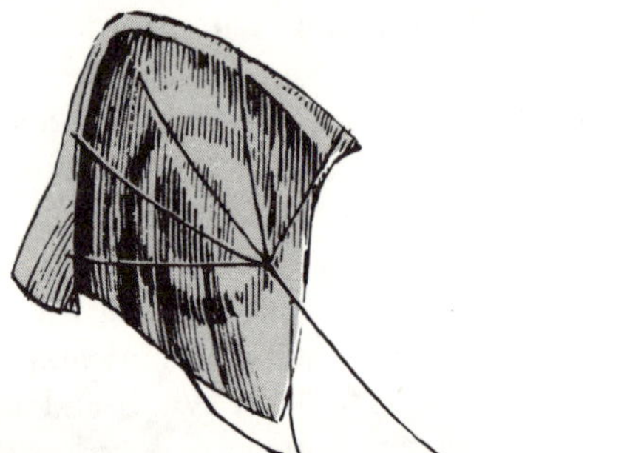

FLEXIBLE KITE

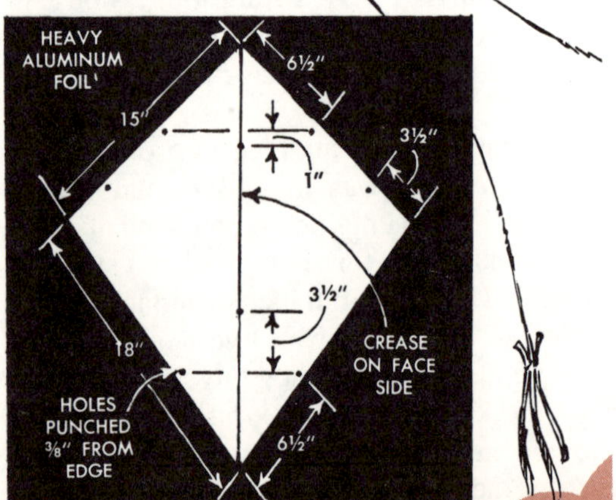

FIGHTER KITE

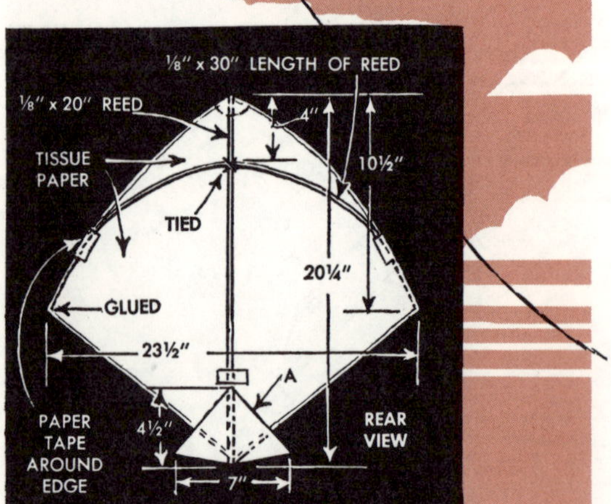

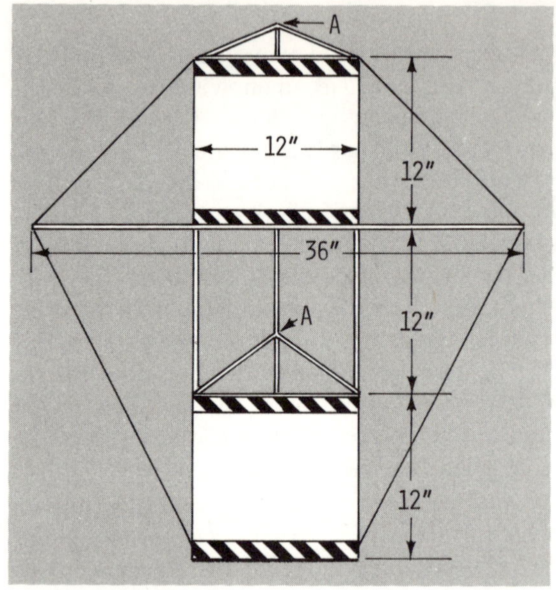

AFTER COVERING this kite's top and bottom (leaving center open), form bat-wing's outline with string and cover it separately. Attach the bridle at point A. The diagram below shows how the rudder version is controlled by lines from the ground.

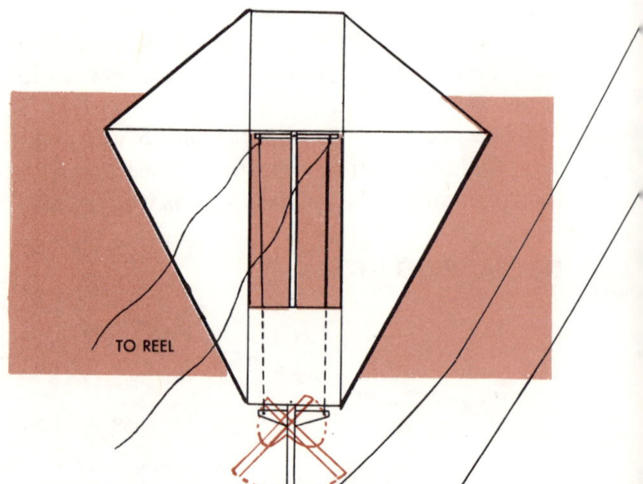

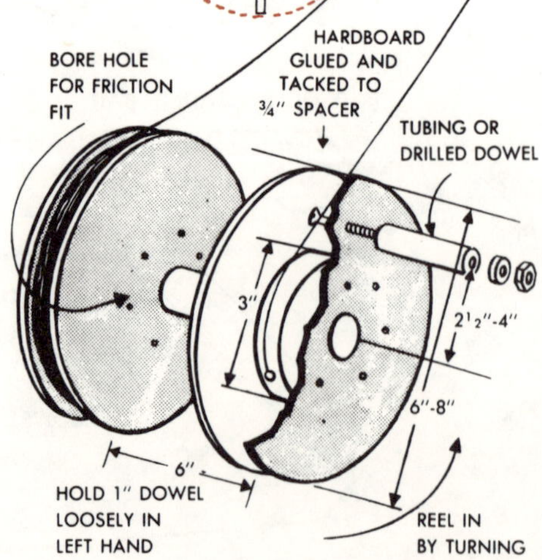

Keep in mind when making a kite tail that it is not the weight of the tail which does the work, but the bulk and the surface which provide balance. The stronger the wind, the more tail needed. Some kites, such as the box variety, don't need tails, but most do, particularly on very windy days.

You can make an unusual tail by folding sheets of typing paper so they are accordion-pleated. After folding, drive a staple through the folds at the center and fan out the paper at both ends. This makes what looks like a pleated bow tie. Attach this bow tie to the lowest point on your kite, using a string about 1 ft. long. Use as many bow ties as necessary to achieve balance, tying each additional bow about a foot below the last one. You'll be pleased at the way the kite looks as it flies high in the wind with a string of bow ties riding beneath.

flying your kites

Most people think that a very windy day is required for kite flying. Actually, kites fly best in a light, steady breeze of from 8 to 15 mph. Have a helper stand downwind, from 50 to 100 feet

THIS MANEUVERABLE VERSION of the triangular box kite is by Roy L. Clough, Jr. The frame dimensions differ from those given for the conventional type, but the main feature of the maneuverable design is the fish-tail rudder at the rear.

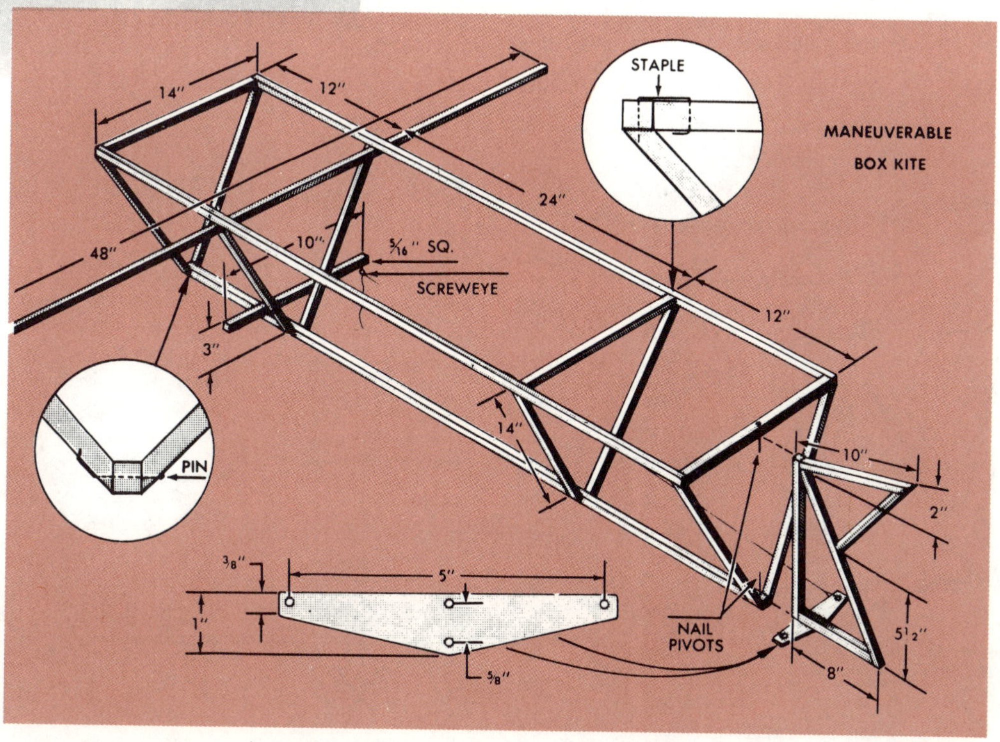

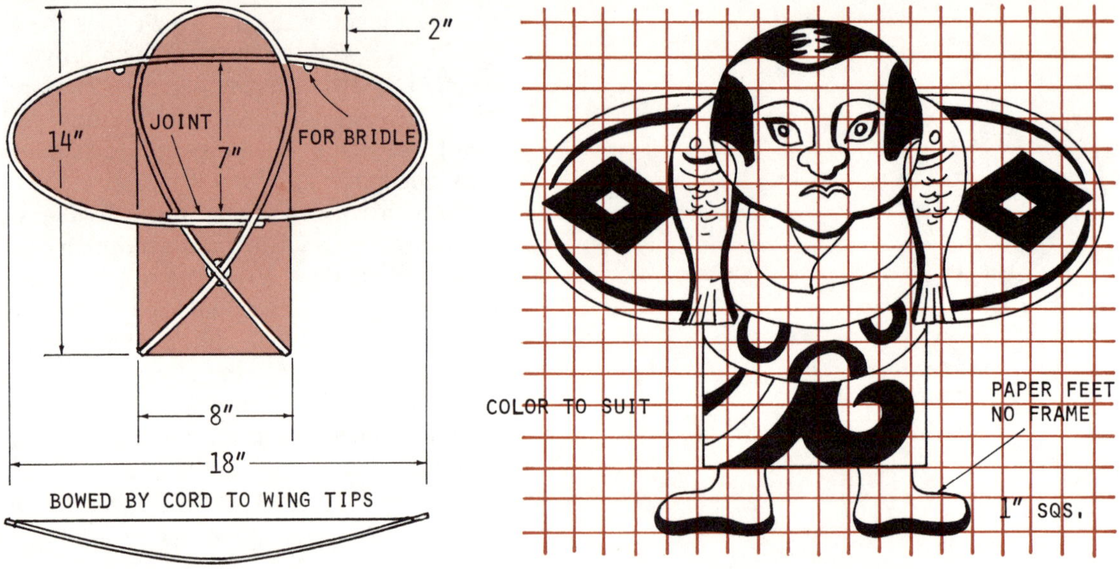

NIKKO KITE

from you. He should raise the kite above his head until he feels it being lifted by the wind and then lightly toss it straight up. At the same time, you should pull *lightly* on the string.

The kite should begin to climb steadily, and as it climbs, you should pay out string at a rate that allows it to keep climbing. If you pay it out too fast, the kite may stagger in the air and fall. To recover control when this happens, pull in the excess string until the kite starts to climb again, and then begin paying out once more—but at a slower rate.

A well-balanced kite should climb with no problems in any light breeze; if your kite doesn't, you can assume that it is too heavy for its surface area, so it can't develop the necessary lift.

The bridle is important in flying a kite. It is usually attached to two or more points of the frame, depending on the kite design, and the flying string is tied to it. Kites fly best when the

THIS HIGH SAILER is a triangular box with wings which are bowed to give them dihedral. Note the pattern for the covering of the top of the kite. Use a lightweight cloth such as cambric or organdy.

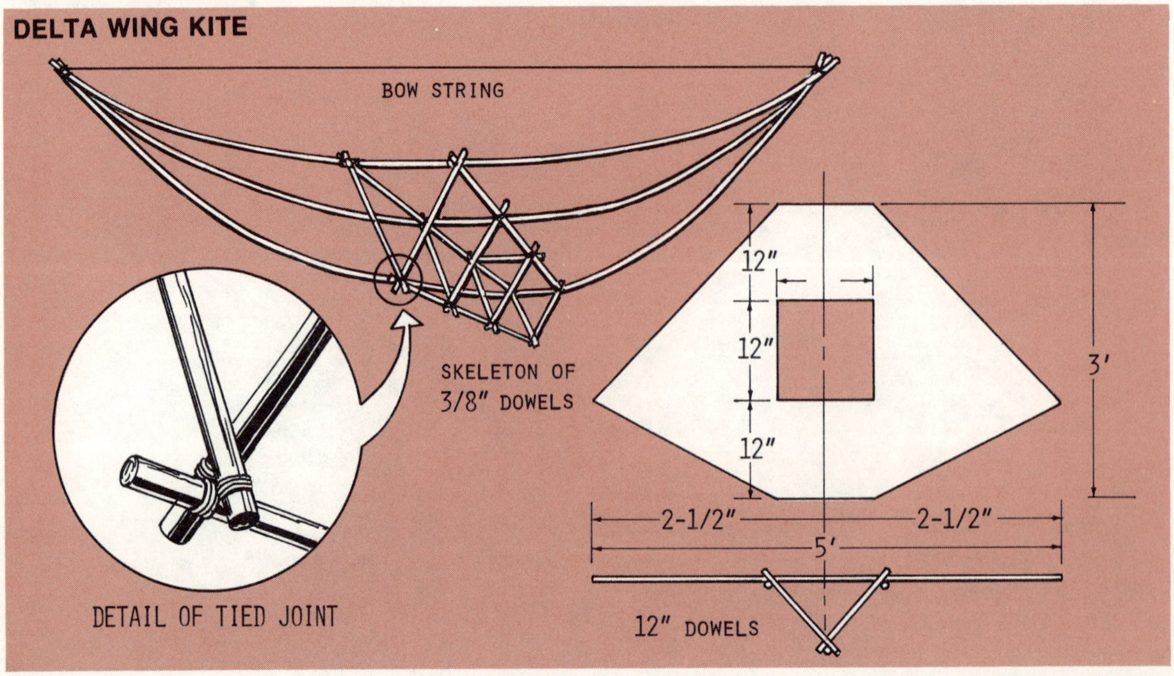

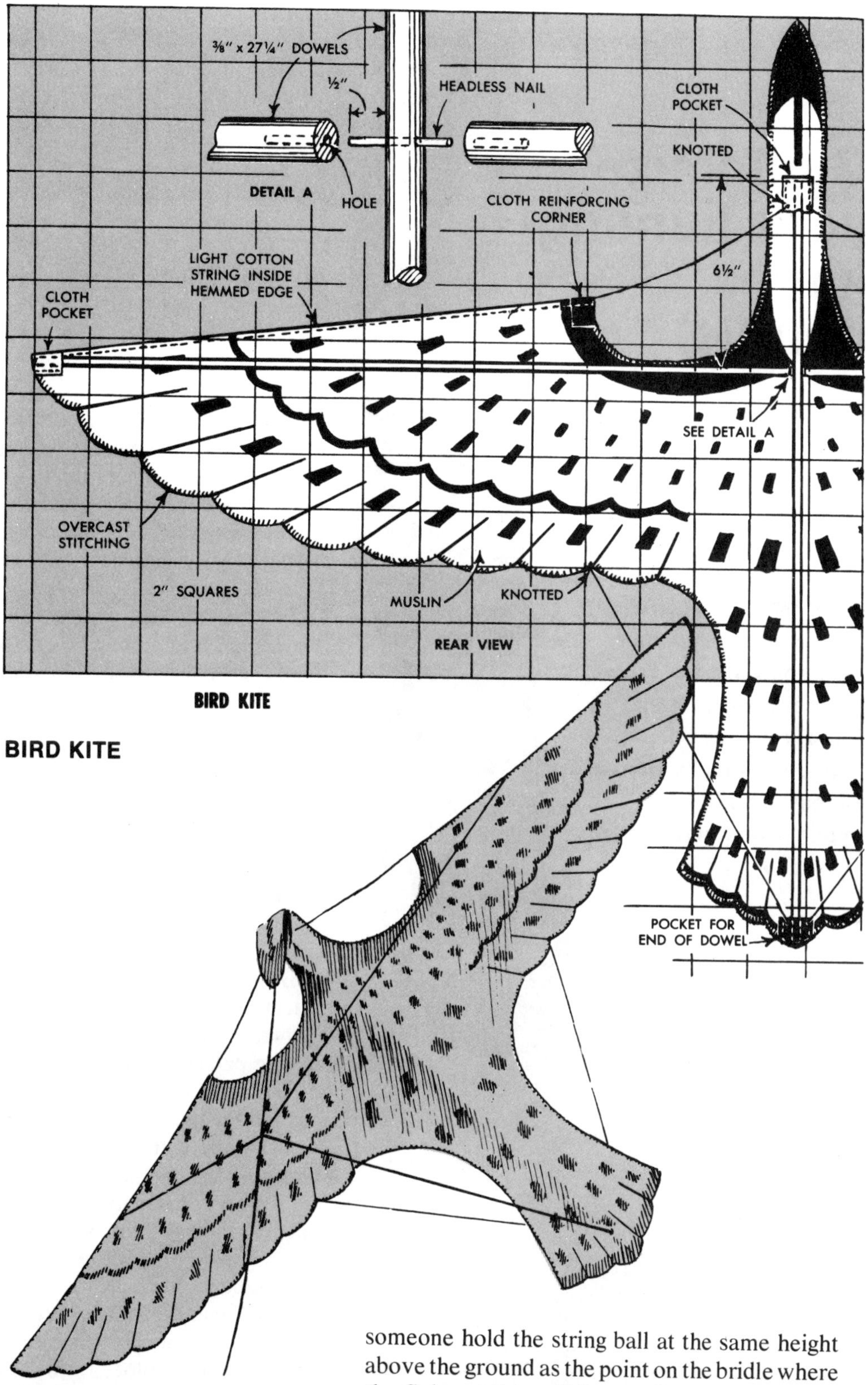

BIRD KITE

BIRD KITE

flying string is attached to the bridle so that the kite is at an angle of 30 to 40 deg. An easy way to determine the angle is to set the kite upright on the ground and then tilt it forward about 30 deg. (This is about ⅓ of the way to the ground.) Have someone hold the string ball at the same height above the ground as the point on the bridle where the flying string will be attached. Unroll some string from the ball and see that it is parallel to the ground. Tie it to the bridle with the kite still in the tilted position. Tie a tight knot so the flying string will not slide on the bridle, and the kite is ready to fly.

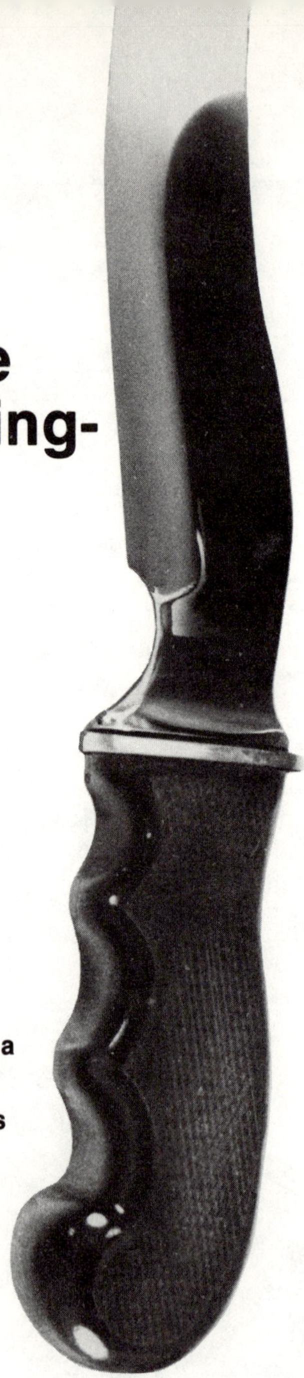

Customize your hunting-knife handle

By MONTE BURCH

There can be a great deal of satisfaction in making your own knife handle. You can order a blade from a mail-order source and make the handle from a variety of materials to fit your tastes and needs

A GOOD HUNTING KNIFE should fit your individual use and needs. And making one is not as difficult as you may think. For starters, good blades today are available from a variety of mail-order sources. A good selection, for instance, can be had from Indiana Ridge Traders, Box X-50, Ferndale, MI 48220.

Almost anything can be used as the handle, including antler, bone, ivory or leather rings. However, one of the best materials and probably the easiest to work with is a heavy mineral wood such as amaranth, vermilion, zebrawood or ebony. These woods will not rot and are heavy enough to balance with the blade. The wood depicted in this article is amaranth—an extremely hard, oily wood that takes checkering or carving and finishes like a piece of fine metal. It is available in the inch thickness required for a good knife handle from Craftsman Wood Service Co., 2727 South Mary St., Chicago, IL 60608.

Best bet is to order a knife-blade catalog and select a blade. While you're waiting for it to arrive, trace its design and make sketches of a handle pattern to fit it.

The pattern shown could be adapted to most any knife, but the "three-finger" handle best suits a knife with a forefinger hole in the blade. Grasping the handle at the rear makes the knife front-heavy, ideal for lopping off tree limbs or hacking through bone when preparing meat. By moving your fingers up one notch, you have good control for delicate skinning operations.

Grind about 1¼ inches off the end of the tang. Make a template for the handle pattern out of cardboard, cut a block from the handle wood and glue the template in position. Make sure the block is absolutely square on all sides. Using a clamp to hold it upright and square, place the block in your drill press and bore for the tang. Be sure to measure the exact length of the tang and bore just a bit deeper. Make sure the hole doesn't

SEE ALSO
Hunting . . . Map reading . . . Sharpening, tool . . . Shooting

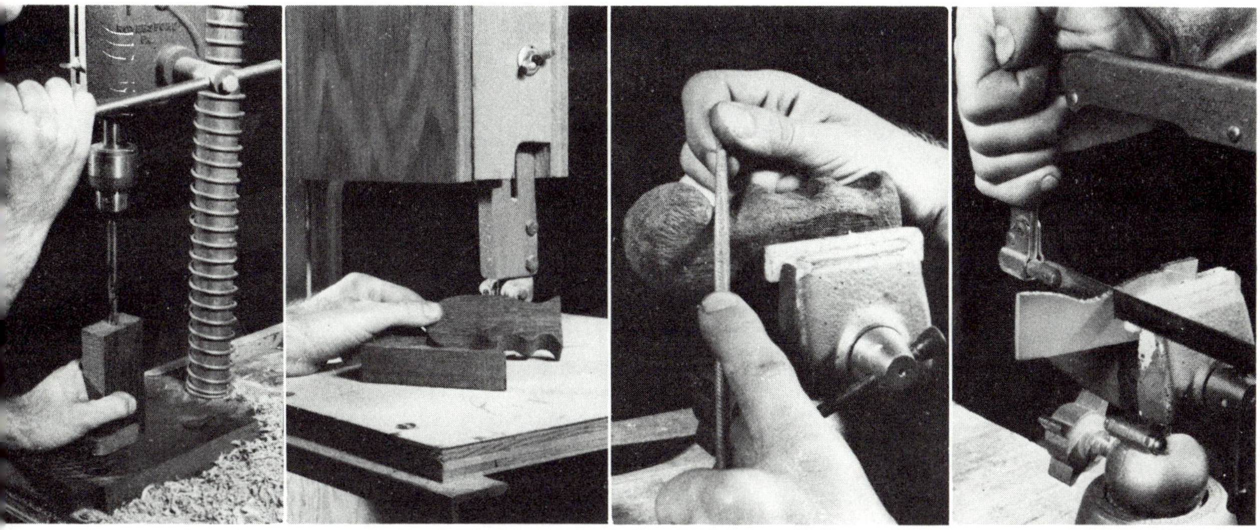

PATTERN FOR HANDLE is traced or glued on squared-hardwood block. Then (from left) block is held in clamp and tang hole bored. Handle shape is cut on a bandsaw or coping saw. Next, the handle is roughed to shape with rasps and files. Spacer guard is cut from brass stock to separate the handle from the forged metal guard.

"lean" to one side. You may have to grind the tang a bit to make it fit properly. When the handle block fits on the tang with just a little persuasion, remove it and cut out the handle.

Next make the brass guard. The one shown was purposely kept small so you could get your forefinger into the notch on the blade. It is needed to butt the handle, providing a smooth transition from handle to blade. The guard should be about ⅛-inch thick and large enough to extend around the handle at least 3/16 inch. Using a hacksaw, cut a brass square the size you wish your guard to be and bore it to fit over the tang. You may have to bore it oversize, as the tang widens at the base of the knife blade.

When you have it bored to fit over the tang and tight against the end of the blade, grind it in an oval determined by the shape of your knife handle. This is a grind-and-fit operation. Grind a bit off, place it on the tang and fit the handle until the oval is centered with blade and tang. Slide the brass guard in place. Mix a batch of epoxy

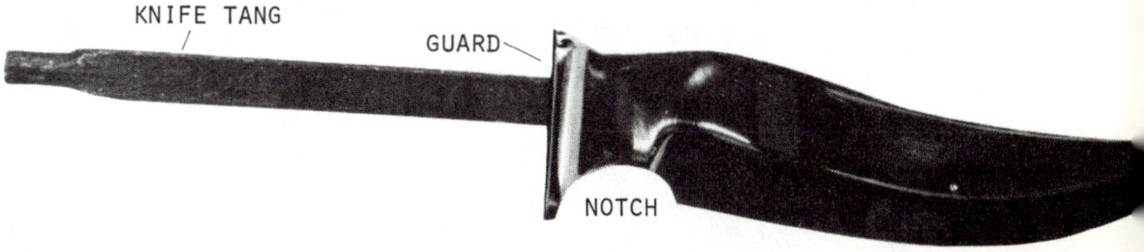

FOREFINGER NOTCH on the forged guard blade makes for excellent skinning control. The knife tang fits into the handle as outlined in the pattern on ½-inch squares below.

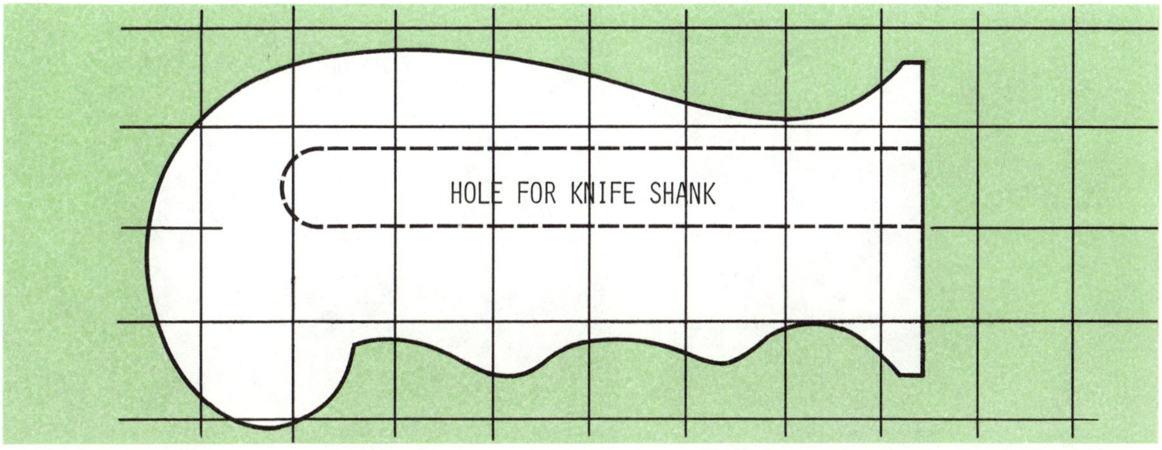

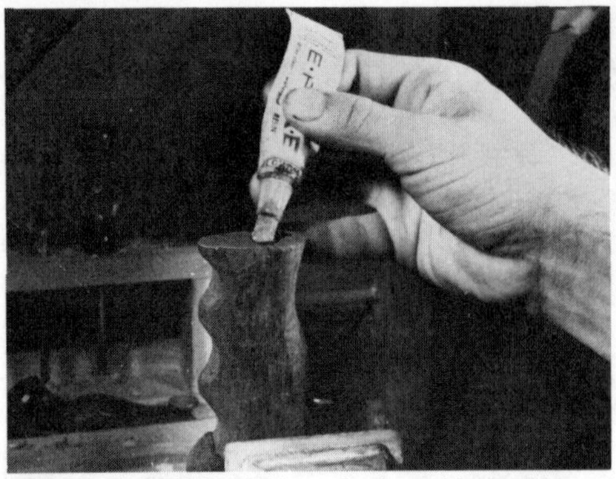

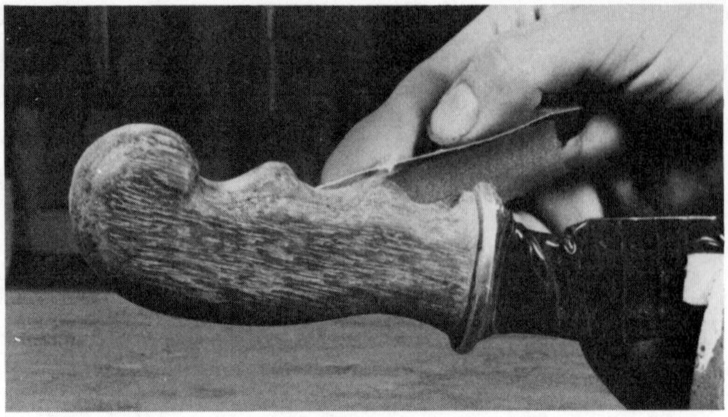

FORCE EPOXY GLUE into the bored hole. Place the brass guard over blade tang and press tang into the hole. Let it sit overnight. Next day, put taped blade in vise, sand handle and brass guard with progressively finer paper.

glue and force it into the tang hole in the handle. Then place the handle down on the tang and examine it from every angle to insure you have the brass guard positioned right and the handle square with the blade. Tap the end of the handle to seat it and let it set overnight.

Using finer grits of wet-or-dry sandpaper, finish the handle and guard. If you have a buffing wheel, polish the handle and guard to a satin sheen. Apply a good quality gunstock finish—oil or spray epoxy—and lightly polish with paste wax and a soft cloth.

You may wish to checker your handle so that it will be much easier to hold when wet or in cold weather. Do not use any checkering finer than 18 lines to the inch. It's beautiful, but won't help much on your grip. A complete set of economical checkering tools is available from Frank Mittermeier, Inc., 3577 East Tremont Ave., Bronx, NY 10465. Amaranth and other mineral woods are especially hard, so hone your checkering tools sharp before you start.

Using a scriber or nail, lay out the checkering design, scratching it lightly into the finish. Using the diamond template, lay out the first line and cut it fairly deep with the single cutter. Switch to the double cutter and score the lines in one direction. When all lines are cut in one direction, find the first line for the other direction with the template and cut it. Proceed as before and when all lines are scored, use the single-line cutter to deepen them and make the diamonds sharp and even.

When the checkering is completed, cut the outline using a fine veiner chisel. Checker the other side of the handle to match the first and with fine sandpaper, knock the sharp burrs off the edges of the diamonds. Apply finish to the checkered handle and polish and burnish it to a fine sheen.

APPLY QUALITY gunstock finish, spray epoxy or oil type. Then checker the knife handle for better grip, spray checkering with the finish and remove black electrician's tape used to protect the blade while you were working on handle.

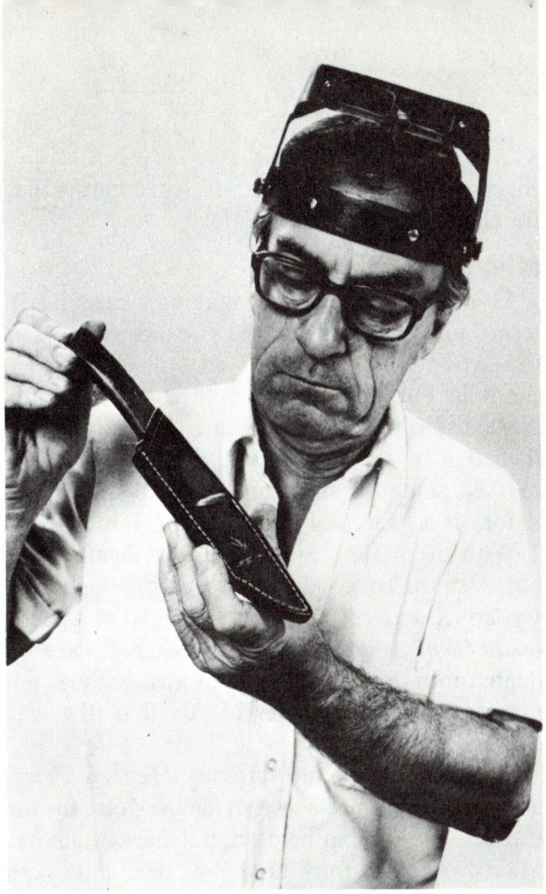

ART AND craftsmanship combine in the knives and sheaths made to order by Jack Barnett.

Customize your knife sheath

Form-fit molding, wax-treating and baking are a few tricks from a master knife-and-sheath maker. Use this technique to make a custom super sheath

By SID LATHAM

JACK BARNETT feels that a fine knife deserves the best sheath possible to protect it. He should know. This Littleton, CO, craftsman is considered by many to be one of the top knifemakers, scrimshanders and leatherworkers in the country.

a creative challenge

Many knife artisans have no interest in leather work. They would rather leave this task to someone else. Barnett finds this part of the job a creative challenge as well.

"I like taking a piece of leather and doing something completely different with it," he says. And his precise construction, artful tooling, plus special wet-forming and hot-waxing techniques result in knife-and-sheath sets that are considered collectors' items.

We asked him to explain to us exactly how he goes about making one of his beautiful custom sheaths.

Choose a good piece of ⅞-ounce vegetable-tanned leather, Jack Barnett advises. This type of leather can be easily formed to the contours of your knife, is excellent for tooling, and provides a better fit than chrome-tanned or other leathers. Because it can absorb water well, it is good to work with, but must be handled with great care. If you happen to touch it with tools or even your

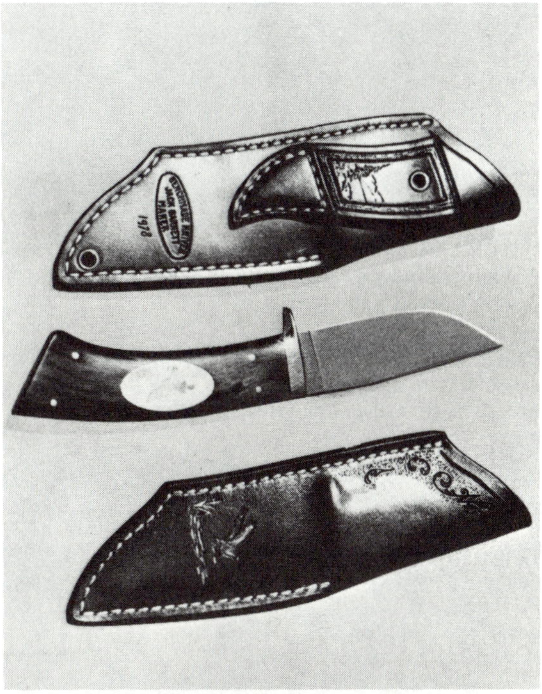

SHEATH HAS hand-tooled decorations, molded front for snug fit, grommet at bottom of back for rain drain, and hole in loop for hanging in display case.

SEE ALSO
Hunting . . . Map reading . . . Shooting . . . Shotguns

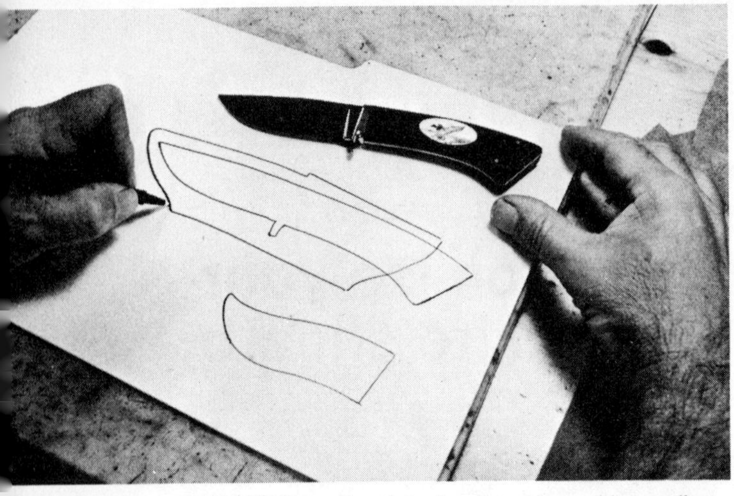

PATTERN for sheath is developed by making outline sketch around knife. Outer edge of sheath is drawn around it. Belt loop must be drawn first, too.

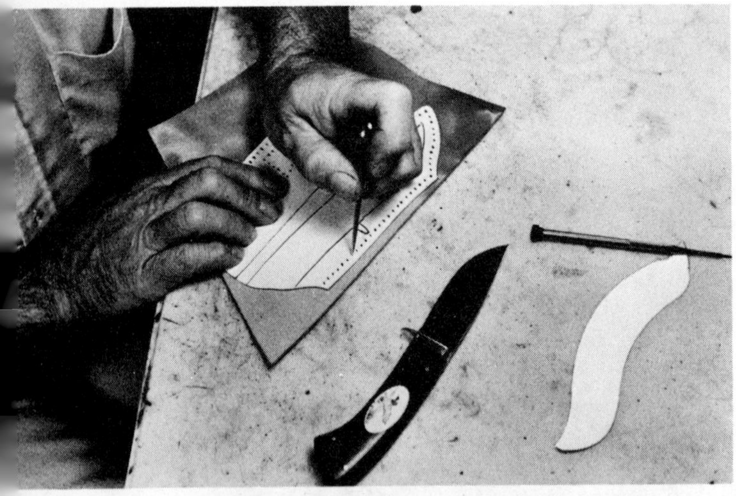

STITCH LINE is first scribed inside outer edge of sheath pattern with dividers. Stitch-hole placements may be marked with fork.

SPACER WELT is then cut and fitted into sheath. It will hold knife in place, keep blade away from threads. Use a small drill for stitch holes.

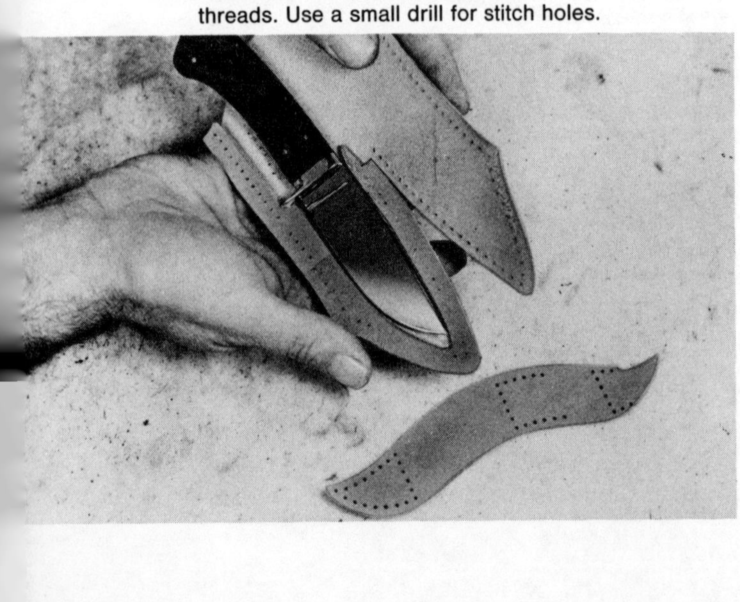

fingers while it is wet, you will leave marks that are almost impossible to remove.

pattern first

Proper fit is the result of making a careful pattern. Take your time and be as exact as possible.

Start by laying the knife on a piece of paper. Draw its outline, plus the outline of the sheath. Next, use dividers to mark a stitch line around the edge of the pattern. Stitch holes are then marked along the stitch line, about ⅛ inch apart. A fork is a good tool to use for this job.

With the pattern as a guide, the sheath is cut out. A sharp knife works fine, but you might also try an X-acto blade, heavy shears or special leather-worker's head knife. Stitch holes are indented into the leather with an awl, but it is not necessary for these holes to go all of the way through at this point.

Barnett prefers hand stitching. He uses a Dremel tool or drill press to provide the holes for the stitches. An awl can be used, but Barnett advises against trying to force an awl or needle through the three layers of leather around the edge. Instead, a small bit slightly larger than the needle should be used. This will make a neat row of stitch holes, and final stitching will be considerably easier.

Edges are now rounded, beveled and trimmed. Fine sandpaper, of 400 to 600 grit, can be used. Rub gently with this to actually burnish the edges down and smooth them off.

Now is also the time to do any decorative tooling, stamping or carving. Artwork and embossing at this stage can add real beauty and value to your knife sheath if done correctly and carefully. For these steps, the leather is dampened, then left until it feels almost dry. Be careful not to spill any paint or scratch the leather as these marks won't be removable.

stitching

Barnett's favorite is a saddle stitch. He uses nylon thread and a needle on each side.

First, the top of the belt loop is sewn to the back of the sheath. Then a hole is carefully punched and lined with a brass grommet. This hole allows for hanging for display in a gun-and-knife cabinet.

Another grommeted hole also goes in the back bottom of the sheath. This second hole serves as a drain hole, in case a hunter or fisherman wearing it should be caught in a downpour or fall in a stream.

The belt loop is grooved slightly at the fold. It is best to shave it down a bit with a skiving knife and stitch it down at the bottom to make a firm, tight loop.

An important part of the sheath is known as a welt. Its function is to keep the top and bottom of the sheath apart and prevent the blade from cutting through the threads. Once the welt is cut, the parts are assembled without any stitching to test the fit.

With holes drilled for stitches and all of the parts stained, they are now laced together. Use tight saddle stitches, as well as a few back stitches to secure them in place. Then a flame should be held to the trimmed end of each nylon thread. This will help prevent it from fraying, and further lock it in.

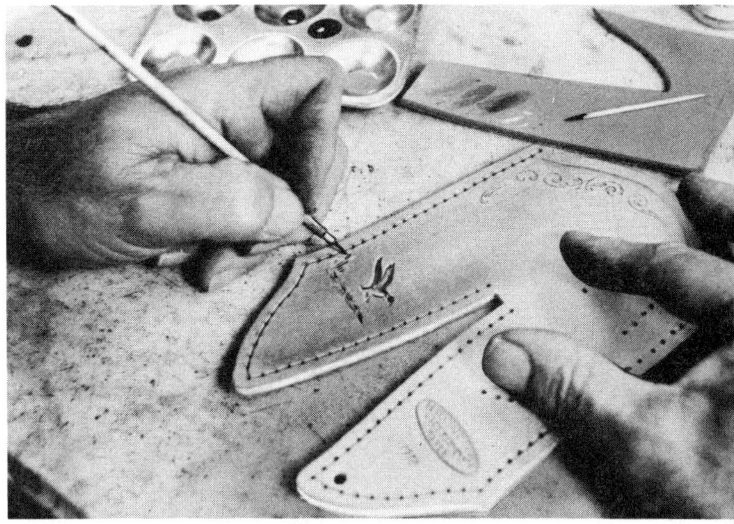

DECORATIVE sketches and tooling, typical of Barnett's craftsmanship, are added. Paint, even fingernail scratches, cannot be removed from leather.

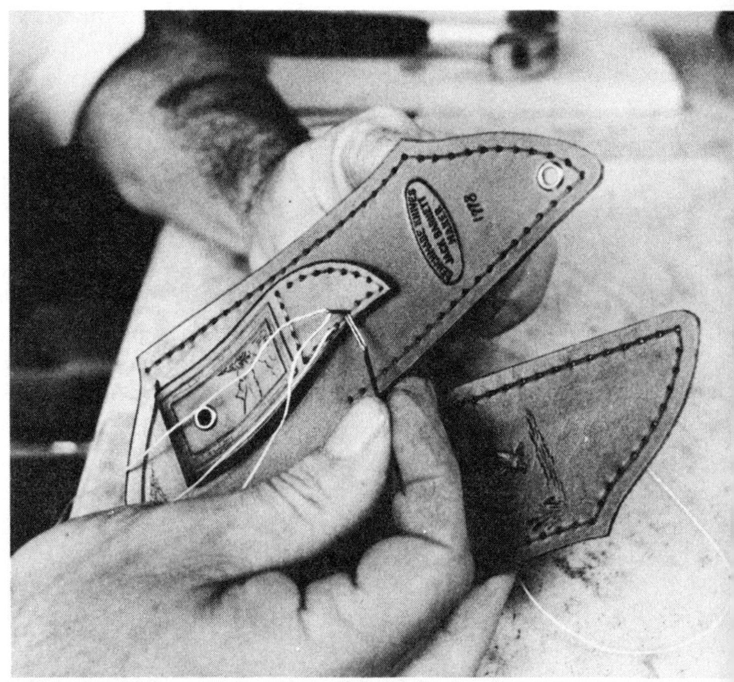

SADDLE stitching, with needles pushed in from opposite sides, secures belt loop to sheath. Top and bottom, with welt, are then stitched together.

forming and baking

Next come more Barnett customizing steps that can give your sheath a professional appearance. Start by trimming all of the rough edges with a very sharp knife. Next slightly dampen these edges and rub them with fine sandpaper. Final polishing is done with a piece of bone, ivory, Micarta or hardwood.

Wet-forming is done to obtain a tight fit. To accomplish this, dampen the leather enough so that, with your fingers, you can form the sheath to the contour of the knife. Again, be especially careful to make no fingernail scratches as they may leave permanent marks. After completing this task allow the sheath to dry overnight.

A final wax process may also be desired. This will give the leather a handsome appearance and make it waterproof. To about four liquid ounces of molten paraffin, add ¾-ounce of saddle oil (a blend of lanolin and silicon). *Heat this mixture carefully, preferably over an electric hot plate, since it catches fire easily.*

Once it is hot and well mixed, carefully brush it on the inside and outside of the entire sheath. Never dip the sheath in the solution; it will absorb too much. (And never coat the mixture on leather boots; it will seal the pores and you might get frostbite).

finishing the job

After the sheath has been brush-coated, place a stick or rod in it and rotate it over a low flame on the stove. This will help melt and draw the wax right into the fibers of the leather. Then set the oven at about 170°. Place the sheath on a piece of aluminum foil and leave it in the oven for 15 minutes. When you take it out, examine it thoroughly. If you see any remaining blobs of wax on the surface or in the stitching, remove and smooth them with a toothpick.

If you have followed the procedure outlined here, you should have developed a fine sheath. Your result may not include the noted embossing and art work that have made Jack Barnett's creations famous, but there is no doubt you'll take pride in your own customized sheath that is a perfect fit for your favorite knife.

Knots everyone should know

You tie your shoes daily, but how many other knots do you know? Here are several that should be right at your fingertips—for tying anything from rope to straps to wire

By W. CLYDE LAMMEY

ROPE, TWINE or cord is of little practical use unless you knot it to something, around something, or tie it to itself. Knots usually are associated with rope or twine, but a good many other materials can be knotted, such as leather straps or thongs, fishline, bandages, thread, even light wire. In fact, anything can be knotted that is sufficiently flexible to be bent or looped on itself without breaking.

When tying a knot, think of rope, cord or twine as having an "end," "bight" and a "standing" part. Think of knots simply as a combination of three basic turns—the bight, loop and overhand (or underhand). Look closely at the details at the right and on the following pages and you'll see how this works out; even in the more involved knots the basic turns are there in each example.

When rope and cord is in more or less continuous use the ends should be whipped, as indicated, with fine twine or tightly wrapped thread; or, the ends may be dipped in glue. The purpose, of course, is to prevent unlaying, or raveling, of the strands. On a rope of, say, ½ in. diameter, the whipping should be laid in shellac or varnish, and should extend at least 1 in. from the end.

Most of the knots are shown loose—that is, in the process of being tied; the purpose is to show the procedure as clearly as possible. In practice, all knots must be drawn tight before being subjected to stress. Don't trust a knot until it is drawn up tightly and tested under stress.

As you will notice most knots are designed so that the parts, or crossings, will bind upon each other as the stress increases; the harder the pull the tighter the knot. In some instances the object

SEE ALSO

Boat camping . . . Camping . . . Canoes . . . Casting, fly . . . Fishing tackle . . . Fly fishing

BASIC TERMINOLOGY

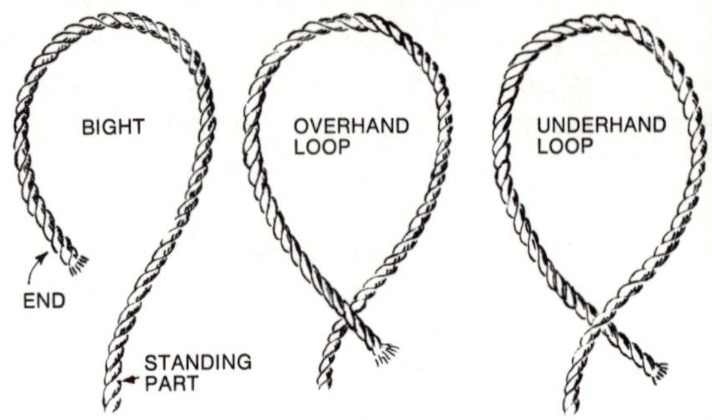

WHIPPINGS, STOPPER KNOTS

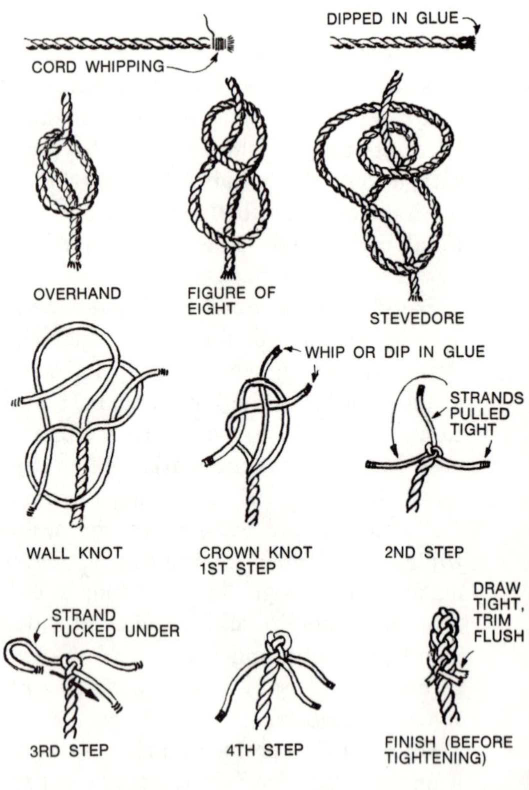

END TO END

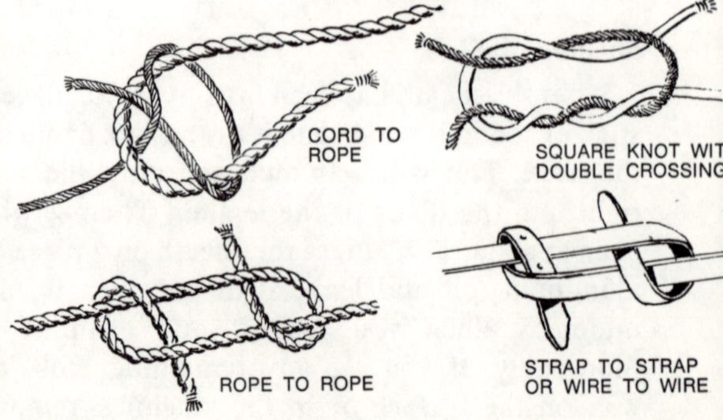

MAKING TIES TO OBJECTS

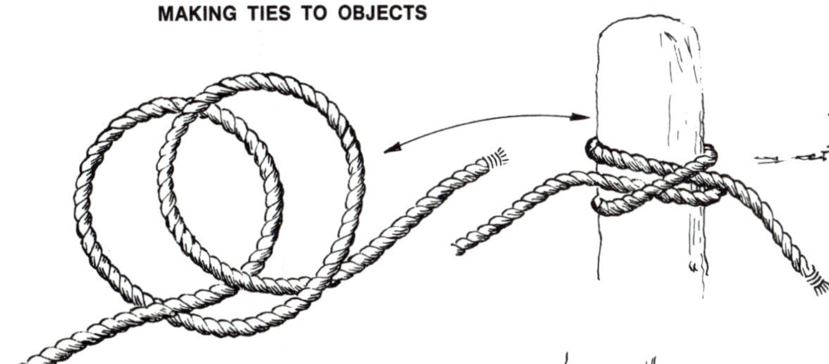

CLOVE HITCH

HALF HITCH

DOUBLE HALF HITCH

SLIPPERY HALF HITCH

SLIP KNOT

HITCHING TIE

ANCHOR BEND (FISHERMAN'S BEND)

TIMBER HITCH

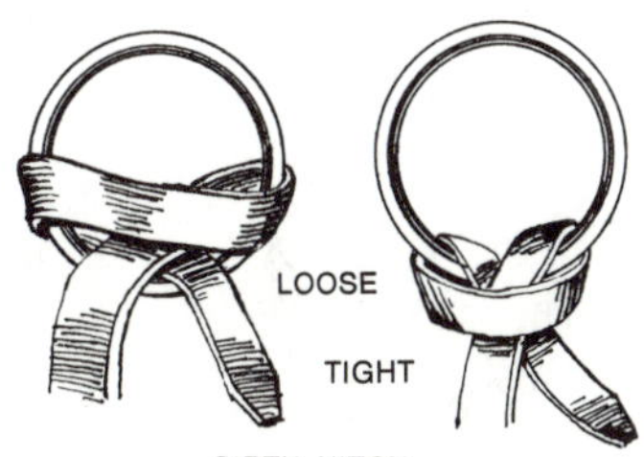

GIRTH HITCH

CORD KNOTS WITH ENDS IN SAME DIRECTION

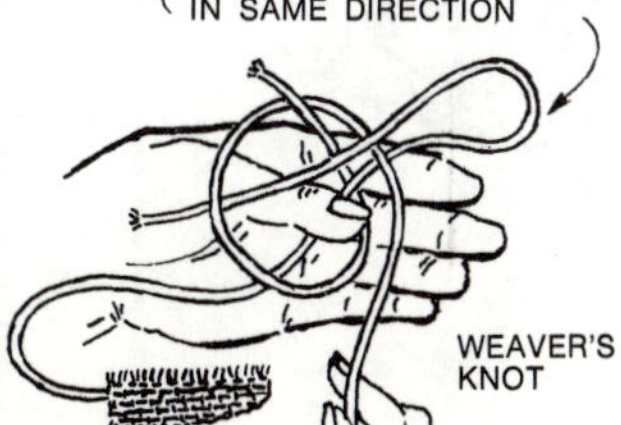

WEAVER'S KNOT

SHEET BEND

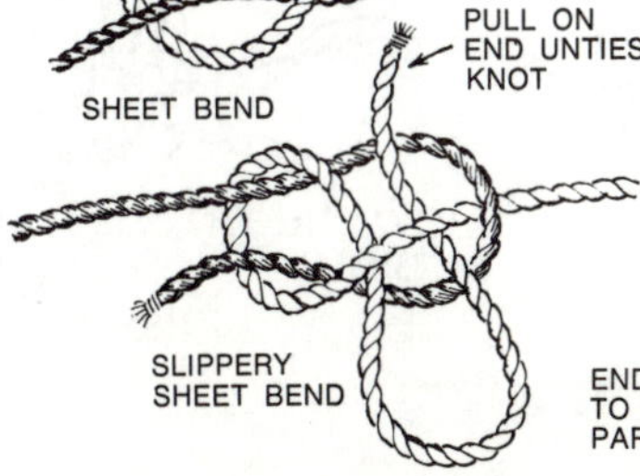

SLIPPERY SHEET BEND

DOUBLE OVERHANG (OFTEN USED BY FISHERMEN TO JOIN LEADERS)

ENDS LASHED TO STANDING PARTS

HAWSER, OR CARRICK, BEND

tied applies the tension necessary to bind the crossings. An example is the sack tie, or miller's knot.

For additional protection, and in some instances purely for ornamental purposes, the ends of a length of rope may be knotted. Typical are the wall knot and the crown knot detailed on page 1640. Note that these are more in the nature of splices than are the common knots and hitches designed for joining rope or cord to objects. The strands are separated and threaded back through the lay as indicated. In the process, the separated strands must be drawn uniformly as the threading, or tucking, proceeds. When threading is finished, the ends of the strands are trimmed flush and the whole rolled between the palms to give a uniform contour.

The single half hitch will hold, given a steady pull on the standing part but may tend to loosen when the stress varies. To assure greater reliability many users tie a "stopper" such as the figure of eight or the stevedore's knot in the end. Other users prefer the double half hitch or perhaps the anchor bend.

Notice that the so-called slippery half hitch can be "locked" by passing the free end through the eye. Otherwise it is easily untied by a pull on the free end. This knot should always be locked if subjected to varying tension. In this it is somewhat similar to the hitching tie. Notice, too, the similarity of the timber hitch, used where it is necessary to tow a log or other long, round object. In some instances the standing part is turned in the direction opposite from that shown, and a second half hitch is made around the object near the end. This tends to steady the log and make towing easier over long distances.

Splicing a rope is quite simple, but it must be done with close attention to procedure as in details A, B and C on the opposite page. When finished, the ends of the strands are trimmed and the splice rolled lightly between the palms or underfoot. The eye splice is handy where it is necessary to hold or exert a steady pull on the rope with the hand. It also is a rather showy example of rope work if done neatly.

Rope and cord that is not used very often should be coiled uniformly and stored in a dry place where temperature and humidity remain fairly constant.

KNOTTING FIXED LOOPS

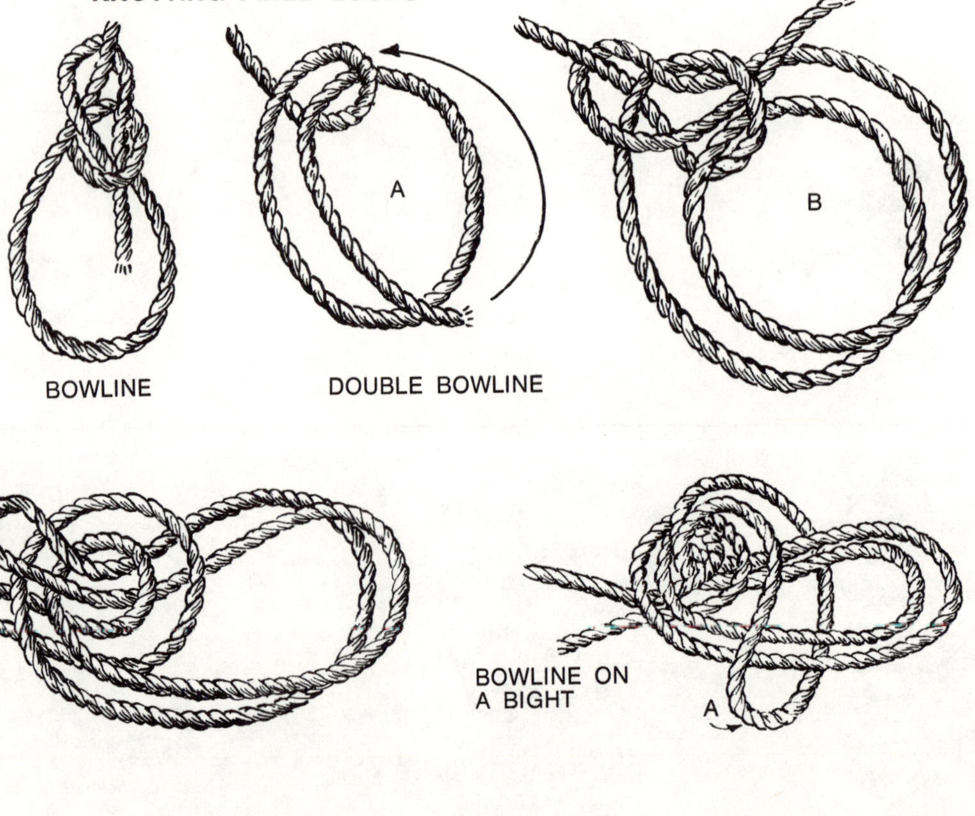

BOWLINE

DOUBLE BOWLINE

BOWLINE ON A BIGHT

FIXED LOOP

HARNESS (OR MAN-HARNESS) KNOT

ROPE SHORTENER OR SHEEPSHANK

WITH DOUBLE HALF HITCHES

PACKAGE TIES

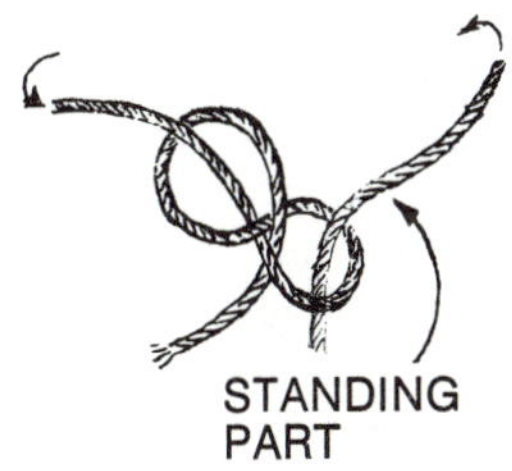

PACKER'S KNOT

SPLICING

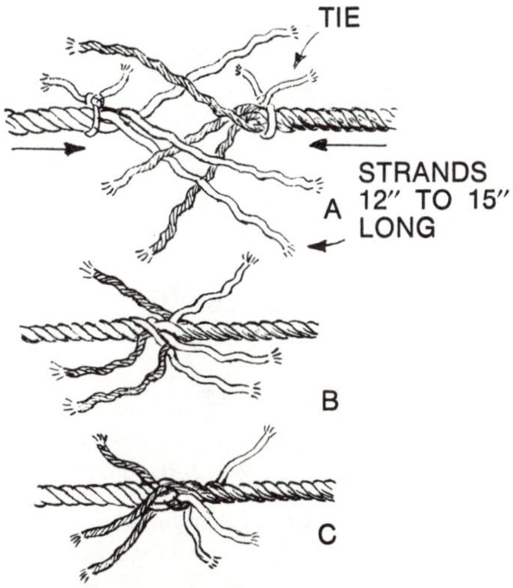

SHORT SPLICE

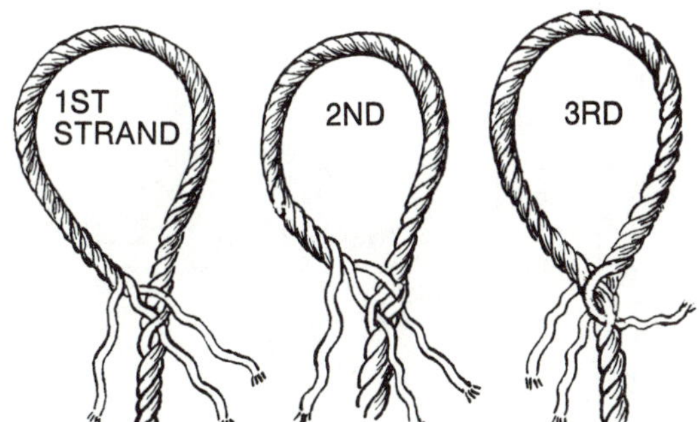

EYE SPLICE

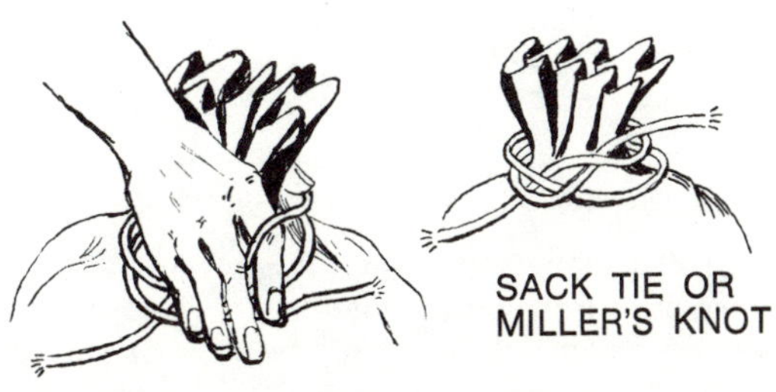

SACK TIE OR MILLER'S KNOT

AN ATTACK ON MY MELONS by pests is prevented by placing each melon atop a glass jar. Perched above ground, the melons are beyond the reach of snails, slugs and the like.—*John Krill, North Lima, OH.*

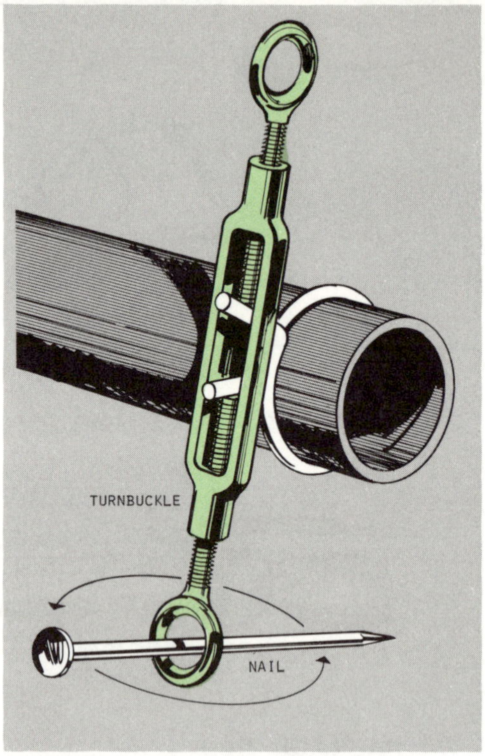

REINSTALLING HOSE CLAMPS, when servicing an appliance, is an easy one-hand operation if you use a turnbuckle as shown. When the clamp takes hold remove turnbuckle.—*John Walker, Walnut Creek, CA.*

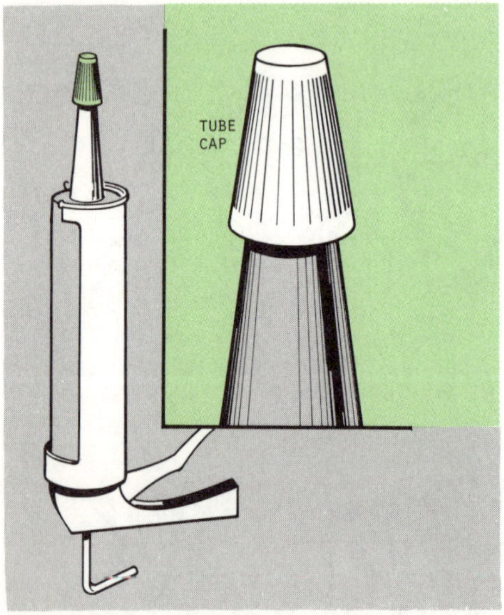

CAULKING-CARTRIDGE CAP can be improvised from toothpaste or shaving-cream tubes to keep remaining caulking usable. Simply twist on the cap tightly to keep air out.—*Victor Lamoy, Saranac Lake, NY.*

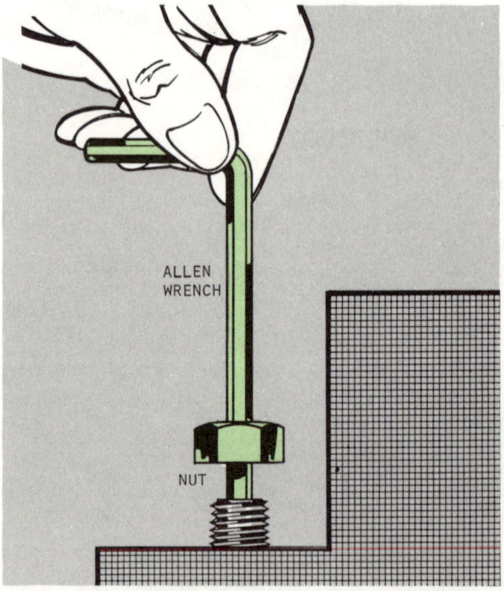

DROPPING NUTS when you're working in tight quarters, can be avoided by using an Allen hex-wrench. Simply rest wrench on the bolt when you have to turn nut on or off.—*Marvin Duchoviner, Brockton, MA.*

A long look at long ladders

By JACKSON HAND

Is that ladder a bargain? Or a shortcut to the hospital? Does it have enough rungs? Enough muscle? Will it give you the usable length you're paying for?

LADDER SHOPPERS too hungry for a bargain risk getting tripped by cheap manufacturing and merchandising methods. In their scramble to undersell each other, many dealers search out ladders they can sell cheaply. At first glance, these rigs seem as good as those costing 25 percent or so more. But let's take a closer look.

The matter of length, for example, is trickier than you might think. A 24-foot extension ladder has two 12-foot sections—the "base" and the "fly" (see drawing, p. 1646). According to the American Standards Assn. (A.S.A.), these

SEE ALSO
House additions . . . Painting, exterior . . . Painting, interior . . . Roofs . . . Scaffolding

A COMMON WAY of fastening aluminum rungs into place in the side rails makes virtually a giant rivet of each rung. The collared rung goes into the rail (left) and is then peened over as shown in the cutaway section.

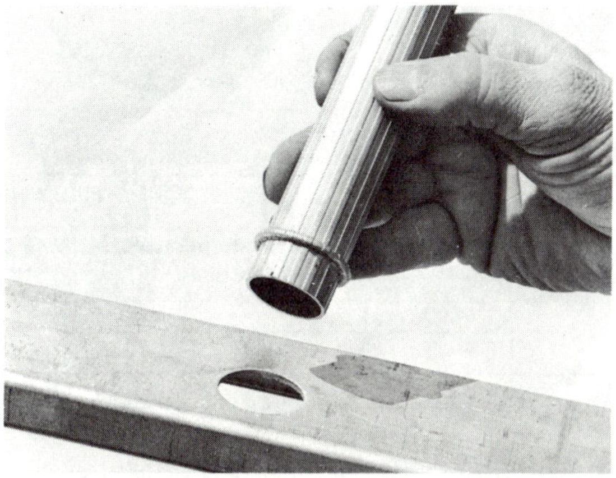

THE RUNGS of magnesium ladders are often welded in place (left). Before buying a ladder, try to twist each rung. They shouldn't budge. Photo at right shows a swivel mount for ladder feet; note the non-skid rubber "soles."

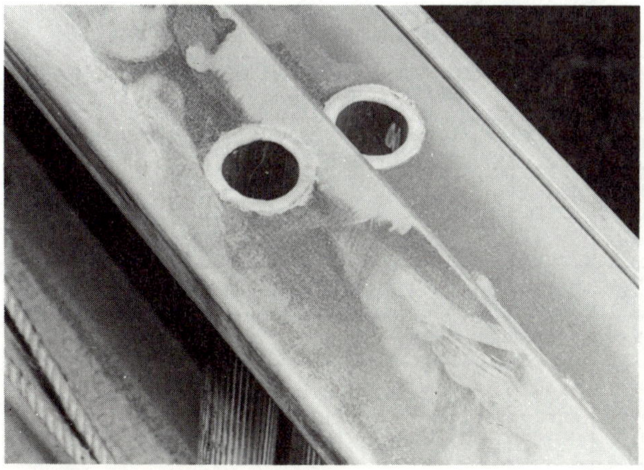

long ladder sections should overlap 3 feet, giving you 21 feet of usable length. Sometimes, especially in cheaper ladders, this overlap is greater to increase rigidity. A tip-off here would be the location of the pulley. Normally, it would be on the top or second rung of the base. On a cheap ladder, the manufacturer may put it two or three rungs away to prevent you from extending the ladder farther than is safe.

The best ladders have one rung per foot of nominal length. For instance, a 12-foot section of a 24-footer has 12 rungs, the lowest one 7 in. from the bottom, the top one 5 in. from the top. Cheaper ladders may have 11 rungs, starting up 1 ft. from the bottom and ending a ft. from the top. This is no great inconvenience, but it leaves 1 ft. of side rail at each end which is not supported by a rung. To reinforce the unsupported rails, some such ladders may have a brace beneath the bottom rung. While the braces may give added strength, check to be sure they don't prevent maximum extension by interfering with the operation of the pulley.

Experts say that the longer a ladder is, the more you should pay for it, by the foot. One ladder-component manufacturer puts it this way: "The longer the side rails, the stronger they must be. The extra strength can come from only one thing—extra metal or wood."

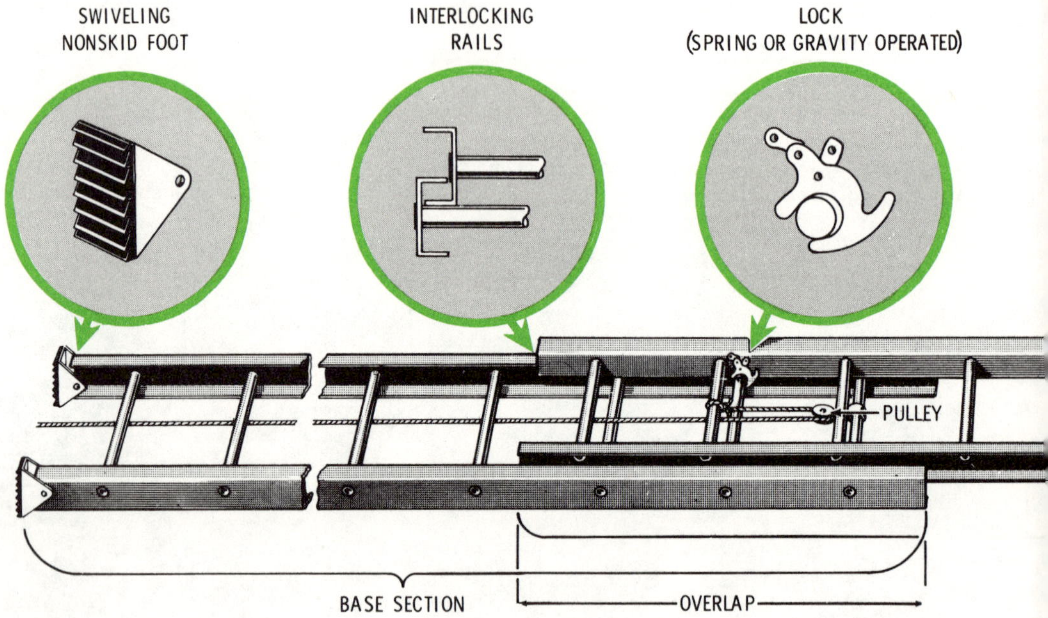

THE DRAWING ABOVE shows basic metal ladder assembly. Many will have rungs and feet shaped somewhat differently from the illustration. Some shorter models may have neither pulleys nor ropes.

THE CHART BELOW lists approximate specifications of well-made extension ladders. Height-in-place is less than nominal height because ladders are used at an angle and the sections overlap.

TYPICAL DIMENSIONS OF METAL EXTENSION LADDERS

		Utility-household grade				Industrial-commercial grade			
NOMINAL HEIGHT	ACTUAL HEIGHT IN PLACE	WIDTH	CROSS SECTION OF RAIL	SIZE OF RUNG	WEIGHT	WIDTH	CROSS SECTION OF RAIL	SIZE OF RUNG	WEIGHT
16′	12′	15″	2½″x ¾″	1³⁄₁₆″	20 lbs	18-20″	3″x 1½″	1⁵⁄₁₆″	36 lbs
20′	16′	15″	2½″x ¾″	1³⁄₁₆″	25 lbs	18-20″	3″x 1½″	1⁵⁄₁₆″	44 lbs
24′	20′	15″	2½″x ¾″	1³⁄₁₆″	30 lbs	18-20″	3″x 1½″	1⁵⁄₁₆″	52 lbs
28′	24′	15″	2½″x ¾″	1³⁄₁₆″	35 lbs	18-20″	3″x 1½″	1⁵⁄₁₆″	59 lbs
32′	28′	15″	2½″x ¾″	1³⁄₁₆″	40 lbs	18-20″	3½″x 1½″	1⁵⁄₁₆″	73 lbs
36′	32′	Not recommended				18-20″	3½″x 1½″	1⁵⁄₁₆″	82 lbs
40′	34′	Not recommended				18-20″	3½″x 1½″	1⁵⁄₁₆″	90 lbs

STRAIGHT GRAIN is important. This typical break followed the grain from edge to edge of the rail.

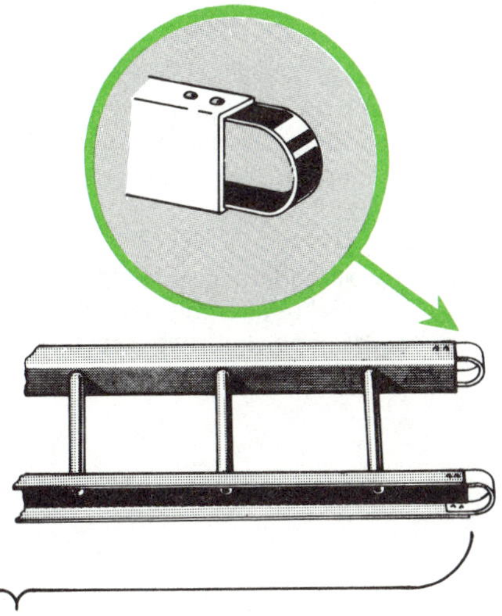

HEIGHT-TO-WEIGHT ratio is a guide to quality in stepladders and extensions. Ladders much lighter than indicated in the charts below and at left may have skimped on strength, stability and safety.

Stepladders: typical sizes and weights		
Light duty	3 feet	6 lbs
	4	9
	5	10½
	6	12
Utility	3 feet	7 lbs
	4	10
	5	11½
	6	14½
	7	18
	8	21
Industrial	4 feet	14 lbs
	5	16½
	6	20
	8	26½
	10	35
	12	42
	14	50

Of course, there is nothing to keep someone from making a cheap 32-ft. ladder using rail stock meant for a 24-footer. As long as such a ladder is never twisted, never set up on uneven ground, never overloaded and never set up at too flat an angle everything may be fine and dandy. But the limitations easily cancel out the low price.

weight per running foot

Metal ladder stock is graded by weight per running foot of rail. A good 24-footer may have rails that go .391 lbs. per foot. A higher ladder or a better 24-footer may go .440 lbs. per foot. Tops for homeowner equipment is around .550. It's hard to measure this weight on the dealer's floor, of course. All you can do is appraise the gauge of the metal by studying the ends of the rails. There are, in addition, two ways you can judge strength intelligently.

First, don't be so all-fired interested in lightness. Any good aluminum or magnesium rig is light enough. If it is too light, it may also be too weak for safety.

Second, here is an A.N.S.I. test for ladder rigidity: Extend the ladder to its permissible overlap. Place it flat on two supports spaced 6 in. from each end. Put a 2 x 4 or something similar across the ladder at midpoint and apply a 200-lb. load. The ladder must withstand the load without permanent bending or other visible weakening. Obviously, few dealers will let you perform this test on their merchandise. But it's worth a try.

Ladder experts agree that you should buy a ladder long enough to reach the highest point around your home. But, think twice about skinning up a 32- or 40-footer to reach the gable ends of a two-story house, especially if you're overweight, under-agile or inexperienced.

How wide should a ladder be? They generally run as narrow as 12 in., which is a bit skimpy. Good ones run 15 in. or more. A worthwhile industrial grade goes 20 in. Extra width, of course, provides greater stability and comfort for the user.

Incidentally, the once common practice of flaring the base section does little, if anything, for stability. It's impossible to flare the interlocking sections of a metal ladder, anyway, and the practice has even grown rare among wood-ladder makers.

Good rungs are important to quality. Wooden rungs should be pretty close to 1¼ in. in diameter. Grain should be straight and clear. Edge grain should face the top of the ladder.

Metal rungs should be closed tubes which may

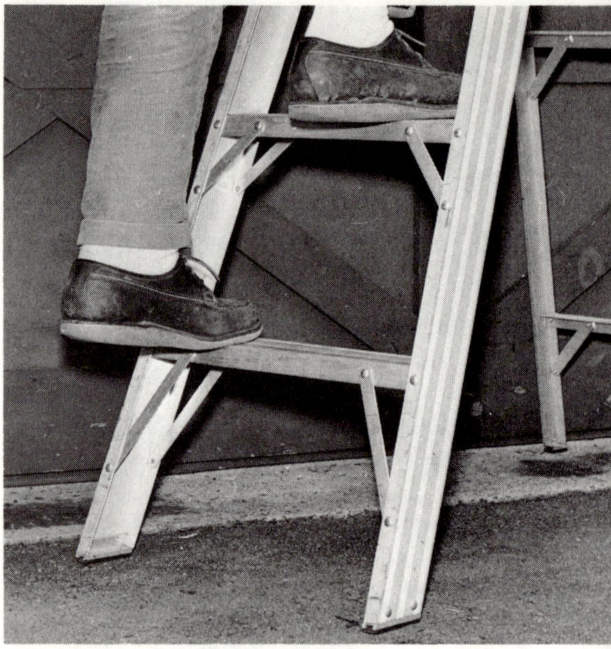

TO STIFFEN the side rails, the bottom two or three rungs of a metal stepladder, depending on its height, should have diagonal braces like these.

BOTH OF THESE wood ladders have straight grain, braced back section, and reinforcing rods under the rungs, but only one has non-skid rubber feet.

continued from previous page

be round or D-shaped, with the flat surface upward. Cheap ladders may have tubular rungs with open seams. A metal rung under 1³⁄₁₆ in. in diameter is too light. Good ladders usually have 1⁵⁄₁₆-in. rungs.

Some ladders have flat treads, riveted to the sides, or tubular rungs with flat treads welded on top. Both are more comfortable than plain rungs. The rivet construction, however, does not give the strength found in properly made round-rung ladders, and should, therefore, be reinforced with braces under several steps.

A ladder derives its basic strength from its side rails. In metal rigs, it's immaterial whether these are channel, I-beam, etc., as long as the metal is properly distributed between flanges and web. In simplest terms, the web provides the strength to keep the ladder from "bellying" when you stand on it. The flanges keep the ladder from bending sidewise. More critically, they hold the web in perfect plane, because the slightest bend or wave might let the web buckle.

Be suspicious of a side rail that measures less than ¾ x 2½ in. overall. Also, compare the dimensions with the weights in the chart mentioned previously, because a rail can be made with good dimensions, but with thin webs and flanges.

Hardware varies greatly from ladder to ladder. Feet should swivel freely, to seat firmly on the ground. In some good ladders, they fasten to toothed projections. In icy conditions, you remove the rubber-soled feet and let the teeth take over. Locks may be gravity-operated or spring-loaded. In either case, try them out. If they are tricky or temperamental, the fly section might crash down unexpectedly as you raise or lower it.

Some metal ladders have little wheels at the top to facilitate raising and lowering of the fly. Make sure such wheels are solidly made. An alternative to wheels is skids, usually in the form of an arch over the top of each rail or a curved nosing at the end of each rail. Sometimes these are covered with plastic to keep aluminum from marking the side of the house. Magnesium doesn't mark, needs no such cover.

So far, we've talked mostly about metal extension ladders. What's the story on metal vs. wood? Essentially, wood ladders cost less and weigh more, as shown by this comparison of typical "homeowner" grade rigs:

	Wood	Aluminum	Magnesium
Height	24 ft.	24 ft.	24 ft.
Weight	48 lbs.	29 lbs.	27 lbs.
Price	$26	$31	$47

check side rail quality

In judging the quality of a wooden ladder, look for side rails of straight-grained fir, hemlock, pine or spruce. Spruce is best, but getting scarce. The edge of the grain must fall on the edge of the rail. Ash or oak (especially red or scrub oak) make the best rungs. There are probably fewer bad wooden ladders on the market than bad metal ones, since there is less price competition.

Is wood safer than metal around high-voltage wires? Well, it is true that you can electrocute yourself by touching a metal ladder to a high-voltage wire, but the antidote is to avoid the wires, not the metal ladders.

Which brings us to stepladders. Because women frequently buy and use them, there has been considerable effort by manufacturers to reduce weights in this group. That should, after all, make their product more appealing to their gentle customers.

But the result is that many stepladders on the market today are virtually worthless—or even dangerous to use. Light weight can hardly be that important.

And anyway, a little lady used to muscling around —say— an 18-lb. turkey or controlling an obstreperous 40-lb. youngster needn't quail at the thought of a 12-lb. stepladder. Yet that's all a good aluminum or magnesium version usually weighs.

Actually, the vast majority of feminine around-the-house jobs can best be handled from a 24- or 27-in. step stool.

The back rails of a good metal stepladder are usually made of channel. Angle can be adequate, however, if the rails are heavy enough. In many cases, you'll find X-bracing between the rear rails, for rigidity, but some products have rungs you could stand on in a pinch. The X-brace breaks up the geometry into triangles—the strongest and most rigid form possible, so the best models have X-bracing as well as rungs.

When you're sizing up a stepladder, open it up and flip down the pail shelf. Then pull down on it. The A.N.S.I. says it should be able to handle a 50-lb. load without failing. And don't be hesitant about checking it out thoroughly; if the retailer isn't confident enough of his merchandise to let you test it, you're better off to get your ladder someplace else. After all, the few bucks you might save with a "bargain" can hardly compensate you for the pain and financial cost of injuries from a ladder that can't handle the job.

The ladder's overall dimensions indicate a lot about its stability. Further, they can help you recognize the product of a manufacturer that has tried to cut corners a bit here and there.

start with the profile

Start out with a look at the ladder's profile. Unless it was especially designed for working unusually close to a wall (a technique that demands special care and is usually better left to professionals), it should follow a minimum spread proportion: The front and back should spread about 5½ in. farther apart for each foot of height. Thus the rear feet should be nearly 36 in. from the front ones for a 6-ft. ladder. The proportion should be even greater for short ladders, to insure enough stability.

Now take a head-on look. The ladder should be at least 1 ft. wide at the top, and each side should spread away from vertical at the rate of an inch per foot. Thus, a 6-footer will spread to around 24 in. at the base. Again, the degree of splay is greater for short ladders.

Finally, a word about a few special-purpose stepladders. At least one—the platform type—is often more comfortable than the standard variety. It has a platform near the top for you to stand on. Such ladders are classified by height. A "No. 8," for example, will be around 8 ft. high, with the platform about 6 ft. from the ground when in use.

The double-front, or trestle, ladder has two fronts instead of a front and back, permitting two people to stand on it simultaneously. Such models are usually strong and stable, and prove handy for such jobs as applying gypsum board to a ceiling.

As you can imagine, there aren't many instances when you'll need this extra versatility. Since there is little call for a double-front ladder in the home handyman market, these are usually available only in commercial or industrial grades. The extra convenience is rather costly.

How to work from ladders

PROFESSIONAL LADDER-USERS will tell you, "If you don't know how to use a ladder wisely, you should stay on the ground." That advice is correct. Ladder accidents can be broken down into three groups:

- A ladder should have been replaced.
- The wrong kind of ladder for the job is used.
- A safe ladder is used improperly.

On these pages, you'll find all the know-how you need to avoid these common errors. And, for extra safety, *always* inspect a ladder before each use.

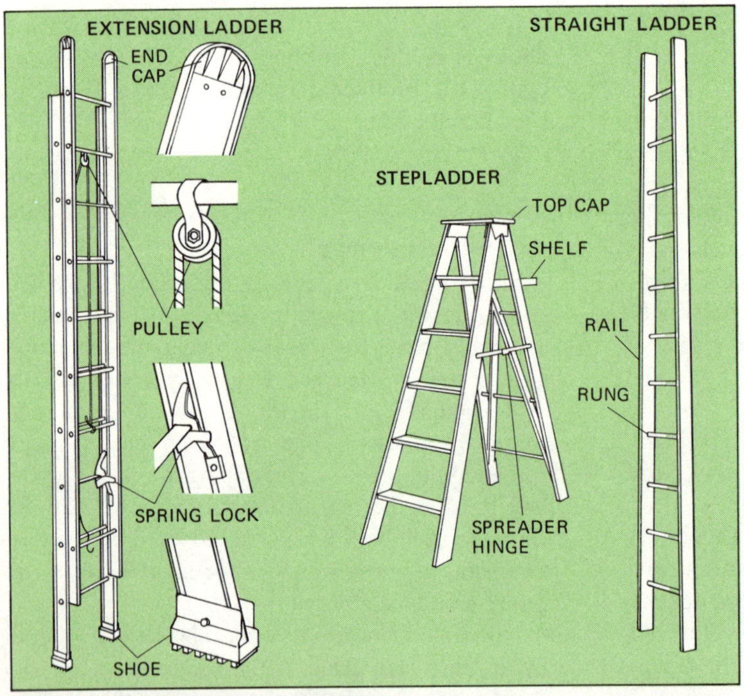

TYPICAL HOUSEHOLD LADDERS
Typical household stepladders come in 4, 5, 6 and 7-ft. heights. Taller ladders available are used mostly by pros. Costs range from about $20 to $30 for wood, with aluminum ladders slightly higher. Single ladder is adequate if you own a ranch home, but for higher altitudes you'll need an extension ladder. These are available in wood, aluminum and (most costly) magnesium.

STEPLADDER SAFETY
Never stand on top cap (step) or tool shelf. If your shins rest against a tread, you have better balance and are working safely. Other tips: Always be sure that spreader hinges are fully locked, and, if you're working indoors on a dropcloth, smooth out the wrinkles before placing ladder.

BE SURE LADDERS ARE LEVEL
Always "try" ladder on its first or second rung with a slight jump or bounce before climbing. This lets you know if the ladder is squarely planted or ground is too soggy. If either condition exists, use a board or ¾-in. plywood under one or both legs.

SEE ALSO
House additions . . . Painting, exterior . . . Painting, interior . . . Roofs . . . Scaffolding

CARRYING AND ERECTING AN EXTENSION LADDER

To raise ladder, brace its foot against base of the house. Standing at opposite end, slowly walk toward base, transferring your hands from rung to rung as you go. (To lower ladder, reverse procedure). To move ladder a short distance, carry it vertically after lowering top portion to maintain better control. If you're using an aluminum ladder, watch out for overhead power lines.

POSITIONING AND CLIMBING A LADDER

An extension ladder must be placed the correct distance from the wall it rests against. If the foot is too far out (sketch, top right), the base will slide away as you move your weight up the rungs; if too close, the ladder may tip backward or slide laterally on the wall. Overlap on an extension ladder is important, too; figure at least 3 ft. overlap for a 36-footer, 4 ft. for ladders up to 48 ft. and 5 ft. for longies up to 60 ft.

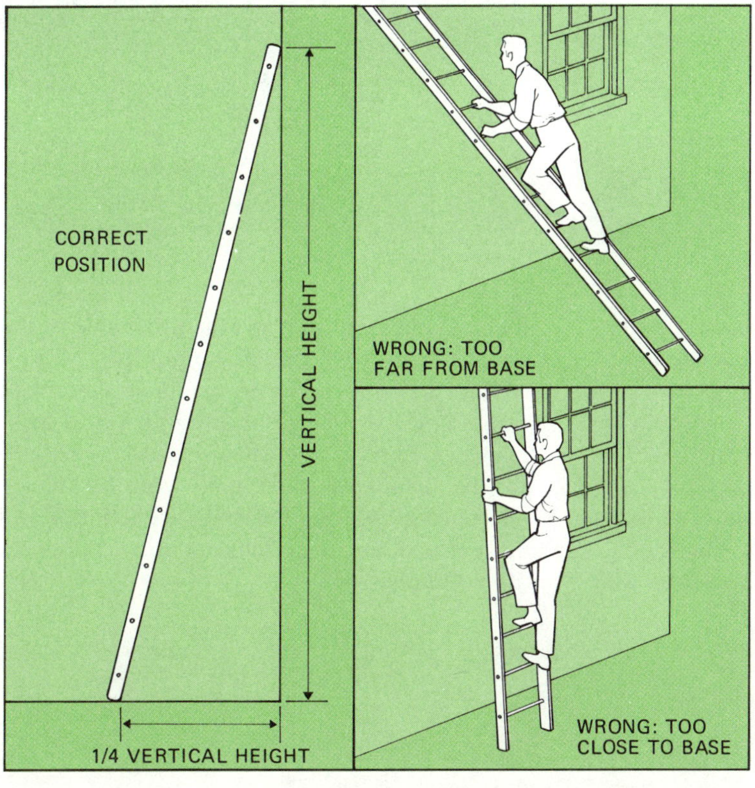

DON'T OVERREACH

Wrong way to work is shown in top drawing; this is uncomfortable and unsafe because user's weight is unevenly distributed, causing overload at one point. Right way to work is shown directly above. Set ladder where object to be painted (or worked) can be reached handily. Don't ever lean out far to one side of the ladder.

The fine art of layering wood

Laminating is the process of combining two or more woods into a project. By using this method, everyday objects can take on a striking new look as you can see in the six handsome projects shown on these pages

By PENELOPE ANGELL

■ COMBINING TWO or more woods into laminations can produce surprising patterns and color blendings. Laminating also offers a chance to experiment with small amounts of exotic woods that would ordinarily be too expensive.

To prepare the laminate, glue the wood pieces together with a thin, even coat of liquid hide, epoxy resin or other wood glue. Clamp the wood tightly with bar or pipe clamps to form a "blank." Place scrap wood on either side of the blank to protect it from clamp marks.

After the glue has cured, plane the blank smooth and saw, carve or lathe-turn it to form the object. Sand it smooth with coarse, medium and fine sandpaper, then apply your finish.

Be sure all mating surfaces are smooth and totally free of imperfections and dust. Purchase dressed lumber.

HERE THE AUTHOR is using a wood rasp to shape the laminated salad scoops.

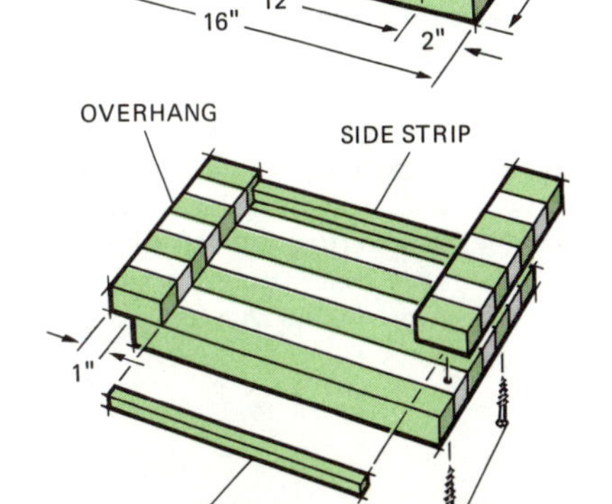

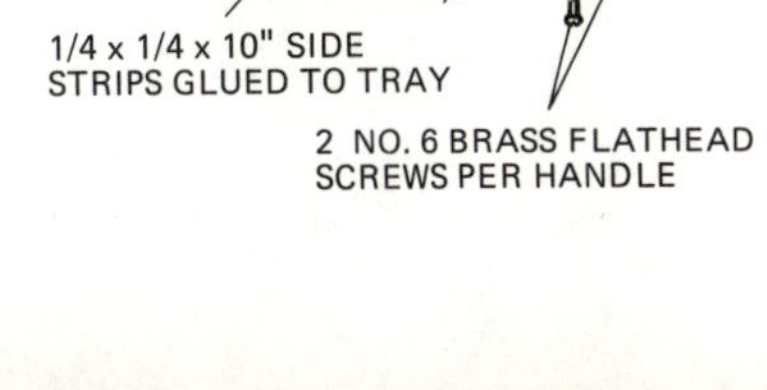

1. Fancy tray

The handles of this poplar and pine tray are cut from the ends of the tray blank to give a continuous pattern effect. The sides are strips of poplar.

Materials: 4 pieces of poplar and 3 pieces of pine, each 16 x ⅞ x 1 in.; 2 strips of poplar, each 10 x ¼ x ¼ in.; glue; 4 No. 6 brass flathead screws, 1⅛ in. long; sandpaper (3 grades); vegetable oil.

Method: Prepare the laminated blank with alternating 16-in.-long pieces of wood as explained on the facing page. After the glue has dried and the wood is planed smooth, saw 2 in. off both ends of the blank for the handles. Attach the handles to the tray with screws by predrilling two holes in the underside of each handle approximately 2 in. from each side. The handles should have a 1-in. overhang. Mark screw placement 2 in. from both sides on the underside of the tray, then countersink them. Glue the poplar strips to the tray sides. Sand smooth, then finish with oil.

2. Rolling pin

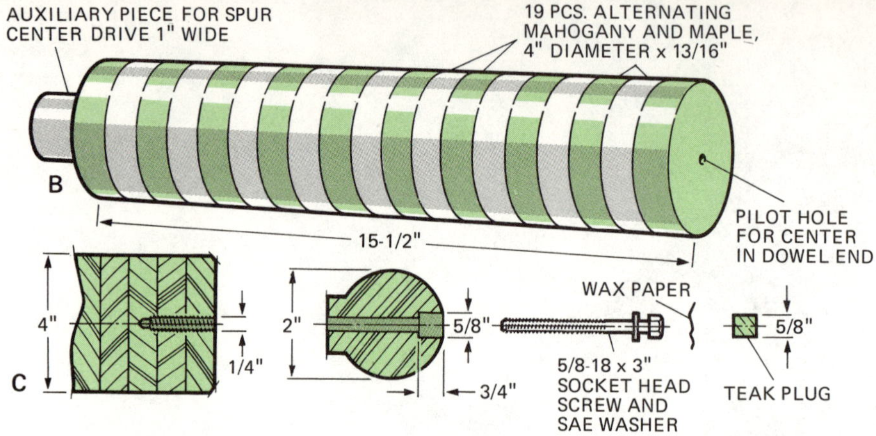

USE A dowel as an axle while you are sanding discs.

THE ROLLING pin is finally ready to be assembled.

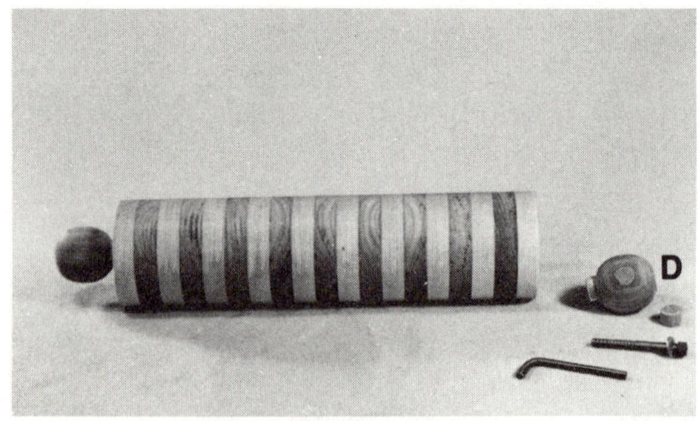

This rolling pin is made of maple and teak discs turned on a lathe.

Materials: 10 maple and 9 teak discs each 4 in. in diameter by 13/16 in. thick; 2½-in.-square teak stock about 8 in. long; glue; ¼-in.-diameter dowel; 2 sockethead screws ⅝-18 x 13 in. and SAE washers; sandpaper; wax paper; peanut oil.

Method: On a jigsaw cut out the 19 discs. Drill a ¼-in. center hole in each (A). Using a dowel as an axle, individually sand the disc edges. Cut the dowel to equal the combined thickness of the discs plus 1-in. Slide the discs onto the dowel and glue together with an auxiliary piece of wood to serve as the spur center drive (B). (You may want to enlarge the disc holes to 9/32 in.) When dry, lay out the center on the drive piece, mount and turn. Remove the auxiliary spur drive and clean the glue from the rolling pin end. Turn the teak stock to a 2-in. diameter and saw crosswise in half for the handles. Drill pilot holes through both handles and make a ⅝-in.-diameter counterbore in one end of each handle ¾ in. deep. Drill pilot hole to 11/32 in. on each handle. Cut two teak plugs ⅝ in. diameter by ¾ in. deep. Drill ¼ in. by 2 in. deep into each roller end and make a 5/16-18 coarse thread tap (C). With a cotton swab place five-minute epoxy glue into the threads in the roller ends, being careful not to get any on the outside face. Add wax paper over the screwheads or the roller may not rotate. Assemble using PVA (polyvinyl acetate) glue for the plug (D). Finish with oil.

3. Salad scoops

These salad scoops are made with five layers of reddish Padouk veneer.

Materials: 5 pieces 9x11-in. veneer 1/28-in. thick; casein glue; lead pipe about 3-in. diameter and 11 in. long (or other cylindrical form); rubber strips for clamping (from an inner tube or rubber gloves); 2 6-in. pieces of leather lacing; vegetable oil.

Method: Cut the veneer pieces, then sponge with water until pliable. Glue them together with an even coat of glue. Clamp the veneer around a pipe, securing it with the rubber bands until the veneer is dry. It will form a nearly complete cylinder (A). Remove from pipe and saw into two equal pieces (B). Trace the full-size pattern (C) on a veneer piece and saw to rough shape with a coping saw. Trace pattern on reverse side of paper as guide for second scoop to produce a right and left-hand scoop. Refine with wood rasp. Sand, then oil. Drill holes for leather hangers.

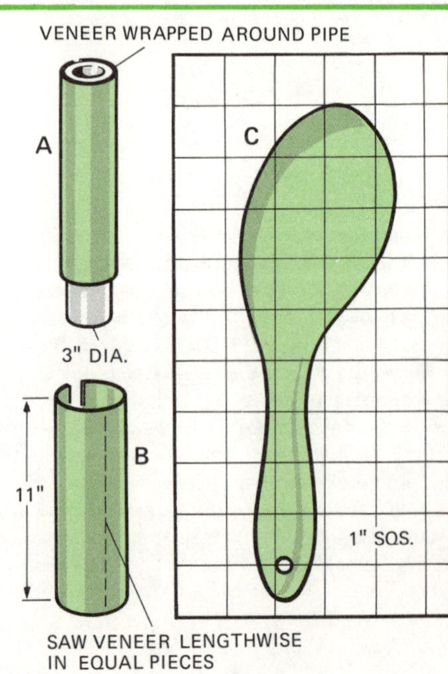

4. Breadboard

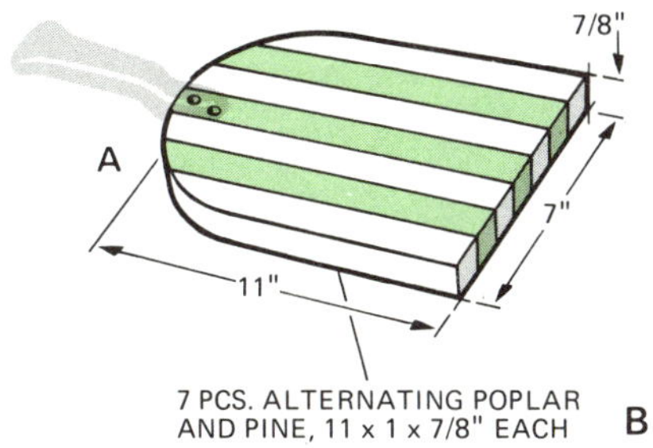

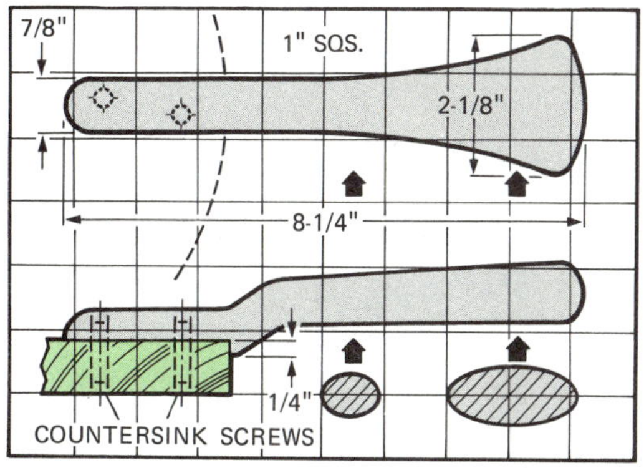

This poplar and pine breadboard has a handle carved from walnut.

Materials: 4 pieces of poplar and 3 pieces pine, each 11 x 1 x ⅞ in.; 1 piece of walnut 10 x 2½ x 2¾ in.; glue; sandpaper; 2 No. 6 brass flathead screws 1⅛ in. long; mineral oil.

Method: Prepare laminated blank with alternating wood pieces. After the glue has dried, plane smooth. Rough-shape the handle end of the board with a saw (A), and sand smooth. Rough-shape the handle with a saw (B). Round with a ½-in. wood gouge and a wood rasp. Sand smooth. Join handle and board by carefully predrilling screw holes in the underside of the handle, marking off screw placement on the underside of the board and countersinking them. Finish with oil.

5. Striped bowl

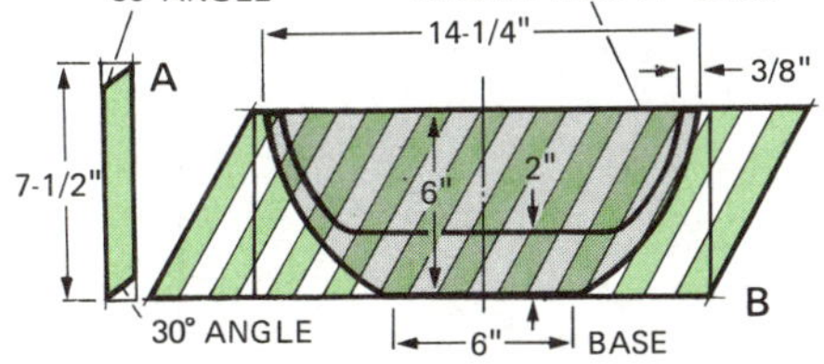

RECTANGULAR blank is bandsawed to form thick disc equal to outside diameter of bowl top (14¼ in.) plus ½ in.

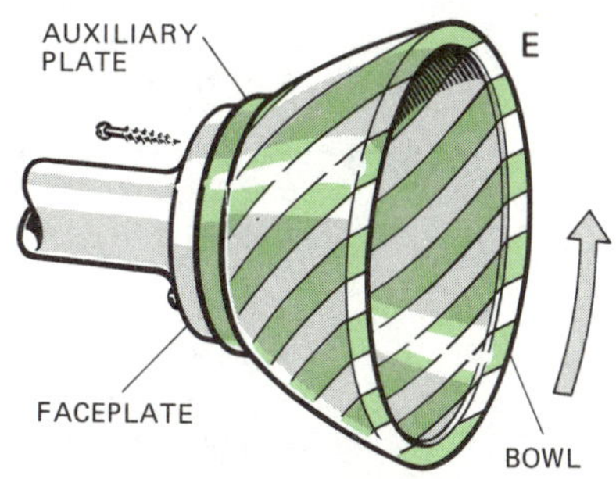

Angled mahogany and maple pieces form a striking pattern.

Materials: 10 mahogany and 9 maple pieces, each 13/16 x 7½ x 13 in.; sandpaper; glue; peanut oil.

Method: To prepare the laminated blank, mark and saw off at 30° angles the ends of the wood on the 7½-in. dimension (A). Glue alternate types of wood together and clamp. The laminated blank will not have vertical sides (B). Saw off the slanted sides to form a rectangle (C). Locate the center of the blank. Mark off both center auxiliary faceplate circle and top outside bowl diameter (14¼ in.) plus ½ in. on the blank. Use a bandsaw to form a thick disc the diameter of the bowl top plus ½ in. (D). Attach auxiliary plate to faceplate and screw to bowl. Mount on lathe and turn the outside of the bowl. Reverse and turn inside of bowl (E). Sand, then oil.

6. Duck

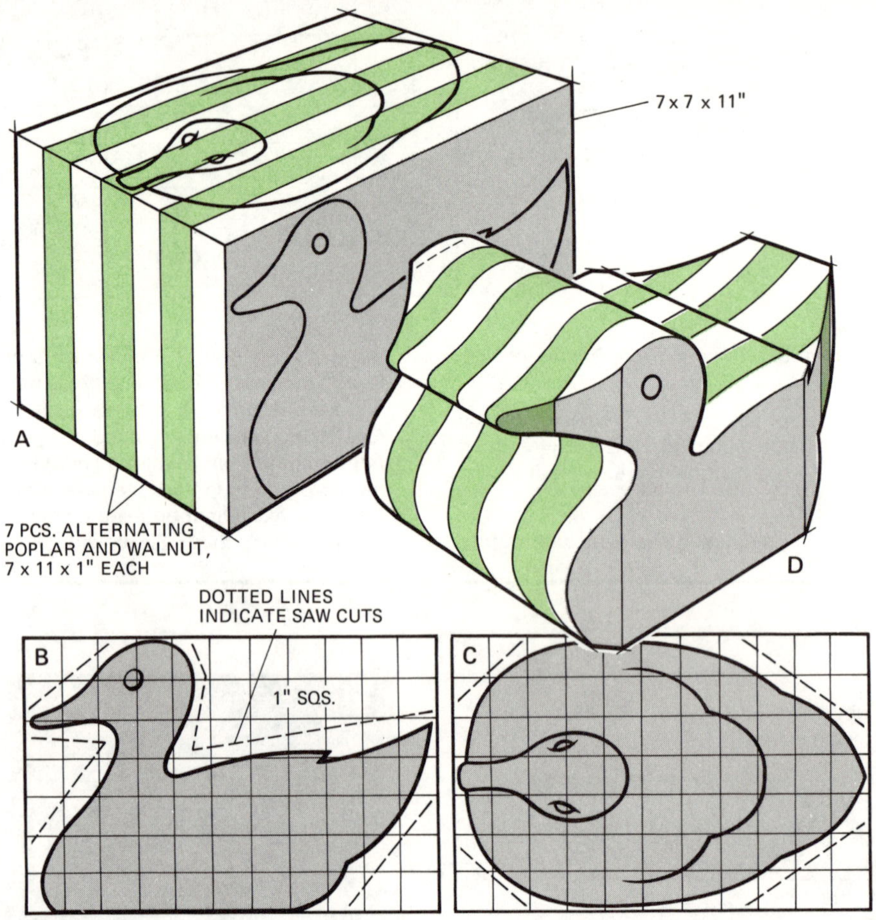

This poplar and walnut duck is a reward for a craftsman.

Materials: 4 poplar and 3 walnut pieces each 7 x 11 x 1 in., glue; 15-in. square plywood; 2 screws; ¾ and ½-in. wood gouges; rasp; sandpaper; linseed oil; butcher's wax.

Method: Prepare the blank and plane smooth. Draw the duck on the blank (A). Form the side of the duck by cutting with a saw (B). Secure the duck to the work surface. Fasten it to the plywood square with screws and clamp the plywood to the work surface. Refine sides with gouges. Redraw and form top (C) with saw and gouges. The rough shape should look similar to the drawing (D). Work toward the back and shape tail. Level bumps and gouge marks with rasp. Sand smooth. Apply three coats of oil. Remove excess oil and apply wax.

FOR MORE INFORMATION ON LAMINATING

Books

- **Glenister, S.H., *Contemporary Design in Woodwork,* Vols. 1, 2 and 3, John Murray, London, 1968.**
- **Nilsson, Ake R., *Woodware,* Drake Publishers, Inc., New York, 1973.**
- **Piepenburg, Robert E., *Designs in Wood,* Bruce Publishing Co., New York, 1969.**

Organizations and schools

- **American Crafts Council, 44 West 53rd St., New York, N.Y. 10019; maintains Museum of Contemporary Crafts at 29 West 53rd St., New York.**
- **National Woodcarvers Assn., 7424 Miami Ave., Cincinnati, OH 45243; for amateur and professional woodcarvers; publishes bimonthly bulletin.**
- **The Woodsmith's Studio, 142 East 32nd St., New York, NY 10016; classes in woodworking, wood finishing and carving.**

Sources of exotic woods and tools

- **Albert Constantine and Son, Inc., 2050 Eastchester Rd., Bronx, NY 10461.**
- **Craftsman Wood Service, 2727 South Mary St., Chicago, IL 60608.**
- **Sculpture House, 38 East 30th St., New York, NY 10016.**
- **Woodcraft Supply Corp., 313 Montvale Ave., Woburn, MA 01801.**

Wood manufacturers' tour

- **Kennedy Brothers, 11 Main, Vergennes, VT 05491; specializes in wood wall hangings. Gift shop; factory open to 4 p.m. weekdays.**

Motor needs oil

I have an old secondhand sewing machine and am sure that at some point grease was forced into the oilers where it hardened. I'm also quite sure the bearings are dry. The nearest service center is miles away. Is there any way I can oil the bearings?—O.L., Minn.

Your service center can give you much better advice than I can at such long range. I suggest that you get in touch with it by phone or letter, giving detailed information including serial number. Or you can detach the motor and send it to the service center, along with a letter of explanation. Be sure to mark the wiring with numbered tabs so that, later, you can rewire the motor correctly.

If circumstances make this impractical, you'll have to try to get lubricant to the bearings temporarily. Old sewing-machine motors have wick-lubricated sleeve bearings and it is possible the lubricant has hardened. Usually there's a small oil hole at the top of the felt retainer. Insert a straight pin into the hole and press down as far as possible. Work with care so that you do not damage the wicking or other parts. Place a single drop of *light* oil (not crankcase oil) in each retainer. Then snip off the point of the pin, insert the blunt end of the pin in the hole already made in the felt and work the pin down as far as it will go. In time the oil should soften the hardened lubricant and reach the bearing. But don't operate the motor until the shaft turns freely. Your best bet, however, is to ask your service center for advice.

Closet condensation

Walls in a clothes closet in one bedroom of my home, especially one outside wall, are sometimes wet and dripping near the ceiling. What causes this, and what can I do to prevent it?—Mrs. I. McClusker, Racine, Wis.

Walls are at a lower temperature than the air with which they are in contact. This causes the moisture in the air to condense on the colder surface, particularly on the outside walls, as you say. Often a cure can be effected simply by leaving the closet door or doors open. Just leaving the closet light on will sometimes do it.

For a better cure; you can insulate the outside wall by nailing furring strips horizontally on 16-in. centers, packing either blanket-type or polystyrene insulation between the strips, and then covering the wall with plasterboard. Seal the corners with Swedish putty.

Some homeowners install a wall outlet in the closet and use an electric strip heater to solve this problem.

Rejuvenating old paintbrushes

I have three old paintbrushes, including a very good one with long bristles, that have hardened due to sheer neglect. Is there any hope now of making them usable again? Can you outline the process?—B.A., Del.

If the bristles are not bent due to their standing on end for a prolonged period, place them in individual cans, pour in sufficient wash-off paint remover to cover the bristles and let them stand for an hour or more. Then remove the brushes, wash off the remover, place them on several thicknesses of newspaper and scrub one way—away from the ferrule—with a wire brush. Put brushes back in the remover for about the same time. Repeat the scrubbing and the immersion in remover; eventually you'll soften all the paint and you can comb out the remainder with a special brush "comb" available from your paint dealer.

The procedure is certainly hard on the bristles but it's the only way I've found reasonably successful.

Unilever faucet leaks

My single-lever sink faucet leaks at a point just below the neck, but only when it's turned on for hot or cold water—there's no leak when it's turned off. Can you tell me what is wrong and how to fix it?—W.W., Mo.

Your faucet seems to be of the type that has two rubber-ring seals called O-rings (or packing) which fit in grooves cut in the sleeve formed at the end on the neck. These seals become worn in time, but you can get replacements from your plumber, hardware store or the manufacturer. Instructions that came with the faucet will tell you how to disassemble it to replace the seals, or your plumber will do this for a nominal charge.

Linseed-oil finish

I've just bought a used sewing machine in a walnut cabinet, so dark the wood is hardly visible. I want to refinish in a lighter color. I'm told to rub on linseed oil in stages to a gloss. Can you advise how to proceed?—C.Y., Va.

If you use linseed oil you may end up with a darker finish than you now have. I'd sand to the bare wood, using a cabinet scraper if necessary to make sure all the old finish has been removed, and then spray-coat with a water-white lacquer over a sanding sealer. This will give you about as near a natural wood color as you can possibly get with ordinary finishing materials. Your paint dealer will rent you a sprayer and supply the necessary finishing materials.

How to apply plastic laminate

Plastic laminate is not as tough to apply as it looks. If you've been afraid to tackle that worn kitchen countertop, these tips will help you do a professional-looking job yourself

IF YOU'VE SHIED AWAY from resurfacing a worn kitchen countertop—or tackling any project that calls for working with plastic laminates—because you felt that applying laminated plastics was beyond your skills, take heart. With average handyman skills, a measure of common sense and the know-how shown on these pages, you'll find that applying laminated plastics can, indeed, be a do-it-yourself project.

In broad terms, working with laminates involves four operations: cutting, spreading the adhesive, bonding, and trimming and finishing. On these pages, we show you how to do all four steps, no matter what tools you may have.

Some basic points to keep in mind:

- Be sure all surfaces are clean. If necessary, dust both core stock and back side of laminate, then wipe surfaces with a rag soaked with lacquer thinner.
- Fill all voids in core surface and edges with rock-hard putty or Plastic Wood. Cut out entirely any large void and glue in a piece of pine.
- Recommended materials for use as core stock are plywood and particle-board. Many pros favor the latter because it's less likely to have voids and thus usually requires less preparation time.
- Applying plastic laminate over a finished surface is not recommended, but occasionally such a bonding will "take." Still, if you want to laminate over a finish, it would be advisable to remove that finish first so that the contact cement will be applied to bare wood.
- Plastic laminate can be applied over old worn plastic laminate if you take precautions. First, test the existing laminate for looseness. It *must be well-adhered*. Then sand its surface thoroughly for good bonding.
- Adhesives. Some contact cements are flammable, and some aren't. If you're using the flammable type, work only in a well-ventilated room and make certain there are no open flames or sparks around. If you're working over a finished floor, protect it with a dropcloth.
- Cutting. Particles of laminate are certain to fly about as the material is cut with power saw or router. *Make it a rule to always wear safety goggles when cutting the material.*

SEE ALSO
**Adhesives . . . Belt sanders . . .
Circular saws, portable . . . Home improvement . . .
Kitchens . . . Routers . . . Sabre saws . . . Tools, hand**

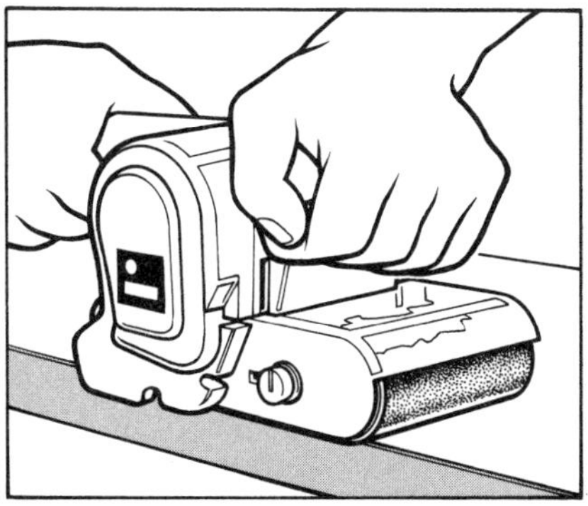

Preparing core stock

The importance of core stock being clean, smooth and free of voids cannot be overstressed. The quickest way to get such a surface is to use a belt sander. Lacking this tool, you can use a finishing sander, or sandpaper wrapped around a block of wood and arm power.

In the above illustration, a belt sander is shown being used to make certain that the top edge of the applied laminate self-edge is perfectly flush with the core top surface. If it isn't, an imperfect glue line between the top piece of laminate and the self-edge is almost inevitable. Such separations are called delaminations. If you use the belt sander to smooth this edge, be sure to keep it moving in order to prevent any chance of "dishing" along the edge.

The quickest method of filling voids (above) is by pushing in a quality wood filler. Left unchecked, voids can come back to "haunt" the project builder. Since the router cutter-guide follows the core edge when trimming, it will follow any unfilled void to cause an indent in the trimmed laminate. Large voids under new laminate can cause cracks or chips in the plastic if it's bumped by a heavy object.

Since most commercial fillers shrink as they dry, plan on two passes with putty knife and filler. When filler dries, thoroughly sand the entire surface and dust off.

About contact cement

Apply contact cement to the core material as quickly and evenly as possible. Unlike most glues, contact cement must be "dry" before bonding the mating parts. Do not use your fingers to test for dryness; use method shown in drawings 4 and 5 below; natural oils from your skin can make the adhesive ineffective.

Always read the manufacturer's instructions on the can label before starting. There are several types of cements available and proper use varies slightly from one maker to the next. The key point is the working time that the adhesive allows: Working time is the period of time after application of adhesive when effective bonding can be achieved. Some contact cements have a greater working time than others; you should know just how much time you have to complete the job.

If too much time is allowed to pass between cement "ready" time and bonding, both the core material and the laminate should be recoated with contact cement. For best results, do not use contact cement at temperatures lower than 70° F. If the air is dry, so much the better; contact cements dry faster when moisture content in the air is low.

When the job is finished, tightly seal can and store in a safe place with other flammable materials. (Away from high heat and exposure to direct sunlight.)

Applying adhesive

There are three ways to apply contact cement. The paint-roller technique shown in drawing 1 is easiest, quickest and best. But make certain you use the right roller cover: Texfab by EZPaintr Corp. applies the adhesive evenly, does not deposit lint on the sticky surface. Drawing 2 illustrates the notched-spreader technique. At one time, contact cement makers gave these away with adhesive purchases; now it is hard to buy one. You can, however, use the edge of a serrated trowel with 1/32 to 1/16-in. notches to do the job. Simply pour a puddle of cement on the surface and spread.

Small areas or strips of self-edge are best coated using a small, clean paintbrush. Though some advocate an animal-hair brush, these do have a tendency to lose bristles. A nylon brush works fine, and a used, stiff one can be rejuvenated for use again with an overnight soaking in contact cement.

To test coated surfaces for readiness, lightly touch adhesive with a piece of brown (kraft) paper. When cement does not stick to paper (5), the surfaces are ready to be bonded.

Cutting laminates

The trickiest part of cutting is making certain that the piece is well supported while the cutting takes place. Damage will occur if the laminate is allowed to "chatter" while the cutting tool's teeth slice the material. Since the surface (decorative) material can be easily chipped off, it should always face the cutting edge of the tool as shown at right.

For example, when using a fine-tooth crosscut handsaw, face the decorative side up (because the saw cuts on the downstroke and cleans the kerf on the upstroke). On a table saw (2), use a carbide-tipped blade, clamp a strip of laminate to the fence to prevent the piece being cut from slipping beneath the fence; cut with good side up. With a sabre saw, use a fine-tooth hacksaw blade—and the sabre-saw shoe insert—while the laminate is well supported on each side of the cutting line. The easiest method is to use a pair of 2x4s across sawhorses positioned below the laminate to straddle and parallel the cutting line. Cut it with face side down. In No. 4, use laminate shears to nip off a narrow section before bonding. With a portable circular saw (5), cut the laminate decorative side down on adequate supports. Use a carbide-tipped blade set to just clear the laminate thickness; thus cutting slightly into the wood support used below.

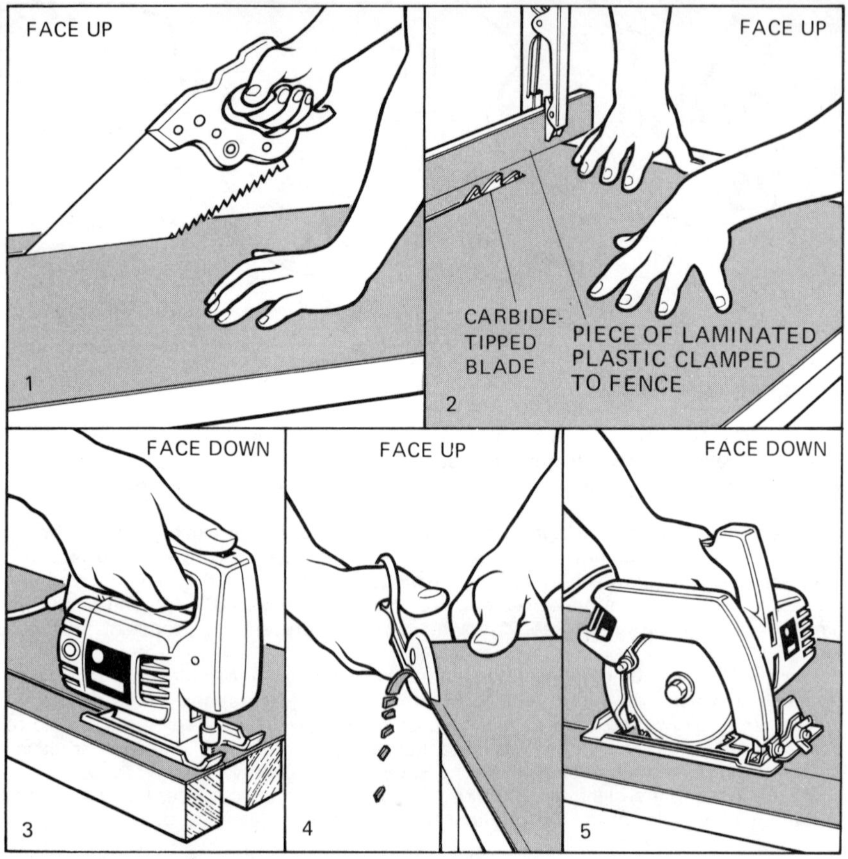

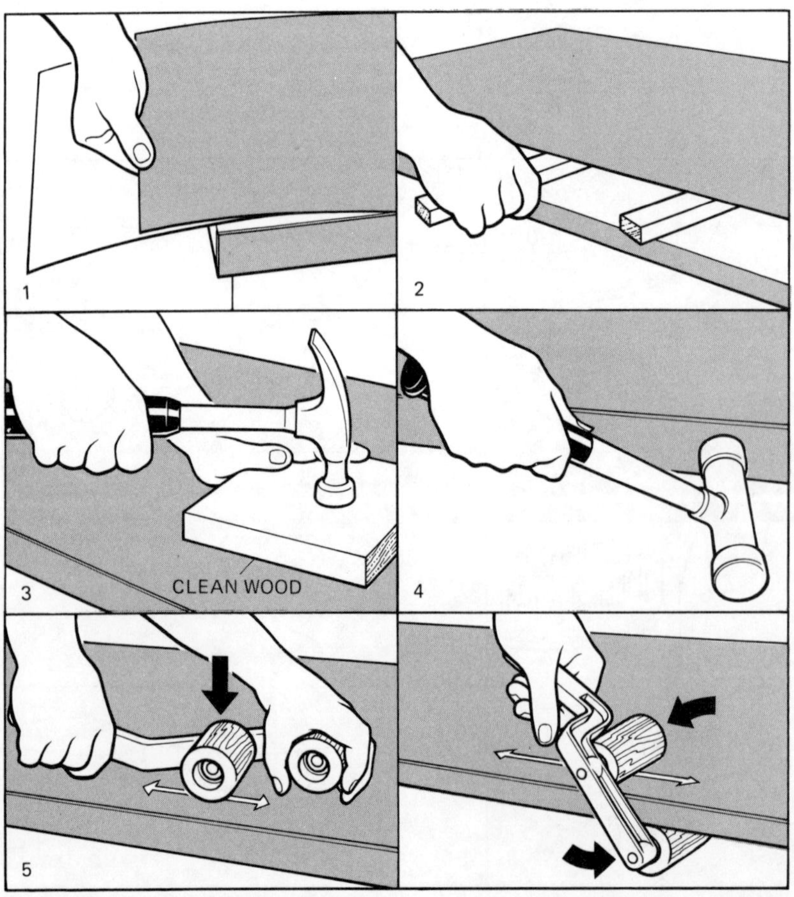

Bonding laminate

When adhesive has dried, it is necessary to keep apart the surfaces to be bonded until desired. Many do-it-yourselfers use a large sheet of brown (kraft) paper to achieve this (1). This method does work, but because the paper can be stubborn to slide out, it often is difficult to keep laminate correctly aligned over core. A better method is shown in No. 2. Here, ¾-in. sticks (or dowels) are spaced about 12 in. apart. Laminate is positioned over the core and sticks are slipped out one at a time. All edges of the laminate should be checked to assure overhang before removing the first stick. Once the bonding process starts, work rapidly—sliding out sticks and pressing laminate into contact with the core material.

When the entire sheet of laminate is in contact with the core, immediately apply pressure to its surface. Most laminates need only momentary pressure. You can apply pressure by any of the four methods shown in drawings 3 through 6. In No. 3, it is by sliding a block of hardwood about and tapping with a hammer. In No. 4, a soft-face mallet is used to apply pressure to a self-edge strip. The double roller in Nos. 5 and 6 applies the best possible pressure—if you use laminates often, you should invest in one. Apply pressure working outward from the center. If the job is done properly, it is not necessary to clamp the workpiece.

Trimming laminate overhang

Since almost all pieces of laminate are cut slightly oversize (larger than the core stock), trimming is usually necessary after bonding. Lacking power tools, you can use a block plane. To avoid gouges, extend the plane iron no more than 1/16th in. Remove excess laminate as close as possible to the core (1); finish trimming with a large, smooth file (2). When filing, remove material on push stroke only.

But power is the easiest way to go. No. 3 shows a router with a carbide straight cutter trimming self-edge. Cutter guide rides the core surface to establish the trimming line. In No. 4, the top piece has been applied and trimmed with a straight cutter; chuck a carbide bevel cutter in router to dress the edge. Laminate trimmer (5) does straight or bevel trimming with one adjustable cutter.

Clean and lubricate bits with pilots after each use to prevent "freezing." Where nonpilot bits are used, apply petroleum jelly to laminate self-edge to prevent cutter scorch marks.

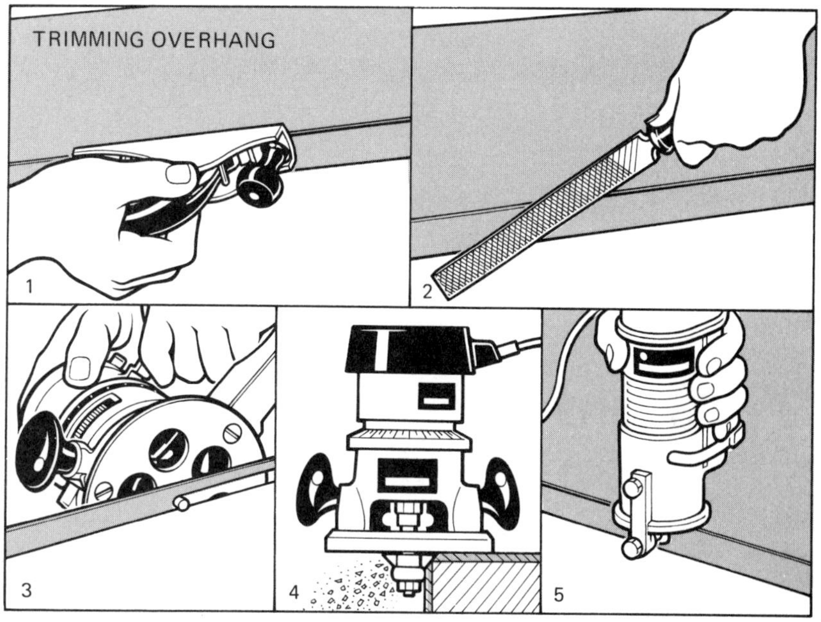

Job cleanup

Never use metal tools to scrape excess adhesive from laminate surface. Instead, use a piece of scrap laminate and a rag soaked with lacquer thinner (or contact-cement solvent). Avoid excessive use of solvent. If it penetrates glue line, it will cause delamination. Soften the adhesive with some solvent, scrape with laminate scrap and wipe clean with dry cloth.

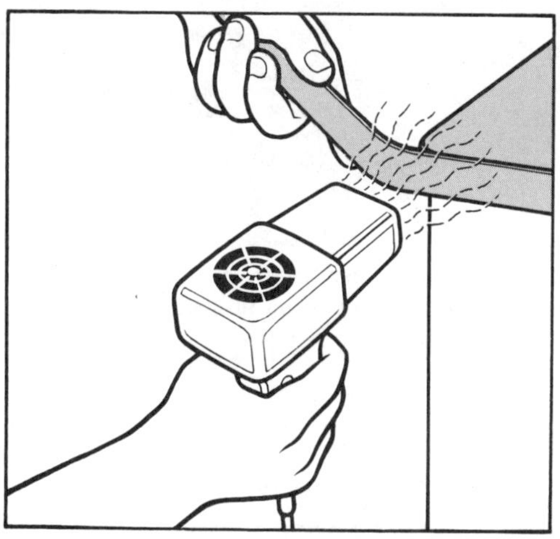

Turning a corner

Conventional plastic laminates have limited flexibility (bend radius). But they can be bent safely around a 7-in. radius at room temperature; tighter if both laminate and core stock are heated. Typical heating instruments are an iron, hair dryer and flameless heater (shown above). Apply two coats of contact cement to the core edge and one coat to the laminate strip. Starting at one end, contact strip to core and work your way toward the bend. When it is reached, heat strip and core and slowly bend strip into contact; hold momentarily. Wear heavy gloves to protect hands from heated surfaces.

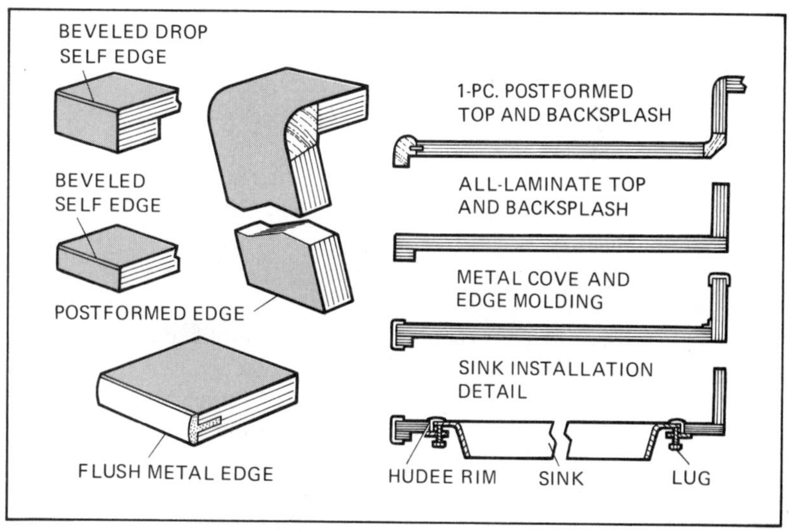

Tips about countertops

Typical kitchen countertop treatments are shown above: The postformed type should be done by pros; do-it-yourselfers can safely tackle the standard type with either metal or self-edging. The latter is better looking and generally preferred.

There are two types of self-edge; one has a thickened edge with ¾-in. square pine or plywood fastened to underside of the countertop using glue and annular-threaded nails. Since the router cutter rides the strip when trimming the self-edge bottom, set, fill and sand smooth *all* nailheads. A backsplash is set in caulk and permanently attached with 1¾-in. wood screws.

Build a Spanish-style lamp

By J. A. LACKNER

With just a few simple hand tools and a couple of shop evenings or a weekend, your choice of ready-made spindles can become a handsome Mediterranean lamp. It's a touch of luxury for your home

THE MEDITERRANEAN lamp's handsome appearance denies its origin as a quick weekend project.

WHY SPEND $50 OR MORE for an imported Mediterranean table lamp, with its customary heavy, large-scale wood base, when you can build this beauty for a fraction of that price in an evening or two?

The lamp's construction is greatly simplified by the use of ready-made spindles. They're available in a variety of styles and sizes at lumberyards and most well-stocked hardware stores.

Begin the project by lining up, measuring and cutting the spindles to desired length. Overall length is not critical; determine it so that it places the lamp at the proper height for the place you want to use it. All four spindles must be the same length.

Because it will be impossible to get inside the

SEE ALSO

Chests . . . Electrical wiring . . .
Fluorescent lamps . . . Occasional tables

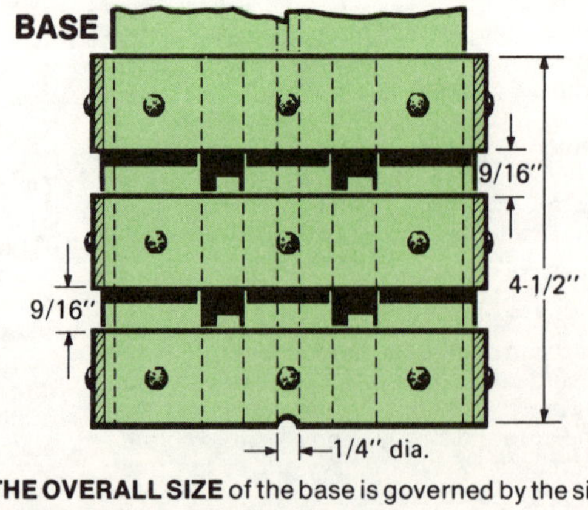

THE OVERALL SIZE of the base is governed by the size of the spindles you choose to buy.

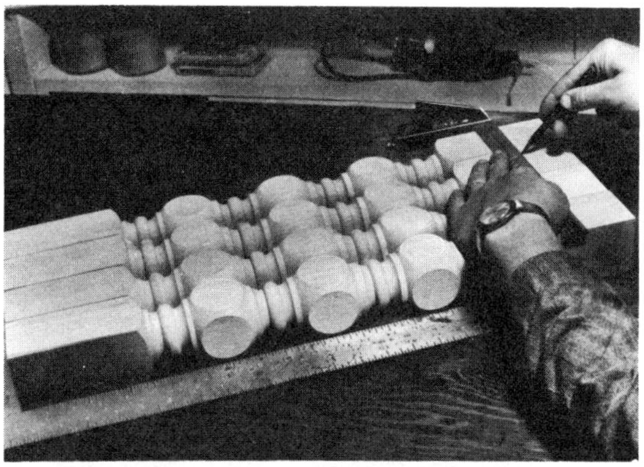

THE SPINDLES are lined up and cut to length. A planer blade will eliminate much sanding.

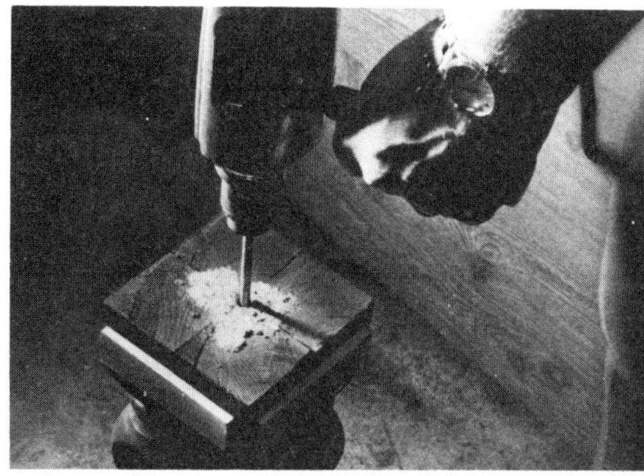

DRILL HOLES through the centers of the top and the base of the column. Use a ¼-in. drill bit.

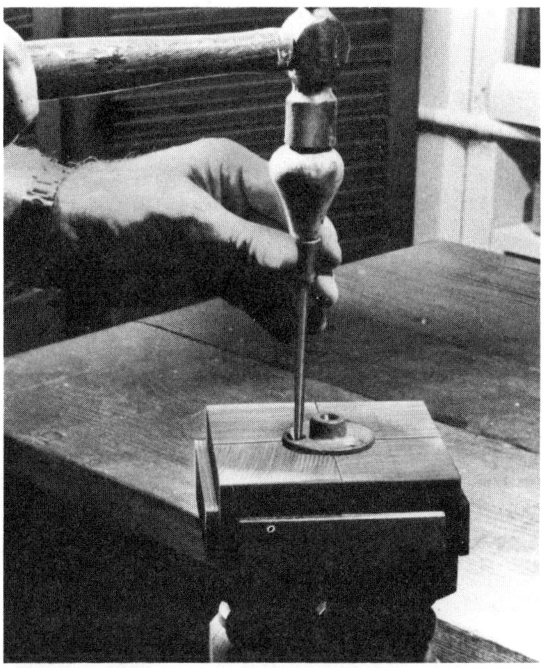

A PIPE FLANGE is centered on top of the column. Mark and punch pilot holes but do not fasten.

VERTICAL SLATS on the base are placed and glued. Measuring isn't necessary; space them by eye.

HORIZONTAL SLATS can be affixed with a hot-melt glue gun (shown parked in a discarded aerosol can cover).

column once it is assembled, each spindle should be stained before assembly. Do *not* stain those surfaces which will mate and receive glue. If you use a hot-melt glue gun, as I did, assembly is speeded up. If you use white glue, it will be necessary, of course, to clamp the pieces overnight before proceeding with the slats and electrical work. The base-surround (slats) is made up of ¼ x 1⅛-in. lattice strips. And once these are added, the lamp should be freestanding. If the lamp wobbles, true up the bottom with a block of wood covered with coarse-grit sandpaper. Dowel buttons were used for accent but, if preferred, roundhead tacks can be substituted. For rustic effect and a more Spanish-looking appearance, these buttons can be painted black.

Drill a ¼-in. hole through the top and bottom of the lamp to receive the lamp cord. Also, for the cord, cut a small half-circle channel in the bottom from the hole to one edge of the base. A pipe flange (painted black) goes at the top of the lamp and you're all ready for the electrical part of the job. If you can't get the lamp parts locally, they're available by mail from Sears or from Albert Constantine and Son, Inc., 2050 Eastchester Rd., Bronx, N.Y. 10461. Lampshades, of course, can be found in department stores. This permits selecting a color and pattern that will blend with your own room decor.

TURNED PARTS can be finished while in the lathe. After turning is completed, sand glass-smooth with extra-fine paper and apply colonial oil stain. Finally, polish with wax and soft cloth while the work is actually spinning.

Build a candlestand lamp

By WAYNE C. LECKEY

Worked on a few too many hammer and saw projects lately? Meanwhile your lathe is sitting idle in the corner? Here's a good-looking colonial candlestick lamp made of cherry that will once again bring you the joy of turning a piece of wood into a beautiful shape

SEE ALSO
Armchairs . . . Candle stands . . . Clocks . . . Fluorescent lamps . . . Lighting . . . Wood lathes . . . Wood lathe techniques

IF YOUR LATHE has become a forgotten tool, maybe it's time to dust it off, oil it up and once again enjoy the fun of watching a spinning chunk of wood turn into a pleasing shape before your eyes.

To start you off again on a lathe project, we built this charming colonial candlestand lamp and photographed it in a true early American setting in Connecticut. Made entirely of cherry, it has the warmth of colonial furniture. Graceful scrolls of black wrought iron add a distinctive touch to its three-legged base.

While a lathe plays a major part in making this lamp, your bandsaw, router and drill press won't stand idly by—you'll need them for making the base and circular table.

The base consists of three identical parts, bandsawed from 1½-in. stock and butt-glued at the center. The top and bottom edges are rounded with a ¼-round bit in your router. Finally, a 1-in. hole is bored all the way through the base at the center.

Rough turning squares for the upper and lower posts are glued up from two dadoed pieces to form a square hole their full lengths for the ⅛-in. running-threaded pipe.

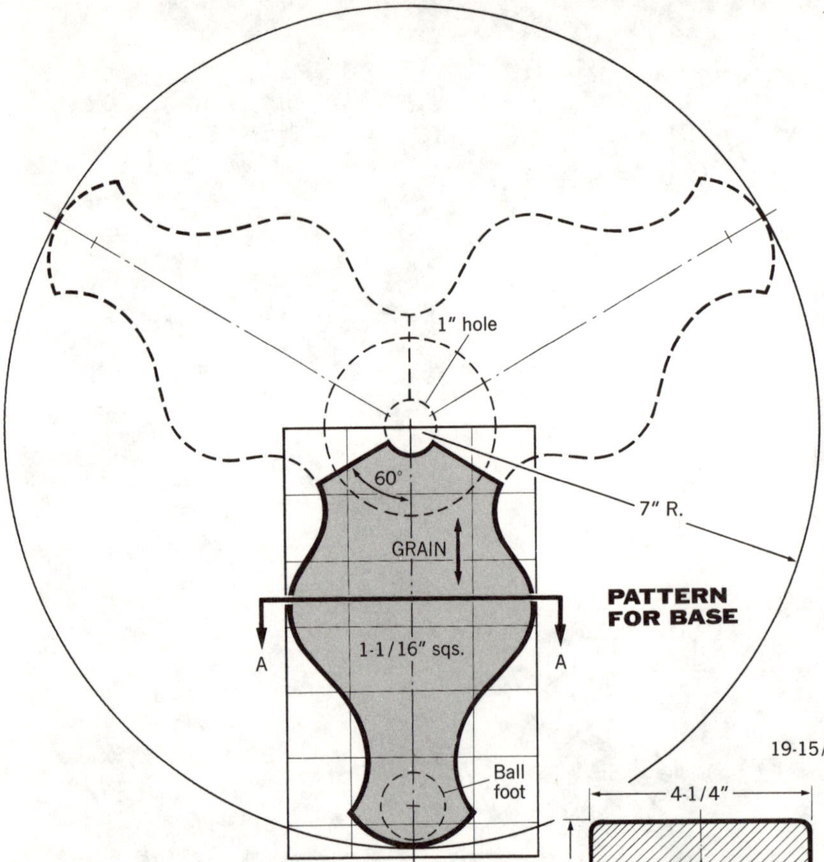

PATTERN FOR BASE

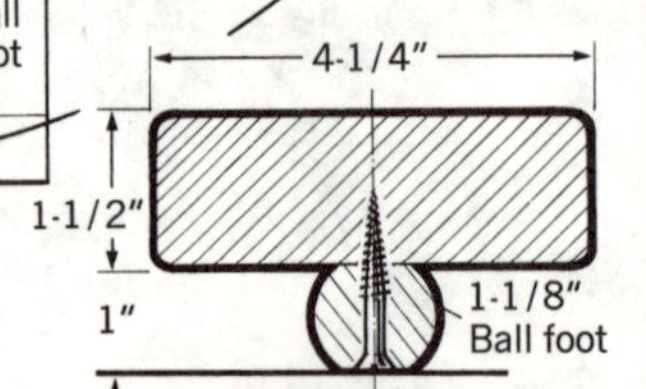

SECTION A-A

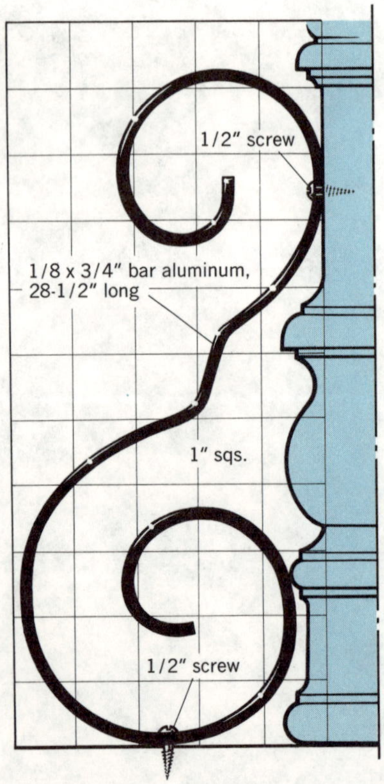

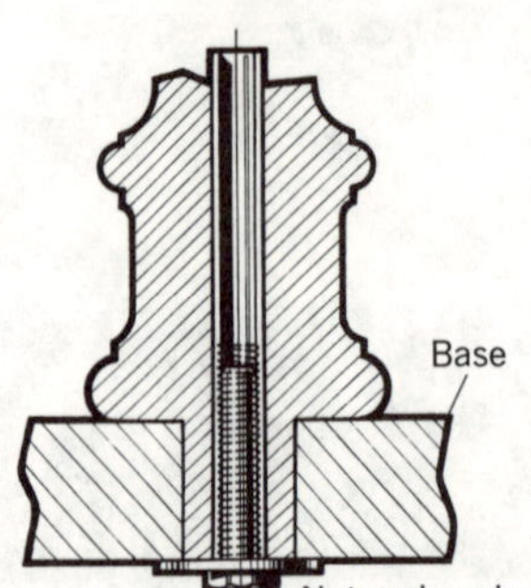

SECTION AT BASE

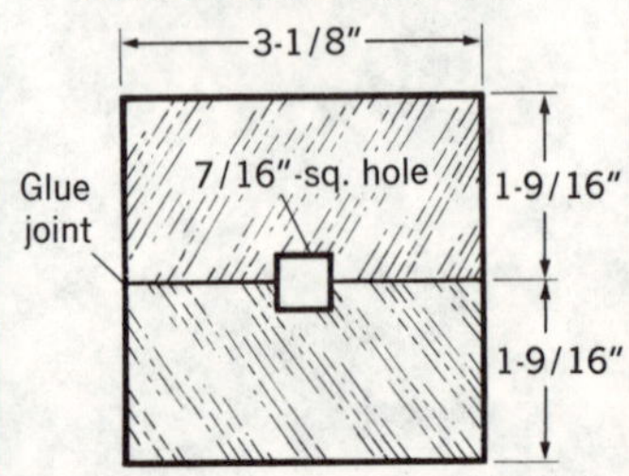

BUILT-UP BLANK
FOR LOWER TURNING

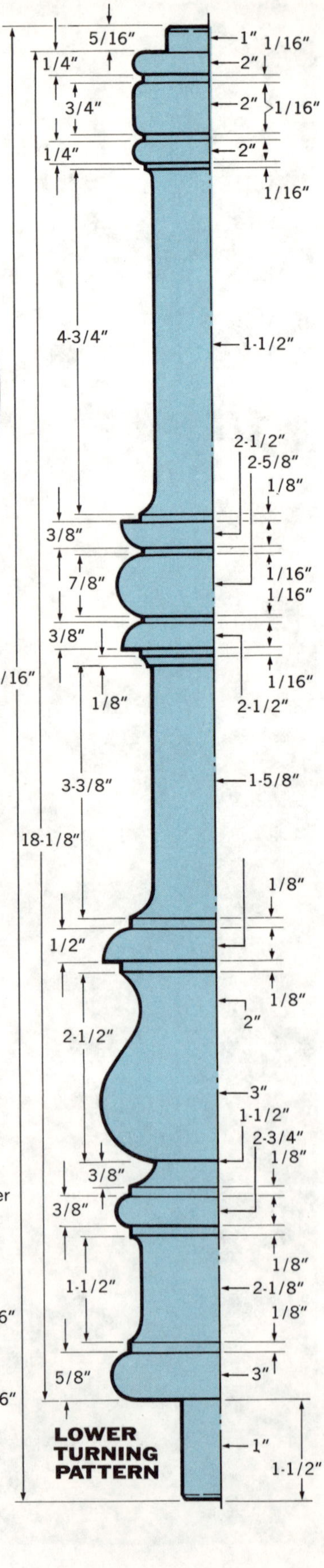

LOWER TURNING PATTERN

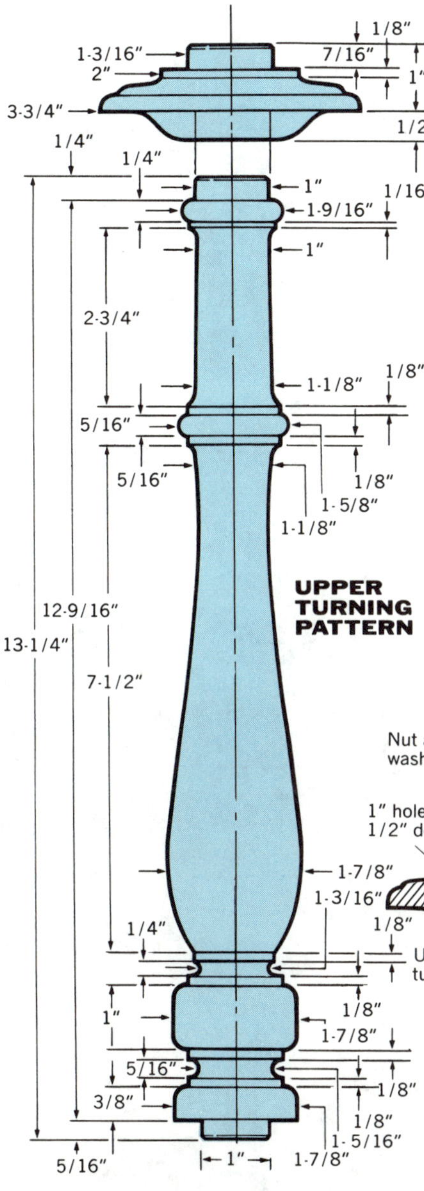

A HEAVY-DUTY bench scroller forms the decorative wrought-iron scrolls quickly. Each scroll requires a 28½-in. strip.

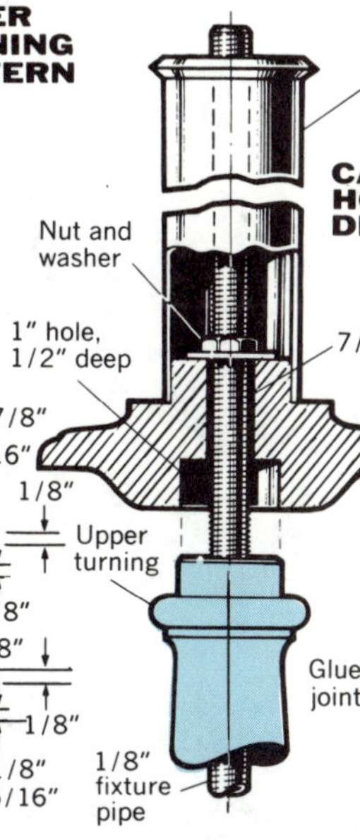

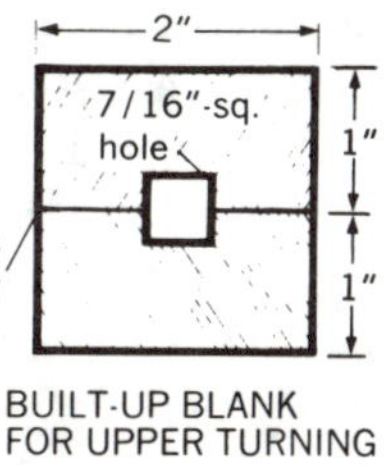

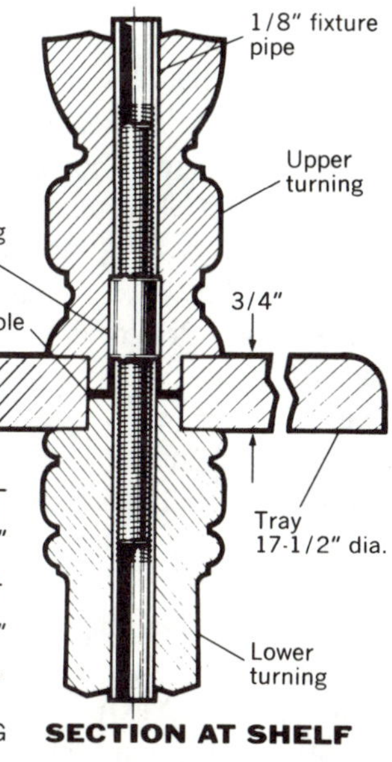

While you only need to turn one of each post, you'll find it easier to work from a full-size pattern from which you can take divider and caliper measurements directly. Notice that 1-in. tenons are turned on each end of both turnings, the longest one being that which passes through the hole in the base.

Inasmuch as you cannot buy ⅛-in. threaded pipe in lengths longer than 36 in., two lengths are joined with a coupling. To accommodate the coupling, the square hole in the upper turning must be drilled larger for a distance of 2 in.

The tenons on the upper and lower turnings meet midway in the hole in the table. A slight clearance between the two tenons will assure a tight fit when all the parts are later pulled together by a nut and washer at the bottom of the pipe.

The candleholder is faceplate-turned to fit over the tenon at the top of the upper turning. Notice that it has a tenon for a 6-in. length of cardboard candle tubing. The brass cap which fits on top of the tubing is a standard lamp fitting. The ⅛-in. pipe should extend about ¼ in. above the cap for a harp, socket and 14-in. linen shade.

The three wrought-iron scrolls are formed from ⅛ x ¾-in. aluminum bar, drilled for ½-in. roundhead wood screws and then sprayed flat black. You'll need to enlarge the pattern and use it as a guide. Three ball feet, flattened top and bottom for attaching with flathead wood screws, are painted flat black to complete the lamp.

Cobbler's bench table lamp

By ELMER VERBURG

■ WHEN YOUR FRIENDS see this charming little table lamp, you won't stop with one—you'll wind up making several. Made in the form of an old cobbler's bench from scraps of clear white pine, the lamp is more than just a lamp. It has a rack for letters to be mailed, a handly little drawer for stamps and a place for a live or artificial plant.

It's a project you can quickly mass-produce with workshop tools. The straight and slanting grooves for the letter rack can be run on your table saw. The 15° holes for the legs can be bored uniformly with a simple jig clamped to your drill press. The flowerpot hole can be cut neatly with a hole cutter, and the hole through the square tapered lamppost can be bored from each end with a ¼-in. wood bit. The upper end of the post is counterbored for a 2-in. length of ⅛-in. fixture pipe turned tightly into an undersize hole. The lower end is whittled round to fit a ⅞-hole. A standard brass pushbutton socket is screwed onto the pipe.

To produce an antique look, round off all sharp edges with fine sandpaper and distress the wood by sanding worn spots at points which would receive wear, like the seat, the drawer front and the letter rack, always sanding with the grain. Then go over the whole thing and "polish" the wood with a worn piece of extra fine sandpaper.

Coat the wood with a brown pigmented wiping stain, let flatten, then wipe off, leaving it heavier in the corners and imperfections. When the stain is semidry, dip a cloth pad in turpentine and add highlights here and there by deftly wiping away some of the stain at the worn spots, the cheeks of the legs, the drawer pull and other places. Let dry overnight, then apply three coats of self-rubbing polyurethane varnish, sanding lightly between coats. Complete by wiring the socket.

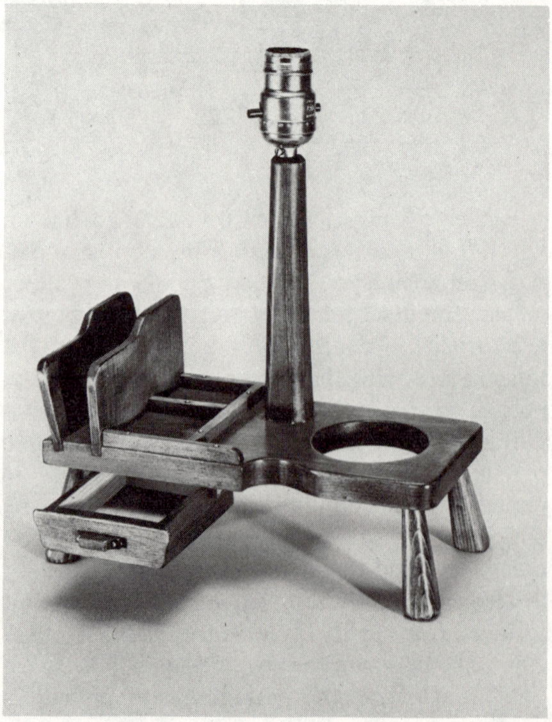

GROOVES in the drawer slide on L-shaped runners. Fit the socket with a 40-w. bulb and 10-in. shade.

SEE ALSO
Electrical wiring . . . Finishes, wood . . . Letter racks . . . Lighting . . . Planters . . . Wood finishes

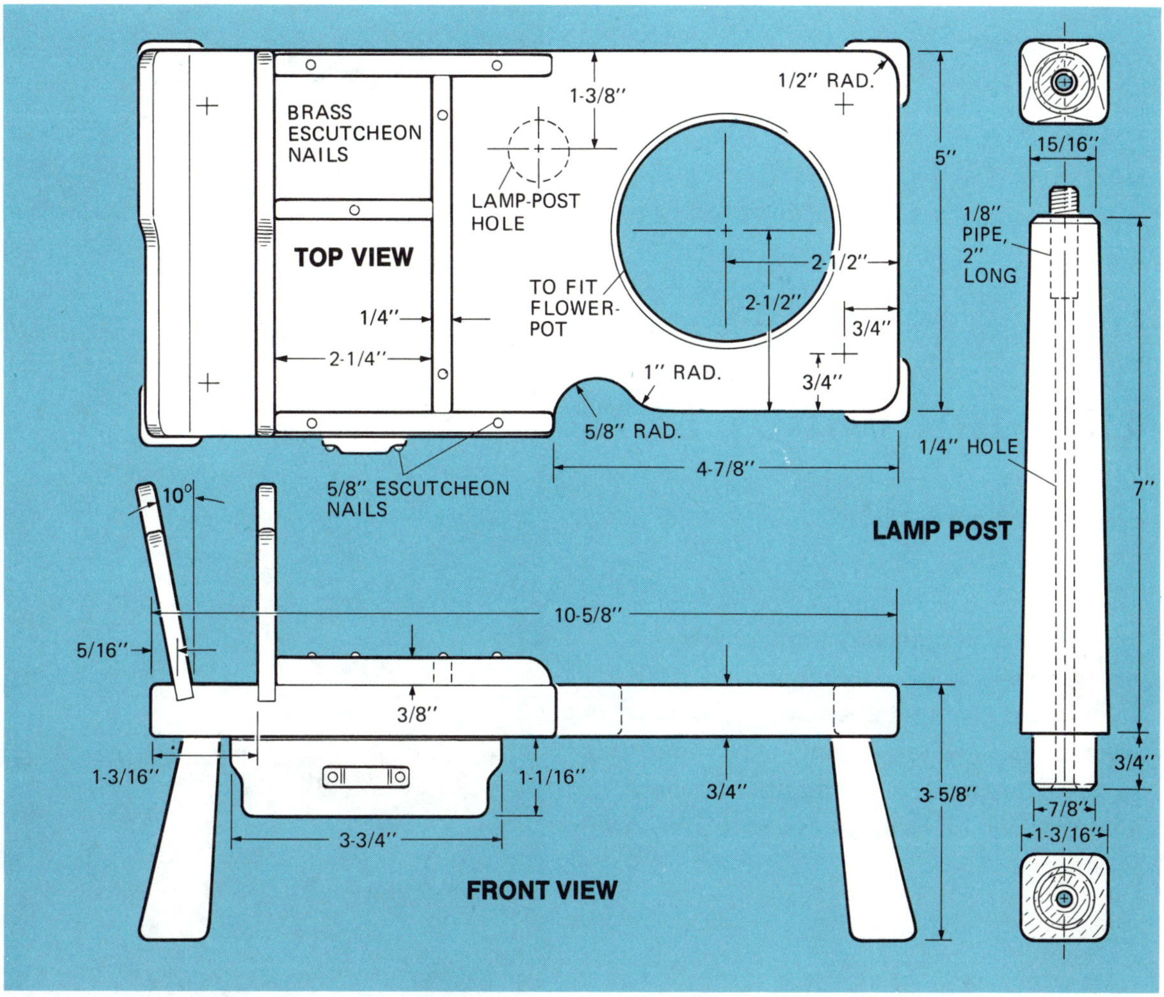

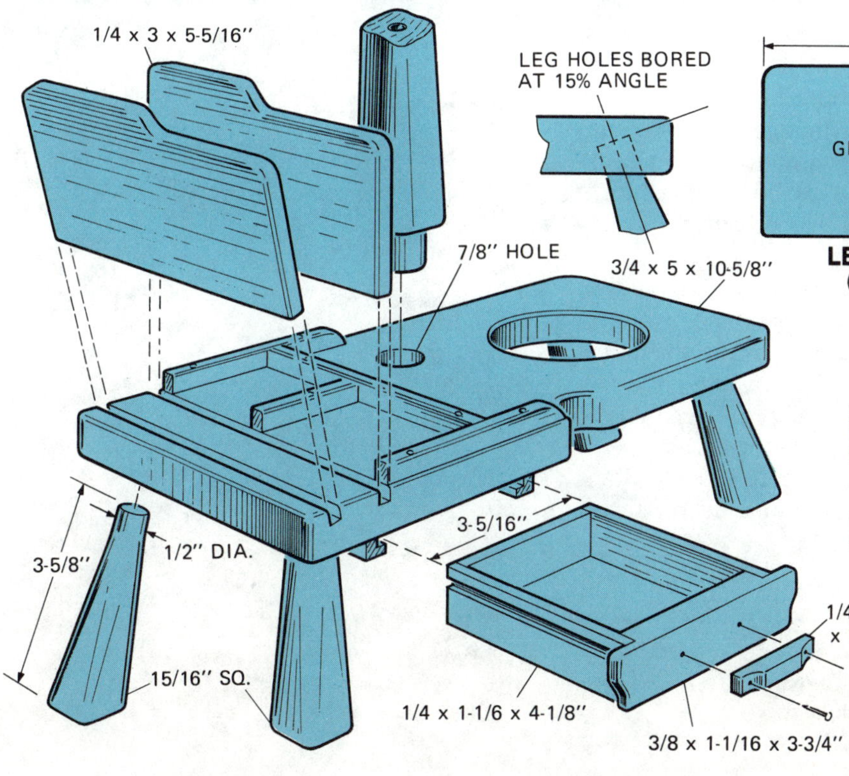

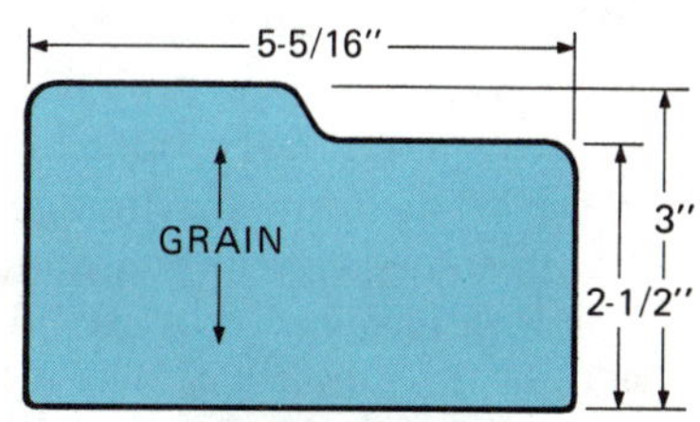

LETTER RACK
(MAKE TWO)

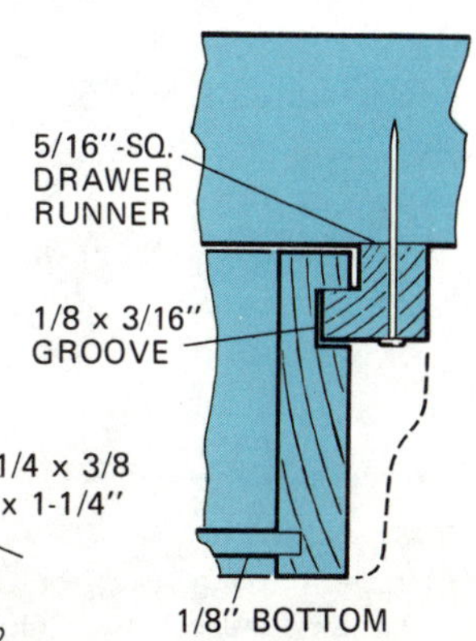

A spoonholder lamp

By WALTER E. BURTON

Here's a striking way to display a collection of spoons—by suspending them from a notched disc that encircles the column of a dining room lamp. Here are directions for obtaining the disc (a saucer), notching and drilling it, and mounting it on a lamp you already may own

A COLLECTION of old or decorative spoons is of little more than sentimental value unless it is attractively displayed. A novel way to keep spoons in view is to suspend them from a spoon-holding lamp on a dining-room table, buffet, or in some other appropriate location. Making such a display is easy and consists mainly of fashioning a slotted disc which is then installed on an existing table lamp.

Lamp design and construction will, of course, pretty much determine the precise position of the disc on the column as well as the size of the center (mounting) hole. When planning the project, bear in mind that usually it is desirable to use a lamp that lets you place the disc at least 3 in. below the bottom of the lamp socket. (Some lamp designs will allow the disc nearer to the socket.)

SEE ALSO
**Electrical wiring . . . Gifts, Christmas . . .
Kitchen accessories . . . Lighting**

The lamp shown had a column consisting of a number of metal tubes, washers and glass knobs strung on a length of iron pipe. Thus it was easy to insert the disc below the top tube and above the decorative glass knob.

The disc here is a 6-in. plastic saucer, colored to match the glass knobs, which I picked up at a five-and-dime store for less than 15 cents. Before buying one, select your lamp and determine what diameter would harmonize best with the lamp's design.

You can make the spoonholding disc from almost any material having a thickness up to ¼ in. if it has a color or can take a paint finish. (Plywood, plexiglass, Bakelite and the like are all good choices.) You could also use a metal, such as brass, but it might tend to mar the spoons unless the notches are carefully finished and padded with a glued-on felt.

When you cut the notches, size them so the spoons will fit snugly. Since spoon designs may vary, it's wise to cut a test template of cardboard or scrap plywood. Each spoon can then be custom-fitted to its matching notch.

The spoons shown are suspended bowls up. The drawing below shows how the notches were cut in the rather tough plastic saucer. Two holes were drilled side by side, ⅜ in. from the rim, and two slots were made from each hole to the rim using a hacksaw. The in-between waste was then broken out. To finish, file each notch smooth to contour.

The center hole was made by drilling a pilot hole and using a tapered reamer to enlarge it to fit over the pipe that forms the lamp-column core.

SPOON HANDLE NOTCHES are roughed out with drill and saw. A file is used to shape and smooth the cuts.

COMPLETED DISC is slipped over pipe. Make certain to allow enough clearance for spoon bowls.

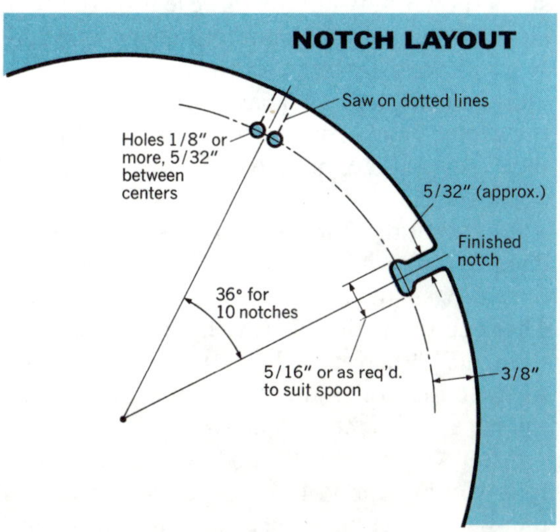

HOLDER is sandwiched between glass knob and tubing. Socket is then tightened to hold it firmly.

Six-in-one wood lamp

Graceful and sturdy, this lamp of contemporary design looks as if it has been carved from a single chunk of wood. In fact, six separate pieces of wood are carefully joined to create the illusion

■ CAREFUL ATTENTION to construction detail makes this lamp give the illusion that it has been carved from a single block of wood. Actually, it consists of six separate wood members. The lamp shown is of walnut with the legs requiring ¾-in. material, the center blocks 2-in. turning-square stock, and the base a 2x10-in. turning block. You will also need a 2-ft. length of ½-in.-dia. brass tubing.

To start, make a full-size paper or cardboard template of a typical leg section using the dimensions shown. Lay out the three legs on the ¾-in. stock and cut to rough contour shape and sand. Next, make a template of the center-block end view and cut these two parts. But before cutting the center blocks, drill a ½-in.-dia. hole through the exact center of both to receive the tubing that houses wiring.

Next, cut the 2-in. base stocks to 9¼-in.-dia. disc. Drill a ½-in.-dia. hole ¾ in. deep in the top of the base to accommodate the brass tube. Then, continue drilling through the base with a ¼-in. drill. Enlarge the hole, from the bottom up, to ⅝-in.-dia. and a depth of ⅝ in. Finally, turn the base to finished shape.

After you sand all wood parts, the base is ready for assembly. Lay a piece of wood across the shaped portion of the center block to serve as

SEE ALSO
Adhesives . . . Clamps . . . Lighting . . . Tubing, metal . . . Wiring, electrical

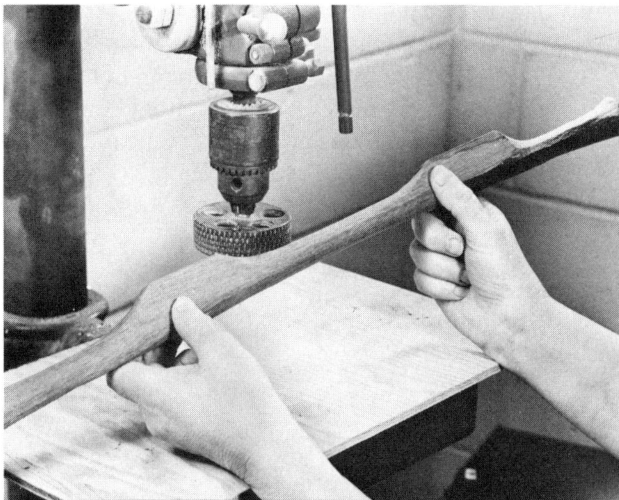

AFTER CUTTING the legs, rough out shape using a rasp (either by hand or with power, above), then complete with Sand-O-Flex wheel (below). Don't touch areas that contact center blocks.

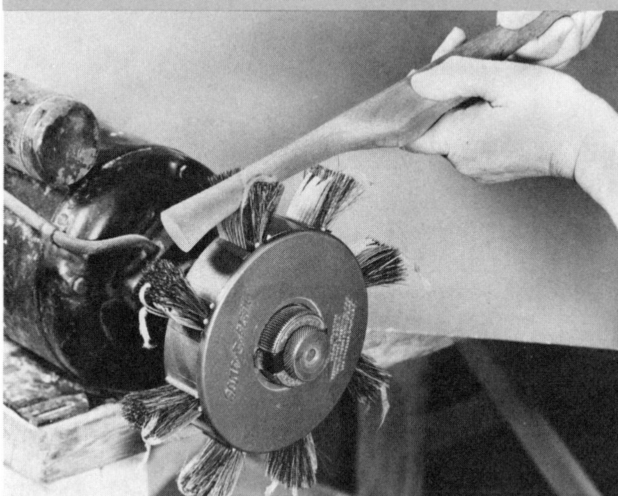

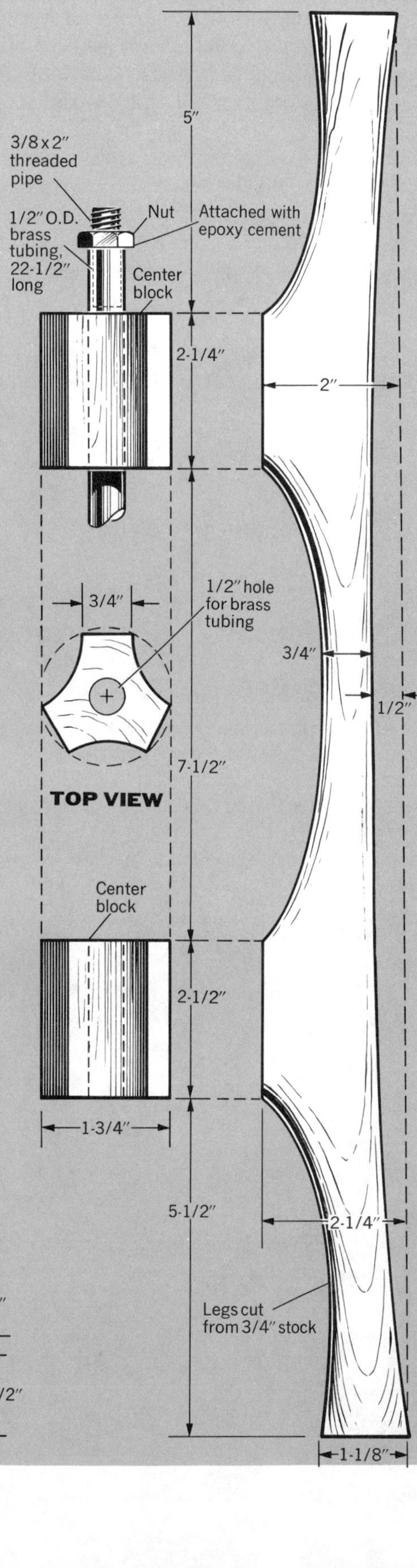

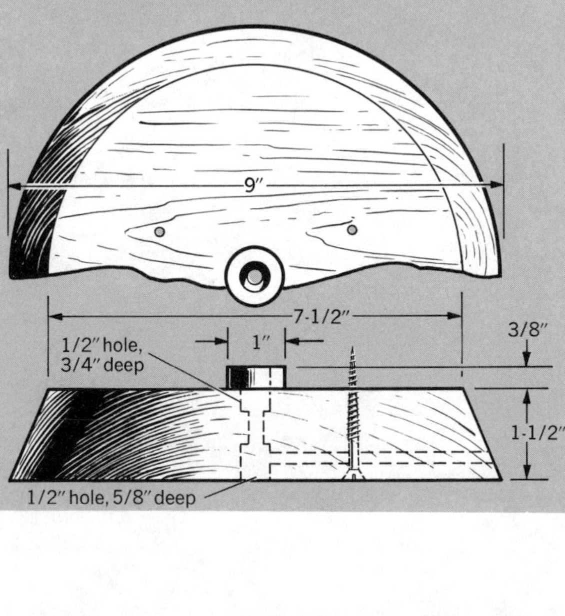

a support for clamping. Glue one flat portion of each block to one leg, clamp and allow to dry. Then glue and clamp the second and third legs.

Cut the ½-in. tubing to an overall length of 22½ in. Then cut a length of ⅛-in. running-thread fixture pipe (⅜-in. O.D.) 2 in. long. Turn on a brass hex nut until the pipe protrudes ¼ in. above it. Fit the longer length of the pipe inside the brass tube and glue the nut to the tube with epoxy cement. Slip the brass tubing through center holes of the leg assembly and push the tube into the "collar" in the base. Drill holes through the base up into each leg and secure with screws.

The cord is threaded through the hole on the base edge and pulled out the bottom hole. After double-looping the end, thread the cord back up through the hole and brass tube until it comes out the top. Attach the cord to a push-through-type socket and pull the cord back down to screw the socket to the threaded pipe above the hex nut.

Finish the piece as desired; it goes a lot faster if done before final assembly.

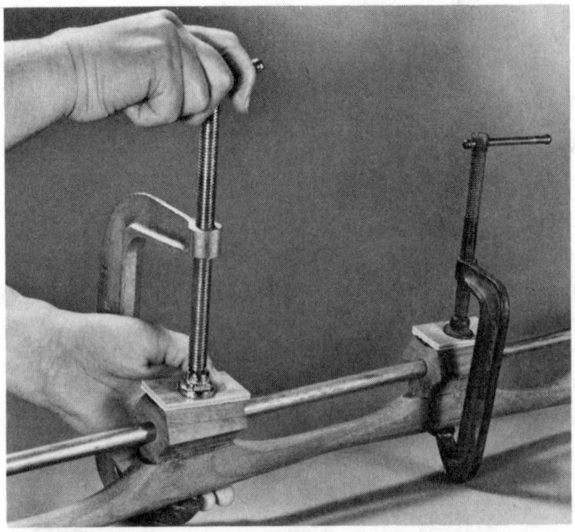

SLIP BRASS TUBE through holes in center blocks, glue blocks to flat surfaces of the legs and clamp.

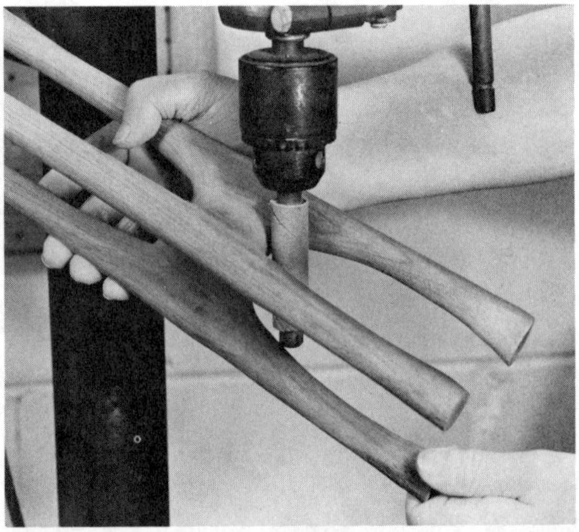

WITH LEGS ASSEMBLED, complete contour sanding between legs. Use sanding drum chucked in drill press.

DRILL ¼-IN.-DIA. HOLE, ¼-in. up from bottom of base, from edge to centerhole for lamp cord.

PILOT HOLES for screws are drilled up through base into legs; assembly is test-fitted before gluing.

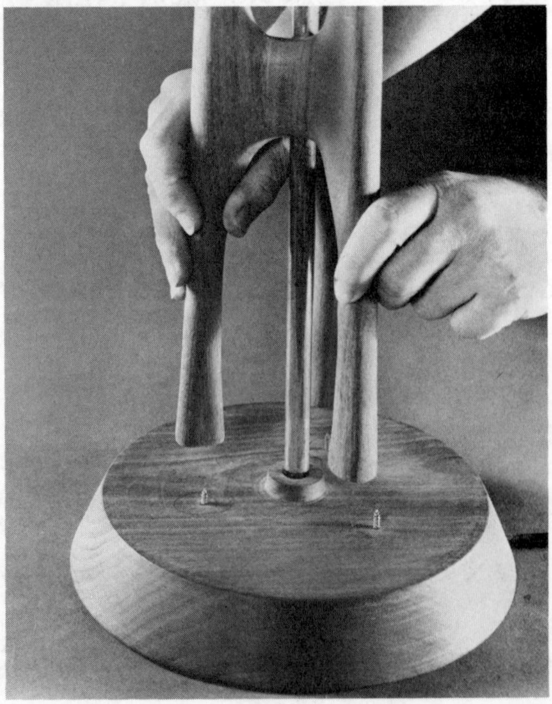

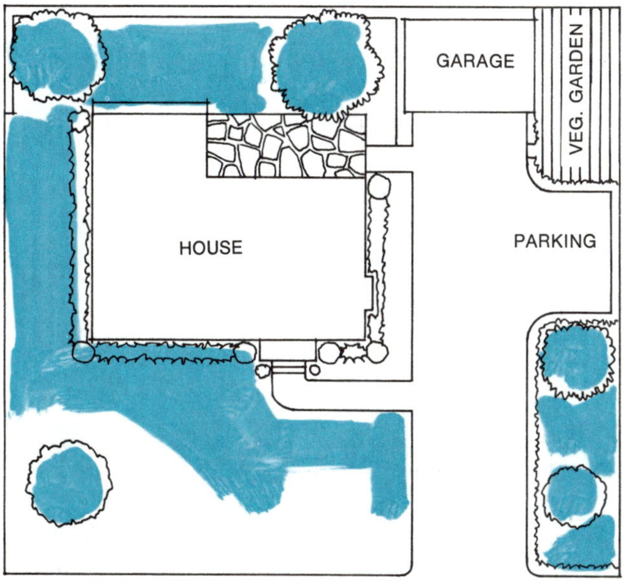

Down-to-earth principles of landscaping

By LEN HILTS

Make your lot serve the life style of your family by planning the different areas—service, living, play, etc.—to match your activities. Then commit the final plan to paper

IF YOU WANT to do an effective job of landscaping—or relandscaping—your home, start by spending a little time analyzing how you use the ground you have. Then design the plantings, gardens, walks and other elements to give you and your family the greatest benefits. The finished product should enhance your life style.

Professionals recognize that there are five general types of use around the average home. Consider these as you think about your own family activities:

Public area. The front yard, the walk to the door, the view of the house from the street.

Living area. That part of the yard you use for outdoor living, barbecues and entertaining. It can include a patio and a screened porch. It is usually at the back of the house.

Play area. The need for a play area varies widely from family to family. The lawn may include a childrens' area with playground equipment, a space for adult games such as badminton, or a swimming pool.

Garden area. Should there be room for a vegetable garden, or a flower garden? Flowers, of course, may be used in beds throughout your plan, but if someone in the family has gardening as a hobby, a special area should be set aside.

Service area. Every home needs an area for certain services: a place to hang clothes, to store the garbage cans, or perhaps to store gardening and maintenance equipment.

After thinking about your family's needs and the different types of yard areas, the next step is to produce a plan on paper. You can buy graph paper at your stationery store. It will help you draw your plan in scale. The easiest scale to follow is ¼ in. on paper equaling 1 ft. in your yard.

Begin by sketching in the permanent structures—your home, concrete walks which are already laid, the driveway. Then draw in all big trees. Locate the trunk by using a small circle on

SEE ALSO

Gardening . . . Grass . . . Hand mowers . . . Lawns . . . Mowers . . . Paths, garden . . . Putting greens . . . Retaining walls . . . Stepping stones . . . Swings . . . Transplanting . . . Trees

the paper, then use a dotted line to indicate the spread of the branches.

The easiest and least expensive way to relandscape is to work your way around existing trees and walks. However, if they present really serious problems, you can consider removing them. There is no point in living with the mistakes made by earlier owners.

Eventually you must arrive at a final plan. The real value of the final plan is that it enables you to plan your work over a long period of time. Once you know exactly what you want to do, you can break the job into parts and spread it over months or even years.

The elements to use. A good landscaping plan is a combination of elements joined together to provide both beauty and practical use.

Open lawn: Large open lawns give a sense of spaciousness, but must be planned for areas which receive sufficient sun.

Walks: You can use concrete, brick, flagstone, railroad ties—any material which provides needed footing. Select your material for appearance and for ease of care. Concrete is easy to shovel clear of snow in the winter, flagstone is not. Brick walks are easier to relocate than concrete.

Fences: Use fences for privacy, for yard division, and for optical effect. Fences, because they enclose, tend to make the yard feel smaller, cozier. An unlimited number of fence designs gives you all the choice you need.

Raised beds: Raised beds, built up with brick, stone or wood, are a good way to break up a flat, uninteresting space.

Structures: Small outstructures, such as gazebos or sheds for maintenance equipment, if well designed, can enhance your yard.

Patios: Poured concrete, brick, stone, wood—nearly every material can be used to lay

WHEN YOU PLANT A TREE, you must consider the long-range effect. Refer to the chart below to get an idea of the eventual height, spread, and overall shape of the tree you select. This chart shows the average measurements of a mature tree—and the age of maturity differs from species to species. However, most trees will occupy near-full space in from 10 to 20 years.

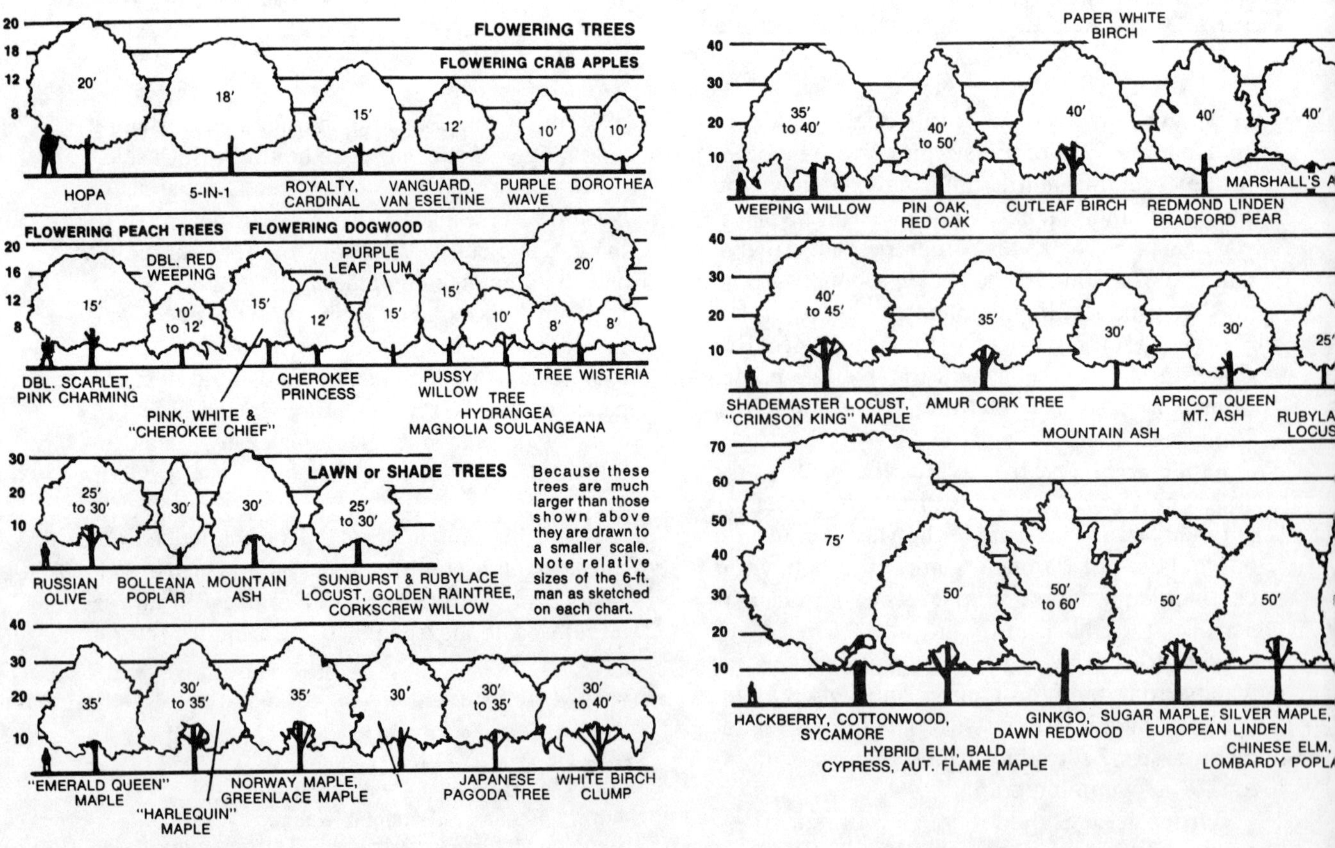

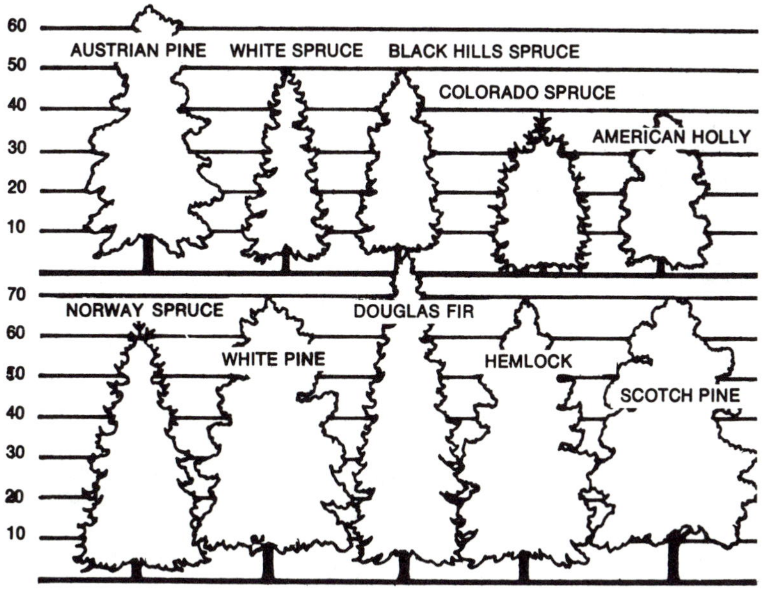

EVERGREEN TREES provide shade all year and are outstanding as a winter windbreaker. Evergreens generally have a smaller spread than deciduous varieties, and so can be planted closer to the house. In time, some evergreens, such as the Douglas fir, will reach great heights—100 feet and more—but they are relatively slow growing. For use near the house, however, it usually is better to plant shorter types.

out patio living space. Begin your design of the living area by laying out a patio, then working out from it.

Steps: If your lot is hilly, steps can be an eye-pleasing addition.

Pools: Tiny concrete pools for flowers and fish offer an interesting method of enhancing your yard.

Bushes and shrubs: Consider these as tools in your landscaping. Use them as foundation plantings, as feature plantings, or in place of fences, as screens.

Trees: Trees are a valuable asset to any home, and increase the sale value. You use them for shade, to frame and decorate the house, and as a screen. Flowering and ornamental trees have an additional decorative value, while fruit trees in many cases add even more value.

Select trees carefully and place them on your lot with even greater care. You must remember that the 6 or 8-ft. sapling you buy now will be a fullgrown tree some day—and you must allow enough room for that inevitable growth. Refer to the tree charts on pages 1781 and 1782 to find the height and spread of various species of trees.

Don't plant young trees too close to your house. They must be far enough away so that when full grown they don't brush against the walls and make painting and other maintenance difficult. If you plan a garden area, remember that it should have full sun for most of each day. If you plant a tree nearby, think ahead to the day when it will cast a shadow. You may end up with no garden if the tree eventually cuts off the sun.

If your plan includes large lawn areas, keep in mind that growing trees will eventually shade the grass, too. Grass is difficult to grow in dense shade, and you may have to change the shaded parts of the lawn—putting in a ground cover in place of the grass.

One of the reasons you plant a tree is, of course, for the cooling shade it provides. One of the important advantages of a landscaping plan is that through it you can recognize eventual changes which must be made—such as replacing grass with ground cover when the time comes.

Talk with your nurseryman about the trees which grow best in your area. He can advise you about disease-resistant trees, growth rates and maintenance requirements, such as annual spraying. Shade trees are undergoing major changes today, brought about by improved propagation techniques and widespread research activities.

The thrust of the research has been to develop trees that grow faster, are disease-resistant, and pollution-tolerant.

In planting trees at the front of your house, try to frame the building. Plant the trees at the sides and slightly to the front. Tall trees in the back yard eventually serve as a pretty background when the house is viewed from the street. Large trees, planted directly in front of the house, can be useful in screening the noise of heavy traffic, and in providing privacy if you live on a busy thoroughfare. But if yours is a quiet residential street, it usually is better to keep the front of the house open.

FILAMENT TAPE, used mainly for such tasks as securing packages, is also handy for holding glued joints immobile while the adhesive sets in either new construction or in repair work. The tape is strong, sticks tightly when applied to a clean surface, and is stretch-resistant.—*B. W. Ervin, Kent, OH.*

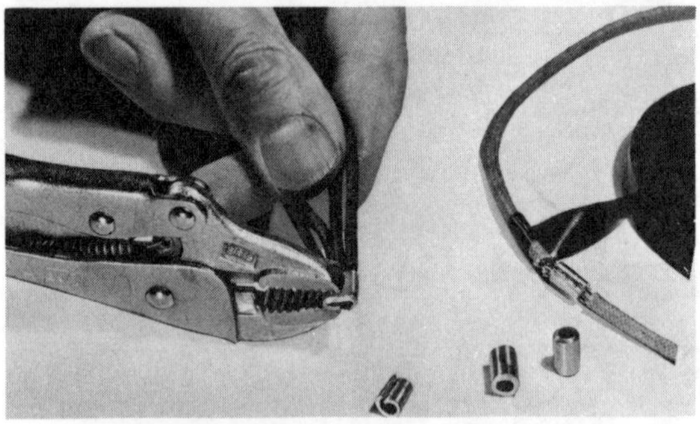

SHORT PIECES of copper tubing can be easily made into electrical-wire connectors. The tubes are slipped over the bared wires, compressed with Vise-Grip pliers, and then the joints are taped. For even greater strength, the connections can be soldered before being taped.—*Burt Web, Skokie, IL.*

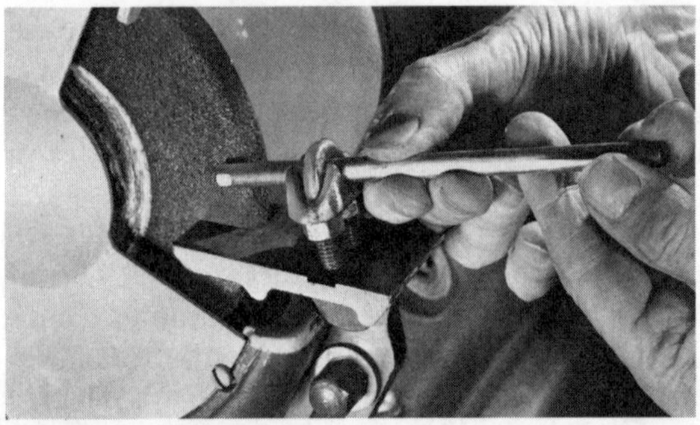

TO GRIND opposing, parallel, flat areas at the end of a metal rod, I clamped a U-bolt near the end, and then placed the threaded ends of the bolt on the grinder's toolrest. This kept the rod in alignment while tilting it forward against the sides of the grinding wheel. —*Walter E. Burton, Akron, OH.*

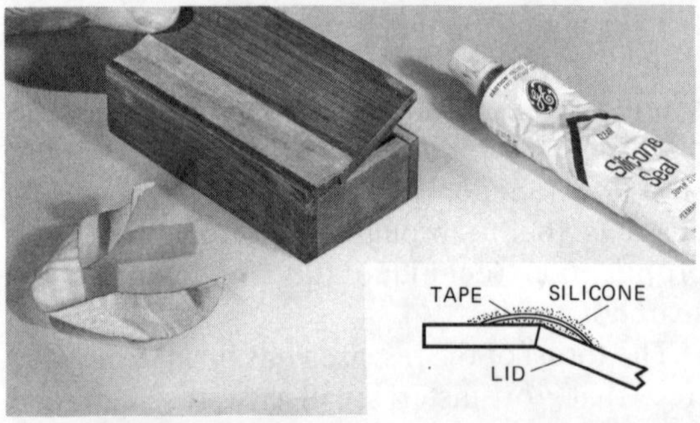

FABRIC TAPE and silicone sealing compound can be combined to make a self-closing hinge for a box lid. Position the lid and adjacent strip to which it will be hinged, so the lid is *overclosed* by about 15°. (Beveling the edges makes this possible.) With the lid closed, apply the compound and immediately press in the tape.—*W. B. May, Oak Park, IL.*

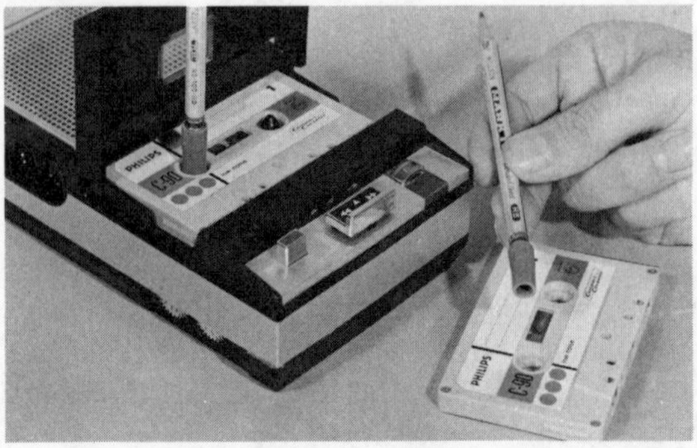

WINDING A CASSETTE TAPE either forward or backward, on or off the recorder, can be simply and effectively accomplished with this easy method. Slip a 1-in. section of rubber hose over the end of a pencil to make the rewinder. With practice you can discover how many turns it will take to locate the appropriate spot on the tape.—*Ken Patterson, Regina, Sask.*

Shrubbery for your landscaping

An amazingly wide variety of flowering and evergreen shrubs is waiting for inclusion in your landscaping plan. Used properly, they'll provide color, massed foliage, foundation plantings—the final touches your home needs

WHEN PLANNING the landscaping for your home, look to shrubs to provide accents, color, low sweeping lines, and year-round interest.

The term "shrubs" takes in a wide variety of growing things and before you complete the final landscape plan for your home, you should become familiar with some of the shrubs available. Tour well-planted neighborhoods and learn to identify the shrubs you see. Visit a nursery and see what kinds of shrubs are available in your area.

You might begin by dividing shrubs into three categories: the flowering deciduous; the broadleaf evergreens; and the needle evergreens.

The flowering shrubs include such colorful beauties as the dogwood, forsythia, honeysuckle, mockorange and spiraea. Most bloom in the spring and there are varieties which thrive in nearly every climate.

Broadleaf evergreens generally favor the southern sections of the country, though varieties have been developed which grow as far north as southern Wisconsin. To learn what types are available to you, visit your friendly nurseryman. The broadleafs include azaleas, euonymous, holly, mountain laurel, and the rhododendron, among others.

Needle evergreens include the whole family of junipers, the yews and arborvitae. Most of these can be grown all the way to the Canadian border.

Look at the chart on page 1680 for a list of shrubs of all three types. In the chart, you'll find the average height each species is likely to reach and the type of light which it prefers. The numbers in the column headed "Hardiness Zone" refer to the zonal map on page 1689 in Vol. 11. But if your favorite shrub isn't listed in your zone, don't despair. Check your nurseryman first, because many new and hardier types are developed each year.

HEDGE	CLIPPED OR INFORMAL	HEIGHT (in ft.)	HARDINESS ZONE	EVERGREEN OR DECIDUOUS
Barberry, Japanese	Unclipped	1½-3	3	D
Korean boxwood	Clipped	2	5	E
True dwarf boxwood	Either	3	6	E
Russian olive	Either	15	3	D
Bigleaf wintercreeper	Either	4	6	E
Japanese holly	Either	3	6	E
Canaert juniper	Clipped	5	3	E
Amur River privet	Clipped	1½-4	4	D
Regel's privet	Clipped	3	5	D
Dwarf honeysuckle	Unclipped	4	3	D
Tatarian honeysuckle	Unclipped	8	3	D
Pachistima canbyi	Either	1	6	E
Dwarf ninebark	Clipped	2	4	D
Colorado spruce	Either	5	3	E
Alpine currant	Either	3	2	D
Bridal wreath spirea	Unclipped	5	4	D
Persian lilac	Unclipped	8	3	D
Hicks yew	Either	4	6	E
American arborvitae	Clipped	5	3	E
Hemlock	Clipped	8	3	E
Viburnum opulus nanum	Unclipped	2	4	D

THE HEDGES SHOWN in this chart are shrubs which are particularly suited for planting in long rows for fencing, to screen an unwanted view, or as a baffle to cut down undesirable noise. Flowering shrubs such as forsythia, lilac or weigela should never be clipped to formal shapes.

SEE ALSO

Gardening . . . Grass . . . Hand mowers . . . Lawns . . . Mowers . . . Paths, garden . . . Patios . . . Retaining walls . . . Transplanting . . . Trees

Shrubs can be used in dozens of interesting ways around your lot. You can group them into small green islands to break up large lawn areas. You can arrange them as hedges, in long rows, with the eventual height being determined by the species you select.

If you have put in trees at either end of the house, the sweeping line of the shrubs at the base of the house will seem to tie the whole picture together.

A row of tall shrubs at the back of your lot is often a better way than a fence to divide your lot from your neighbors. If you don't want the curtain between the two properties to be too much of a wall, keep the shrubs trimmed to four feet.

use shrubs as hedges

The idea of using shrubs for hedges can be important, depending on the landscaping problems you have to solve. You can grow hedges ranging from as little as one foot in height up to 15 or more feet. You can allow a hedge to grow in its natural shape, or you can clip it to the shape you desire.

The list of hedge plants on page 1679 includes the majority of the most popular shrubs used for hedges. Some are deciduous, some are evergreen. Some will flower, some will be festooned with colorful berries.

The very smallest hedges provide an interesting and natural way to divide your yard without really breaking it up. You can set apart a patch for a garden by surrounding the area with a tiny privet. It shouldn't be high enough to break up the view across your yard or to shade the sun from the garden, yet it should have the effect of setting the area neatly apart.

Tall shrubs planted behind a flower garden provide a green backdrop which shows off your flower blooms to great advantage. If you have flowering shrubs, you will be rewarded with a burst of color in the background planting early in the spring, followed later by the color of the garden itself. When planning this use, place the shrubs so they don't shade the garden too much. A flower garden on the south side of a planting of shrubs is best.

In planning the use of shrubs, particularly at the front of your house, think in terms of what the eye sees—lines, and color and mass. You have the vertical lines provided by the trees, the vertical and horizontal lines of the house itself, and the low horizontal lines provided by shrubs to work with. For mass, when you need it, you can group shrubs of different heights. For color you have not only the green of the lawn and the color of the exterior of the house, but you have a variety of greens, blue-greens and yellow-greens among the shrubs—not to mention reds and grays.

Your objective is to blend these lines, colors and masses into a harmonious whole. Through plantings you tie the house to the ground and make it a part of the natural environment—instead of a foreign structure superimposed on it.

Ground covers. Ground cover plants, though not actually shrubbery, must also be included in your landscaping plan. They provide answers in problem areas, for example, where grass is difficult to mow or grow.

They also can be used ornamentally, in beds beside walks and at the base of the house, or even in small islands in the midst of the lawn. Ground covers provide an interesting variation in texture and color when you need it.

Good ground cover plants thrive in a wide range of soil and moisture conditions, and are relatively free from pests and disease. Three very hardy and popular ground covers are myrtle (Vinca major), pachysandra, and English ivy.

Other good evergreen ground covers worth investigating are ajuga, Cornus canadensis, lilyturf, sedum, heather, euonymous fortunei, and the creeping junipers. Look, too, at the dwarf spreading English and Canada yews.

plant where mowing is difficult

Plant ground covers in areas where mowing would be difficult or inconvenient—the narrow area between the foundation of the house and the edge of the driveway, for example, or along a lot line between houses. If you have problems with growing things on the north side of the house, ground covers can solve this problem, too. Many of them do very well in areas where there is little or no sun.

Plant them around the base of a tree as a good substitute for the grass which refuses to grow there—or at the base of a fence, to make the fence more attractive and to eliminate the hand-trimming of grass which otherwise would grow there, too close to the fence for the mower to reach.

As with trees, when you plant shrubs keep in mind the size they will attain when mature. Give each shrub ample room to develop and to take on its attractive natural shape. Once a shrub has reached its mature size, it should be pruned or trimmed annually.

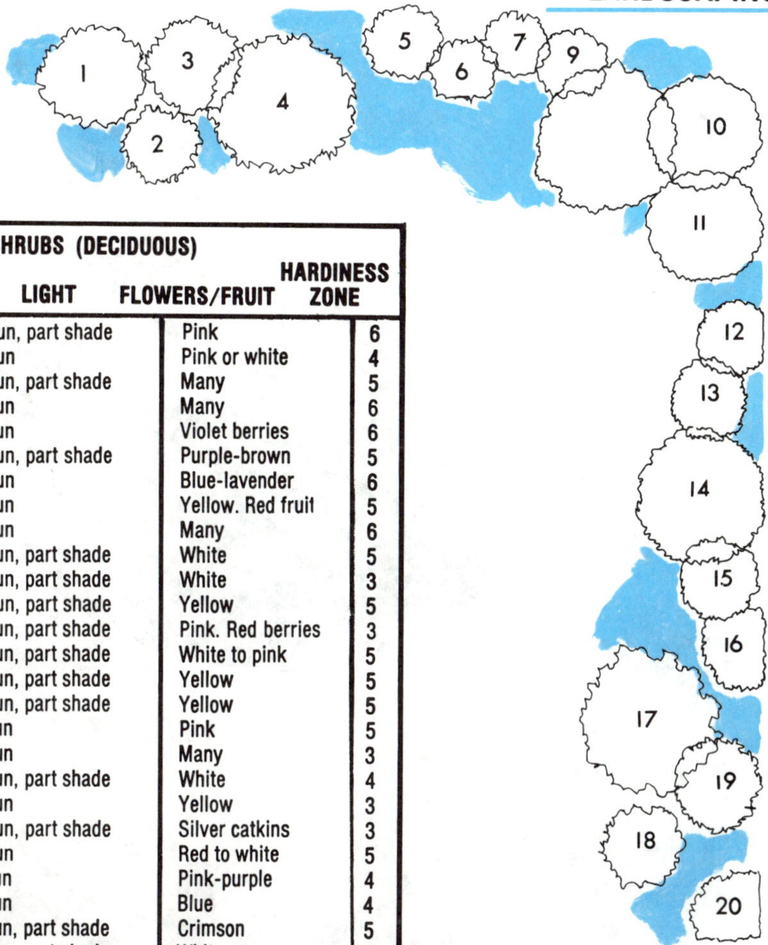

NAME	HEIGHT (in ft.)	LIGHT	FLOWERS/FRUIT	HARDINESS ZONE
FLOWERING SHRUBS (DECIDUOUS)				
Abelia	5	Sun, part shade	Pink	6
Almond, flowering	4	Sun	Pink or white	4
Althaea	10	Sun, part shade	Many	5
Buddleia	8	Sun	Many	6
Callicarpa	5	Sun	Violet berries	6
Calycanthus	4	Sun, part shade	Purple-brown	5
Chaste tree (vitex)	9	Sun	Blue-lavender	6
Cherry, Cornelian	15	Sun	Yellow. Red fruit	5
Crape-myrtle	5-25	Sun	Many	6
Deutzia	3	Sun, part shade	White	5
Dogwood, red-twig	6	Sun, part shade	White	3
Forsythia	10	Sun, part shade	Yellow	5
Honeysuckle, bush	8	Sun, part shade	Pink. Red berries	3
Hydrangea, Peegee	5	Sun, part shade	White to pink	5
Hypericum	2	Sun, part shade	Yellow	5
Kerria	5	Sun, part shade	Yellow	5
Kolkwitzia	8	Sun	Pink	5
Lilac, French	8	Sun	Many	3
Mockorange	10	Sun, part shade	White	4
Potentilla	3	Sun	Yellow	3
Pussy willow	20	Sun, part shade	Silver catkins	3
Quince, flowering	2-8	Sun	Red to white	5
Smoke tree	12	Sun	Pink-purple	4
Spiraea, Blue Mist	2	Sun	Blue	4
Spiraea, red	3	Sun, part shade	Crimson	5
Spiraea, Van Houtte	5	Sun, part shade	White	4
Tamarix	15	Sun, part shade	Pink	5
Viburnum carlesi	6	Sun, part shade	Pink	5
Viburnum, doublefile	8	Sun	White fls. Red fruit	5
Weigela	7	Sun	Red to white	5
BROADLEAF EVERGREEN SHRUBS				
Azalea, Glenn Dale	5	Sun, part shade	Many	7
Azalea, Flame	6	Part shade	Warm colors	6
Barberry, wintergreen	5	Sun	Black berries	5
Boxwood, English	20	Sun, part shade		6
Boxwood, littleleaf	3	Sun, part shade		6
Cotoneaster, bearberry	1	Sun, part shade	Red berries	6
Daphne, rose	1	Sun, part shade	Pink. Fragrant	5
Euonymus japonica	10	Sun	Pink berries	7
Euonymus, spreading	6	Sun/shade	Pink-red berries	5
Holly, Burford	6	Sun, part shade	Red berries	6
Holly, Japanese	5-10	Sun, part shade	Black berries	6
Holly, Oregon grape	4	Sun, part shade	Yellow. Blue berries	5
Laurel, Mountain	6	Sun, part shade	Pink to white	5
Leucothoe	3	Shade	White	5
Osmanthus ilicifolius	8	Sun, part shade	White	7
Pieris japonica	10	Part shade	White	6
Pyracantha	8	Sun	Orange berries	6
Rhododendron	8	Part shade	Many colors	5
NEEDLE EVERGREEN SHRUBS				
Arborvitae, globe	3	Sun/shade		3
Juniper, Andorra	1½	Sun, part shade		3
Juniper, Keteleer	12	Sun, part shade		4
Juniper, Pfitzer	4	Sun, light shade		4
Pine, Mugho	5	Sun		3
Yew, Hicks	6	Sun/shade		6
Yew, Japanese spreading	5	Shade		5

SHRUBS CAN PROVIDE flowers or berries almost year-round. The typical border plan shown here needs a sunny place about 10 x 60 feet, and will provide spring-to-frost flowers and berries. Shrubs are l. doublefile viburnum; 2. abelia; 3. pyrancantha; 4. Andorra juniper; 5. lilac; 6. callicarpa; 7. tamarix; 8. buddleia; 9. forsythia; 10. crape-myrtle; 11. smoke tree; 12. Blue Mist spirea; 13. potentilla; 14. mockorange; 15. hypericum; 16. pussy willow; 17. Japanese holly; 18. red spirea; 19. red-twig dogwood; and 20. deutzia.

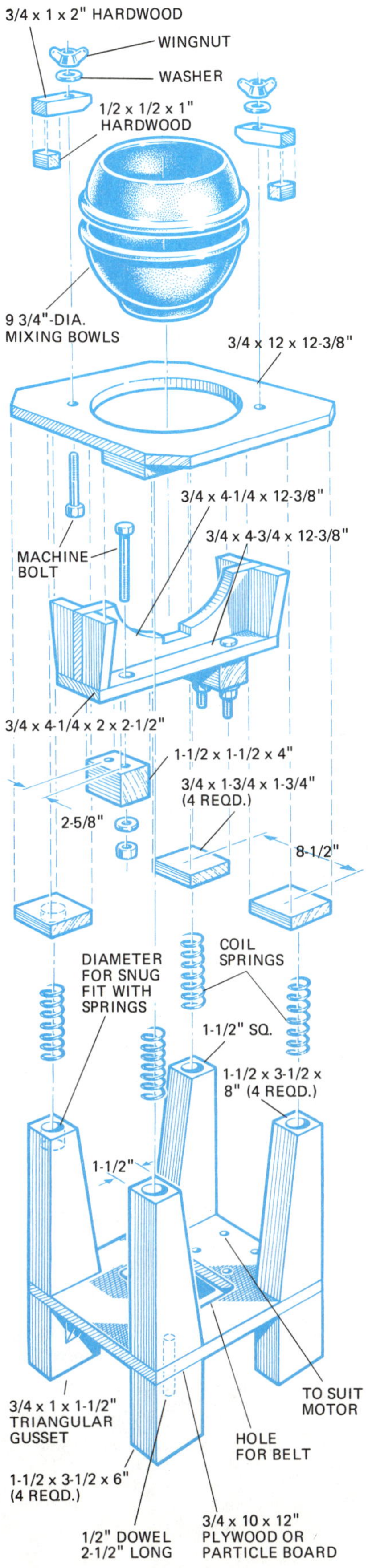

Make glowing gemstones in this shop-built polisher

By R. S. HEDIN

■ BY POLISHING the rocks you collect with progressively finer grades of abrasive, you can turn them into glowing gemstones. Inexpensive tumblers do the job well enough, but slowly—requiring at least one month per load. Vibrating rock polishers do it in one-quarter the time.

Commercial versions cost $200 and up, but you can build this one for about $50. It is basically a shaker table, with a platform, which holds the rock bowl, suspended on four coil springs and vibrated by eccentric weights on a rotating shaft attached to its underside.

The rock bowl is made from two Melmac mixing bowls (No. 118 by Texas Ware) fastened mouth-to-mouth. The bottom of the upper one is removed. Grinding is the best method—use eye, nose and mouth protection. Pencil a cutting line on the outside of the bowl and grind with the corner of the wheel. Silicone-rubber caulking is used to cement the bowls together (sand the glaze off the rims) and to line the lower one. One tube of caulking rubber will do the job. Apply it with a caulking gun in concentric circles, and

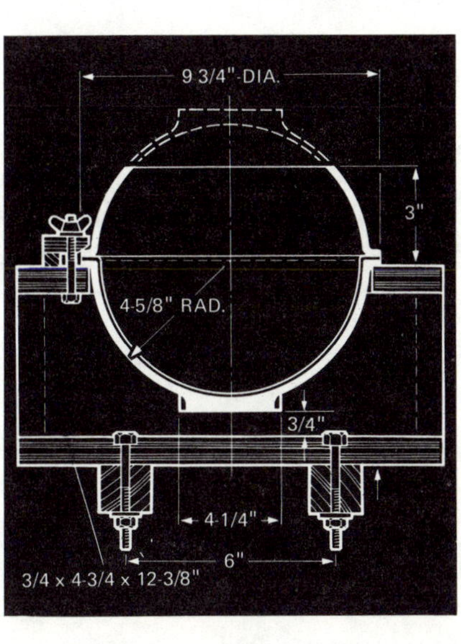

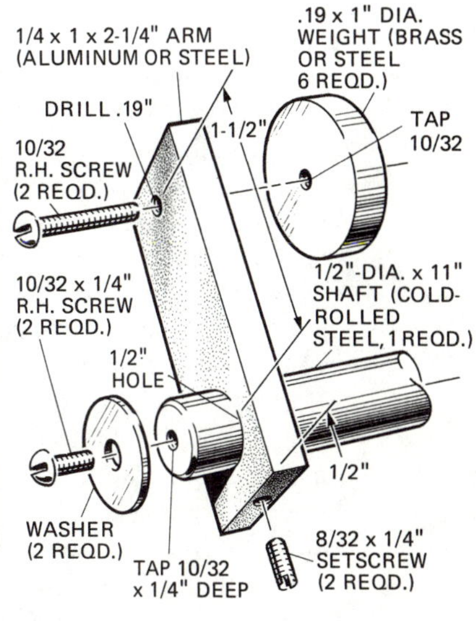

SEE ALSO

Art glass . . . Bottle craft . . . Hobby centers . . . Internal carving . . . Jewelry . . . Marquetry . . . Potter's wheels

HERE IS THE complete polisher with the bowl in place. The second holddown clamp is hidden.

THESE ARE THE major assemblies. The platform is inverted to show pillow blocks, shaft, arms and pulley.

HARDWARE REQUIRED

2 10-32 x 1" RH machine screws
2 ¼ x 2½" machine bolts
4 ¼ x 3" machine bolts with nuts
4 ¼ x 1½" machine bolts with nuts
2 ¼" wingnuts
2 pillow blocks, Fafnir PB½
2 3/16" or ¼" V-belt pulleys; 3" dia., ½" bore
3/16" or ¼" V-belt, 22" long or to suit
¼-hp split-phase motor, 1725 rpm
2 8-32 x ¼" setscrews
2 10-32 x ¼" setscrews
4 coil springs, approx. 1⅛" O.D. x 4" long; 10 coils, .090" dia. wire.

spread with a wet wooden spoon. The rubber needn't be smooth, but pockets that could trap grit should be filled. The lining should be about 1/16-in. thick.

Springs specified in the hardware list are just about right to support the load and isolate the base from vibration. If they're too stiff, the base will tend to walk; if too light, they may buckle under the load.

The pillow blocks for the shaft include ball bearings and can be bought most conveniently from a bearing supply house or well-stocked hardware store. Weight arms are held to the shaft with setscrews. Tapped holes in the shaft ends are for screws and washers that act as safety stops in case the arms loosen.

Defer buying pulleys and belt until the polisher has been assembled, then measure the distance between shafts—from this and pulley size you can determine belt length. *Without* the bowl and rocks in place, it should be necessary to compress the springs about ¼ in. to install the belt.

setting up the first run

For a first run, set the weight arms 90° apart, two weights on each. Fill the lower bowl with 10 lbs. of rocks (to assure correct motion and circulation), a cup of water and a few tablespoons of detergent, and, if starting with rough stones, ¼ cup of 120 or 220-grit abrasive. Get the abrasive from your local rock store or hobby shop, which can provide more information on technique than can be presented here. To begin in lapidary, you can use this basic guide: Rough grind—120 to 220 grit for one to 1½ days; fine grind—400 to 600 grit for two to three days; prepolish—levigated alumina for one to two days; mirror polish—tin oxide for two to three days.

Don't use too much water; it will only splash out. Always start with a full load of rocks to get proper action. The rocks should circulate, rising to the top of the center of the bowl, traveling to the edge and then going under again. The pattern of their motion can be varied by changing the angular relationship of the weight arms, while the speed of rock motion can be varied by adding or removing weights. Although the polisher is not very noisy, it can be made quieter by covering the bowl with an old bath towel doubled up.

Shabby redwood table

My redwood picnic table has weathered to a dirty gray color. How can I make it look like new?—J. Lindsey, El Paso, Tex.

"Like new" may not be entirely possible, but you can rejuvenate it with a thorough sanding, starting with a coarse grade of sandpaper and working up to a fine sandpaper. Give the picnic table two coats of a redwood stain that's made especially for the purpose.

Cleaning basement floor

My concrete basement floor is dirty—I mean ground-in dirt. Detergents, household bleach or scrubbing just don't clean it. I want it cleaned to the original color. Any suggestion?—E. Roth, Cleveland.

Yes, that you forget it and resort to painting. Ground-in dirt is difficult to remove from concrete. Clean the floor by scrubbing, allow it to dry, then etch with a prepared (paint-store) solution and apply a coat of paint that's approved for use on concrete floors.

Cleaning fireplace flue

I think my fireplace flue needs cleaning, but how? The chimney is about 25 ft. high and so far as I know has never been cleaned of the sooty coating at the top. Also, is it true there's a downdraft in the flue at all times? If so, what prevents the fireplace from smoking?—C.A., Ill.

If you burn resinous woods or fireplace coals, the flue is probably coated with the sticky, resinous material mixed with soot. The former is difficult to remove, the soot less so. If you use the "cleaner" woods exclusively, the flue may not need cleaning. But dust and debris collect in time on the sides of the flue and on the "wind shelf." The latter, just above the damper in a properly built fire opening, will probably need cleaning to maintain its efficiency.

To clean the flue, pack a cloth bag with straw or similar resilient material and weight it with a brick or two. Tie a long cord to the bag and lower bag into the flue. It should just fit so that as you lower and raise it all sides of the flue will be scrubbed thoroughly. Keep the fireplace opening covered while doing this. Then open the damper, reach up inside the opening and remove the accumulation from the shelf.

There is always an up-and-down draft in the chimney. When the house is closed this equalizes the air pressure. The shelf turns a good portion of the downdraft back into the updraft and thus prevents the smoke from being blown into the room.

Bubbles?

My new basement wall is very smooth, having been poured in plywood forms, but there are several holes on the inside surface (caused, I suppose, by air bubbles in the mix). I want to apply a waterproofer, but how do I fill the holes?—N.E., Pa.

I think perhaps you would do best using a concrete patching mixture. I'm assuming that the holes you describe are not more than an inch deep and are of the oval shape that would be formed by an air bubble (also that there are no cracks running through the wall).

Before mixing and applying the patcher, undercut the edges of the openings with a small cold chisel to form a "key" for the new material. This must be done with care to avoid chipping the edges of the opening and enlarging it. Be sure to remove all loose material after undercutting. Then mix the patcher according to the instructions on the container. Take care not to get the mix too thin, as this would make it unmanageable on a vertical surface.

With a small trowel, build the patch a trifle over-flush with the wall surface. Then before the mix sets, smooth the area flush with a whiskbroom or paintbrush and wipe off any excess with a damp cloth. Usually it's advisable to keep the patches damp until the mix has hardened.

'Longer look' with narrow siding

I live in a small ranch house that is sided with wide boards. I'd like to make it appear longer and lower. Can such an illusion be created?—L. Powers, Little Rock, Ark.

In some settings and depending a bit on the architectural detail, a darker-colored paint will give the effect of greater length.

For a better way, apply narrower siding, such as 4-inch widths over the existing 8-inch boards. There are also 8-inch-wide sidings to be applied in such a way that you end up with the appearance of 4-inch siding.

Stain painted shingles?

Shingled walls of my house are painted. Can I use a stain on them?—R. Blanchard, Portland, Me.

No. Stains commonly used on shingles won't "take." You risk flaking of the stain and peeling of the paint. Some homeowners use a chalking paint on previously painted shingles. This gives a rather flat surface similar to stains in appearance, but it has a tendency to run as it chalks, thus discoloring different-colored window trim.

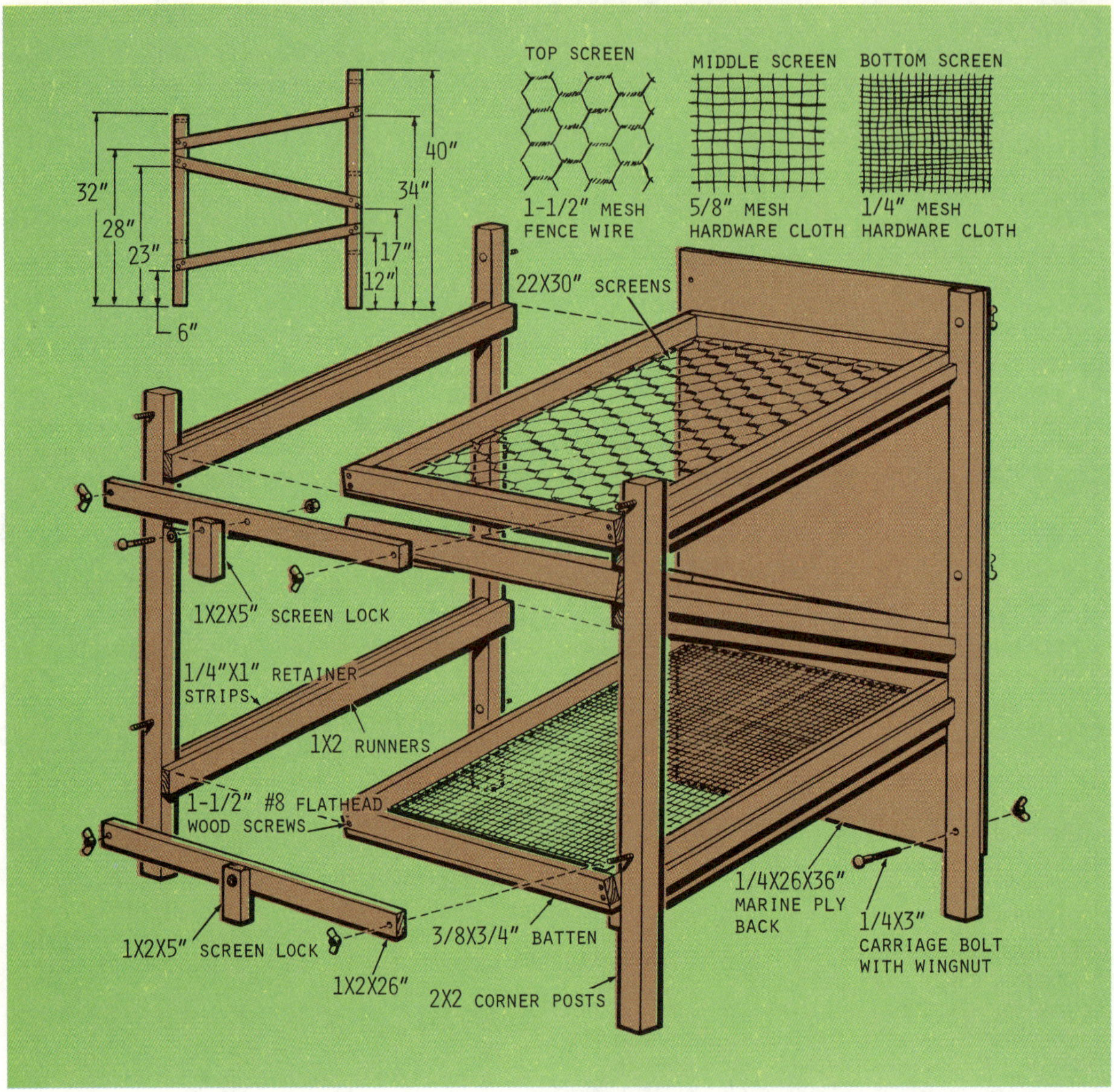

A triple-screen sorter for rockhounds

You can make this unit yourself and it disassembles easily for transportation to your collecting area. Once you have it set up, let gravity do the work for you. As the stones gather at the lower ends of the screens, keep your eyes open for the gems

By CARL FISCHER

SEE ALSO

Jewelry . . . Potter's wheels

WHETHER YOU'RE an old hand or an enthusiastic beginner, this easy-to-make sorter is bound to make your rock-hunting field trips more rewarding. Using gravity alone, it separates the gemstones from their overburden and grades them according to size. The whole thing weighs only 30 lbs. and disassembles.

ONE BIG advantage of this low-cost sorter is that it lets you dig and screen large amounts of promising material instead of just scratching the surface.

KEEPERS GATHER at the lower ends of screens along with the debris. Once you've picked them out, slide screen into place and shovel on more material.

To keep the weight down, use white pine for the 2x2 corner posts. Nail the 1x2 screen runners on the inside of each pair of posts, locating them according to the dimensions given in the detail on p. 1686. Add a ¼ x 1-in. batten to the outside of each runner, elevating it about ½ in. above the upper edge of the 1x2 to form a guard rail.

The screen frames are made of 1x2 white pine and assembled with two 1½-in. No. 8 wood screws at each corner. Mesh sizes listed on the plan are suitable for most gem collecting areas. Tack the screens to the bottoms of the frames. To keep the screens from sagging, it's a good idea to reinforce them with lengths of galvanized wire. Just stretch three evenly spaced strands lengthwise under each screen and three strands crosswise. Tack these to the bottom of the frame, then nail battens over all these screen fastenings so the screens will slide smoothly.

The ¼-in. marine plywood back should be mounted flush with the tops of the rear corner posts. This will allow a little ground clearance, making it easier to use the sorter on an uneven surface.

To assemble the unit, you'll need ten ¼-in. carriage bolts, six 2½ in. long for the rear and four 3 in. long for the front. Use washers and wingnuts with all these assembly bolts. Cut the 1x2 front crossbars and mount the pivoting screen locks on them, then drill holes for the assembly bolts and the sorter is completed. If you plan on using it in water, such as working a stream bed, it's advisable to give the unit a couple of coats of paint.

using the sorter

There are no special tricks involved in using the sorter. The inclined screens feed one into the other, classifying the gravels almost as fast as you can shovel them. Stones will gather at the lower ends of the screens where you can inspect them at a glance, lifting out the "keepers" and discarding the debris.

The screens slide out easily and may be shuttled back and forth rapidly to dislodge stubborn sand and clay from your specimens. The sorter has no trouble handling wet material from stream bottoms, but it's wise to add an occasional pail of water to accelerate the separation.

The biggest advantage of this sorter is that it lets you screen large masses of material, digging down instead of just searching the surface. The more material you can inspect from a likely area, the more stones of gem quality you are likely to find.

How to have the best lawn in your neighborhood

A thick, green, beautiful lawn isn't the result of hard work—but of smart work. You just need to know when and how to seed, feed, water, weed and mow

By CLIFFORD B. HICKS

THE NO. 1 PROBLEM of most lawns is not scraggly weeds, grasping crabgrass or hungry insects. The No. 1 problem is human nature.

Come spring, most homeowners can hardly wait to get in the warm sun and begin rolling the still-soggy turf, reseeding bare spots, spreading fertilizer, and swinging the first punch at crabgrass. Their enthusiasm carries into summer.

But come fall, most homeowners have had it. Mowing has become a tiresome chore, and crabgrass is fighting back. Besides, there are storm windows to hang and the kids are beginning to holler for help with their homework. Suddenly it's much easier to forget everything that needs to be done, including lawn work.

Yet fall is the prime time for renovating a lawn. A little work invested then will pay off in a vastly improved lawn the next year. Lawn care is a round-the-calendar operation, but fall offers real opportunity.

- Nature is shedding seeds herself, and offers a big boost to your own efforts.
- Grass has come out of its summer dormancy and is growing vigorously in an unconscious urge to prepare itself for winter.
- Weeds are again growing vigorously, and thus are prime targets for weed killers. If you kill weeds in spring and summer, the resulting bare spots are likely to be infested with an even worse enemy—crabgrass. If you kill weeds in the fall, crabgrass has begun to go dormant, and fine grasses will spread to fill bare spots.

Furthermore, seedlings established in the fall are much more likely to survive. Heat, not cold,

SEE ALSO

Gardening . . . Grass . . . Hand mowers . . . Landscaping . . . Mowers . . . Paths, garden . . . Patios . . . Playgrounds . . . Putting greens . . . Retaining walls . . . Swings . . . Transplanting . . . Trees

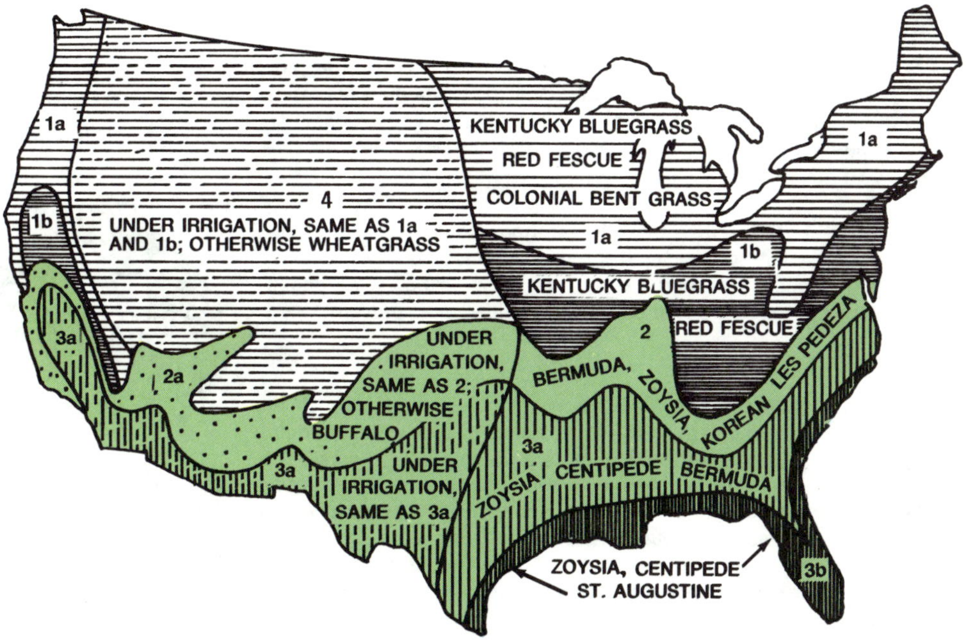

is the biggest environmental threat to a seedling. If you reseed in the spring, some of your tender new plants will inevitably be killed by summer heat and drought; on the other hand, if you sow seed in early fall, seedlings will be well established by the time they are covered with an insulating blanket of snow, and will emerge healthy and vigorous in the spring, when they will have three or four months to mature before they are exposed to the summer sun.

Autumn may be the best time to give your lawn rehabilitation treatment, but you don't have to wait until then to start applying good practices. You may be able to improve its health considerably by changing your mowing or watering habits, or by feeding it now. And if the weeds are using it for a picnic ground, you can dampen their enthusiasm now—and totally wipe them out later.

There is no such thing as the perfect all-around grass. If there were, it would be disease-free in all situations, would grow in all parts of the country, thrive in both the sun and the shade, survive long droughts, and put up with constant trampling. Alas, the best we can do is to select the best grass for each situation.

The grasses which do best in the southern states are quite different from the stellar performers of the north and northwest. Check the map above for the best grasses for your areas. As a rule, dealers feature seeds and mixtures tailored for the local climate.

Read the labels as you shop. These days they tell you a lot. And look for "mixtures." These are formulations of four to six different grasses put together by seed companies to give you the best possible combination of grasses.

The box will list any type of seed present in excess of five percent. Beware of mixtures containing very high percentages of annual grasses, usually annual ryes. These won't grow the second year. Their chief value is that they germinate quickly and serve to shelter the slower-starting perennials during the early weeks after seeding. This is important if you are sowing a new lawn, but of little value if you are reseeding an old one.

The label also shows the amount of weed seed present in the mixture. Compare labels and look for the lowest amount of weed seed and the highest amount of perennial grass seed. You'll pay more for the better mixtures, but you buy more good grass and less weed grief when you do.

Always buy fresh seed. When grass seed is on sale, find out why the price has been cut. Perhaps the dealer wants to attract new customers, which is a legitimate reason—or perhaps he wants to move some older seed, which isn't good. The reason is that the older the seed, the less of it you can expect to germinate.

The label gives you two important clues to the freshness of the seed and its ability to germinate. The first is the figure showing the percentage of germination of each seed in the mixture. This tells you how viable the seed was at the time of testing. Good seed runs 88 percent or better.

ARE YOU MISTREATING YOUR LAWN?

PROBLEM LAWNS have become problems in most cases because they are mistreated. Over many years, experts have found that most problems are caused by a standard group of errors. If you have a tired, disloyal lawn, you probably are committing one or more of these seven sins.

IMPROPER USE OF FERTILIZER. Too little nitrogen starves your lawn; too much weakens the root structure. See the section on feeding your lawn, page **1692**, and also check the chart, "Best Grass for Your Lawn," on pages **1692** and **1693** for the recommended amount of fertilizer for your turf.

IMPROPER WATERING. Wait to water your lawn until the grass actually shows signs of wilting; then water to a depth of 6 in. Sandy soils require frequent water in small amounts; clay soils require infrequent watering in large amounts. Never apply less than an inch of water to an established lawn. To know how much water you are applying, place coffee cans around the sprinkled area and wait for an inch of water to appear in them. This is the minimum amount. If you live in Area 1A (map on page **1689**), your lawn won't stay green in midsummer even if you water as directed, because virtually all cool-season grasses go dormant in midsummer. They'll turn green again in the fall.

POOR SEED MIXTURES. Buy only seed that is fresh and that is right for your area. Read "How to Buy Seed" on page **1689** and don't try to save money on cheap mixes which contain undesirable seed types. Check the germination data and the seed formula on the box.

POOR MOWING PRACTICES. Don't mow too low because when you do you don't leave enough leaf area to provide for good root development. Never remove more than half the blade at one time. See recommended mowing heights on the chart on page **1693**.

TOO MUCH TRAFFIC. Most of us believe that lawns should be played on and enjoyed, and normal activity won't harm a good lawn. But heavy traffic in certain areas, particularly during the winter ana early spring, compacts the soil so it can no longer support grass. Don't fight the system. Pave or lay stone in areas which always get heavy traffic.

TOO MUCH SHADE. Most grasses are not adapted to shady areas, and those that are recommended for shade still must get some sun. To help grass in shady areas, fertilize frequently but lightly. Prune tree branches when possible to allow a bit more light through. Then fertilize the trees four to five ft. deep so they won't steal food from the grass, and apply lime to the shaded soil, which is more likely to become acid. Finally, remove leaves and clippings frequently from these areas.

POORLY DRAINED SOILS. Grass plants will drown in those depressed areas of your lawn where water gathers in puddles. Soil in these areas becomes compacted quickly, too. Fill these depressions with layers of top soil added a little at a time. Slopes also are a problem because the water runs off so quickly that the grass gets little water. There also may be erosion. The best solution is to regrade the lawn.

The second clue is the date of the germination test. The law requires that the seed be shipped within five months of the test. Reputable seed companies are careful to replace aging stocks in stores—but check the date anyway. If several brands are available, check one against the other and buy the freshest. More of it will sprout.

You'll find two basic types of mixtures, one for a beautiful "picture" front lawn, and another for play areas which receive rough wear. The show lawn has fine-bladed grasses which produce a lawn of exceptional color and texture. The play grasses are tougher, broader-bladed, and not as deep a green.

If you always believed that rye grass was a poor lawn grass, you must now change your mind. The old ryes were wide-bladed, coarse annual grasses. The new turf-type ryes are perennials which mix well with bluegrass. They were bred especially for soft fibers, to provide clean cutting. Common rye, when mowed, gets frayed ends which turn brown. The new ryes cut as nicely as bluegrass, with no browning, and their fine blades don't give the lawn a coarse look.

You'll also find a variety of seed mixtures tailored for sowing in shady places—but don't be misled. All grasses need some sun. The more dense your shade, the less likely you are to grow grass. Shady lawn mixtures actually are for lawns which receive partial or filtered sunlight. They will grow where bluegrass won't, but they won't grow without some sun.

Finally, when shopping for grass seed, keep an eye open for new varieties. A lot of research is being carried on to develop new types of grasses, for the seed producers are still searching for the perfect grass. Read the labels and literature carefully, to find out what improvements the new seed offers. Expect such features as better resistance to disease, richer color, better drought or shade survival, or the ability to form a more dense turf in a single growing season.

feeding your lawn

To have a healthy lawn which grows vigorously, has rich color, and renews itself, you need to see that its grasses get enough nourishment. This means that you must make periodic applications of fertilizer. But not just any fertilizer. The element which makes grass greener, promotes good growth, and helps to build roots is nitrogen—so the fertilizer must be rich in nitrogen.

Most soils have too little nitrogen, and when you apply it to the soil in any form, the nitrogen washes out in time. This is why continued applications are necessary. The amount of nitrogen needed varies with the type of grass. Common Kentucky bluegrass and fescues need about 3 pounds per 1000 square feet of lawn per year. Some of the improved bluegrasses need 5 pounds. Bent grass needs about 4 pounds.

You can feed two or three times a year, applying about 1 pound of nitrogen per 1000 square feet each time. After the long winter, your grass

YOUR LAWN-CARE CALENDAR

(For regions 1A, 1B and most of region 4. Warm-season grasses grown in regions 2 and 3 require care only during the hot summer months.)

Early fall—If your lawn needs a complete renovation, do it now (see separate section). Apply herbicide to eliminate broadleaf weeds. Apply lime if needed. In September, apply half of your fall fertilizer allotment. Rake bare areas and reseed; water lightly but often.

Late fall—In mid-October, apply the other half of the fall fertilizer allotment. Continue mowing as long as the grass grows; do not leave the grass tall for the winter months. Mulch the leaves as they fall, or if they tend to clot on the lawn, rake and remove them.

Early spring—Rake trash from lawn. Apply lime if needed, and if you were too lazy to do it last fall. Apply a pre-emergent crabgrass killer. In late February or early March, spread a light application of fertilizer, or a heavier application of slow-release fertilizer. Reseed any bare spots you missed last fall. If the soil has heaved from frost, use a light roller but not a heavy one. Apply a herbicide for chickweed if that weed is a problem in your lawn.

Late spring—Give your lawn another light shot of fertilizer. Kill the broadleaf weeds. Mow according to the recommended practice for your type of grass. You should have used a pre-emergent crabgrass killer months ago. If you didn't, do it now.

Summer—If you have a zoysia or Bermuda-grass lawn, feed it in July and again in August. Mow frequently enough that you remove no more than one-half the total leaf length. If you have a bluegrass lawn, don't worry if it turns brown—it's dormant as nature intended it to be. In long periods of drought, water deeply once a week. Take a vacation. When you return, if the grass is so long that the clippings may smother the lawn, remove them as you mow.

is hungry and active in the spring—and so should be fed in April. It grows vigorously until early June (early July for improved bluegrasses), and takes a nap until September, when it wakes up and starts feeding for the winter ahead. Experts advise feeding the second meal around the first of June, just before nap time. They tell you not to feed in July or August unless you have a bent grass lawn, which could use a snack about the first of August.

The big, important meal comes in the fall—anytime in September. If you cut out any feeding, skip the June application. But don't miss the fall feeding, whatever else you do. This is the one which determines how strong your lawn will be next spring.

Now—about buying your fertilizer—there have been so many claims and counterclaims about lawn foods that most homeowners are confused. They buy bags of anything labeled as great for lawns, without thinking about nutritional values. And often they spend unnecessary money doing it this way.

A complete fertilizer contains three elements: nitrogen, for stimulating leaf growth; phosphorous, for the formation of strong roots; and potash, to give plants stamina and disease resistance. Every bag of fertilizer is labeled with the percentages of these elements it contains. Thus, a 10-6-4 fertilizer consists of 10 percent available nitrogen, 6 percent phosphorous, 4 percent potash—and 80 percent inert carrying material.

Since nitrogen is the most vital of these elements, and also the most expensive, the *first* figure on the label is the one which you should pay most attention to. Simply divide this figure by 100. The answer is the number of pounds of fertilizer you must buy to apply 1 lb. of nitrogen to 1000 sq. ft. of lawn; it's a good idea not to apply more than 1 pound of nitrogen per 1000 sq. ft. of established lawn at any one time.

You can buy organic or inorganic fertilizer. Organic fertilizers are processed from such plant or animal materials as sewage sludge and bonemeal. Soil bacteria cause them to break down and release nutrients into the soil. Their action is slower, and during decomposition they become a part of the soil.

Inorganic fertilizers, urea-form and resin-form mixtures, are synthetic fertilizers which slowly release nitrogen into the soil as a result of rain and moisture. They begin feeding quickly, which is an advantage, but it is easy to overfeed a lawn with these. Overstimulation causes spindly top growth and weakens the lawn. Plan your feedings with these materials carefully.

The chart on page 1696 shows various combinations of inorganic fertilizers as well as some of the more common organic materials. It indicates how much total fertilizer you have to buy to apply 1 lb. of nitrogen per 1000 sq. ft. of your lawn.

When buying any kind of fertilizer, don't shop for the lowest-priced bag on display, because in use its contents may actually be the most expensive. Fifty pounds of one fertilizer may be needed to provide 1 lb. of fertilizer for a 2000-sq.-ft. lawn, while 100 pounds of a cheaper fertilizer may be needed. Be a smart buyer and do a quick computation. Divide 100 into the nitrogen number on the bag—and then compare prices. You may find that a $9 bag is cheaper than a $6 because the $9 bag puts a pound of nitrogen on more square feet.

NAME	GEOGRAPHICAL AREA
1. KENTUCKY BLUEGRASS	
Common	1A, 1B, 4 under irrigation
Merion	1A, 1B, northern 2
Park	1A, 1B
2. RED FESCUES	
Common	1A
Pennlawn	1A
3. ASTORIA	1B
4. ZOYSIAS	
Meyer	southern 1A, northern 2
Emerald	2
Manilagrass	2
5. BERMUDAGRASSES	
Everglades 1	southern 2
Ormond	southern 2
Texturf 10	2 and 3 in Texas
Tifgreen	2, 3
Tiflawn	2
6. ST. AUGUSTINES	
Floratine	2
Bitter blue	2
7. BAHIAGRASS	2
8. CENTIPEDE	2
9. BUFFALOGRASS	southern 4
10. BLUE GRAMA	4
11. WHEATGRASS	northern 4

HERE YOU'LL FIND THE BEST GRASS FOR YOUR LAWN

CHARACTERISTICS	MOWING HEIGHT	BEST SEEDING OR PLANTING TIME	NITROGEN, LBS./ 1000 SQ. FT. ANNUALLY
Excellent cool-area grass; withstands abuse; not good for heavy shade.	1½-2″	Fall	3-4
Low-growing, short leaves, good color; thick turf; leaf-spot-resistant.	1½-2″	Fall	6-8
Vigorous and resistant to rust, particularly in far north.	1½-2″	Fall	3-4
More tolerant of shade than bluegrass, narrow leaf, good color.	1-2″	Fall	2-3
Better turf than common red fescues, more tolerant of leaf spot.	1-2″	Fall	2-3
Beautiful bentgrass lawn, but requires continuous and expensive care.	¾″ or less	Fall	4-6
Dense turf able to withstand hot, humid summer.	¾-1″	Spring	5-10
Dense, relatively weed-free turf. Very slow to establish.	¾-1″	Spring	5-10
Very dense, stands considerable shade.	¾-1″	Spring	5-10
Dark green, fine textured, vigorous; excellent for Florida.	¾-1″	Spring	5-10
Blue-green, slow growing; resists leaf spot, but not dollar spot; excellent for Florida.	¾-1″	Spring	5-10
Medium texture, dark green; makes early spring recovery; slow spreading.	¾-1″	Spring	5-10
Dark green, fine texture, disease resistant.	¾-1″	Spring	5-10
Dense, weed-free turf; tolerates heavy wear, used on many football fields.	¾-1″	Spring	5-10
Thick growth; adapted to sandy soils; year-round color.	2-2½″	Spring	4-5
Blue-green; excellent ornamental turf, but does not withstand heavy wear.	2-2½″	Spring	4-5
Coarse, relatively unattractive turf, but easy to maintain.	2″	Spring	4
Easily maintained, good for heavy soils; has unattractive brown winter color.	1-1½″	Spring	2
Best grass where water is unavailable; thrives when mowed low.	1-2″	Spring	Seldom required.
Bunch-type grass, not as desirable as buffalograss, but drought-resistant.	1-2″	Spring	Seldom required.
Withstands long, dry periods and heavy traffic if not mowed closely.	2″	Fall	Seldom required.

who needs weeds?

The battle to keep your lawn free of weeds seems unending. The creepers sneak in among the grass stalks, the dandelions spread their leaves and pop their yellow heads. Sometimes it seems that if you take your eyes off the grass for 10 minutes, some weed sneaks in and establishes himself.

There are three ways to win this battle: Keep the weeds out in the first place; slaughter them in the spring, before they get moving; or fight them throughout the growing season.

The best way is the first way—and you keep weeds out by building a thick, healthy, vigorous stand of grass. Strong, thick grass crowds out the weeds, or smothers them before they can take hold. If you have a good thick lawn, don't mow it too close, because this allows the weeds to get in. And when you water, do it thoroughly because light waterings, which don't soak into the soil, will water the weeds near the surface, but won't water the deeper grass roots.

The next best method of fighting weeds is to clobber them with a pre-emergent herbicide. Your dealer has a number of these, which you must apply early in the spring, before weed seeds have a chance to germinate. A good rule of thumb in many areas is to apply them before the lilacs bloom or the magnolia petals fall. By killing the weeds before they start, you can save yourself a lot of labor later.

Finally, there is the old method of day-by-day hand-to-hand combat. Today's herbicides are pretty good and take out some of the work, but this type of treatment is still a season-long nuisance. If you can identify the unwanted visitors in your yard, you can buy a herbicide specifically designed for them. If you have a fine collection

ESTABLISHING A LAWN

SEEDING IS THE EASIEST and least expensive way to establish a lawn. For even distribution of the seed, broadcast it with a mechanical spreader. Rake the area after seeding, then mulch lightly with straw.

PLUGGING IS A GOOD WAY to start zoysia and similar grasses. The plugs are small squares or cylinders of sod and usually are set about 12 in. apart. Set them closer if you want more rapid coverage.

SODDING IS EXPENSIVE, but is the quickest way to an established lawn. Prepare the surface as you would for seeding, then roll it lightly. Dampen the soil then lay the sod over it. Butt the sod strips closely. Roll the completed lawn, then water regularly.

SPRIGGING IS INEXPENSIVE and an excellent way to start Bermuda and zoysia lawns. In this method you propagate individual runners which are broken from established sod. A neighbor with a good lawn may be willing to contribute the sprigs. If you want fast coverage, set the runners close together. Firm the soil over each sprig with your feet, and keep the sprigged area moist for several weeks or until the sprigs take hold and begin to spread. This is a good job for very hot weather because the sprigs spread very fast at this time, but you must keep them well watered or you will lose them.

of weeds, with nothing predominant (including the grass), get an all-purpose weed killer.

Herbicides come in liquid concentrate form, which you mix with water and spray on, and in dry form, which you apply with a spreader. You can buy pre-emergent weed killers mixed with fertilizer, so you can both weed and feed your lawn with one shot in the spring. This is probably the handiest way to get both jobs done.

Note that herbicides will kill any type of broad-leafed plant or flower. Be careful as you spread or spray the stuff not to let any of it drift into the flower beds. And reserve any sprayer used with weed killer for weed killing use in the future, because it is extremely difficult to get rid of all traces of herbicide. Get a second sprayer for spraying insecticides.

crabgrass confrontations

Crabgrass is a tough adversary, but we finally have good ways to control it. To understand what you are up against, you have to know a little about crabgrass.

Throughout the summer and fall, the crabgrass in your lawn produces seeds. These seeds lie dormant until early spring, when they start sprouting. By midsummer, you can see the plants—coarse, broad eyesores, unwanted islands in an otherwise nice lawn. Each plant dies in the fall, but by then has left behind its own legacy of seeds. Unfortunately, we now know that crabgrass seeds can stay dormant for as long as 50 years.

Fortunately, pre-emergent crabgrass-killing herbicides do a great job of killing the seedlings just after they sprout. This means that with some smart action in the spring, you can stay free of crabgrass through the growing season. But you still must go on with the pre-emergence treatment the following spring, because older seeds may germinate. In time, perhaps after two or three years, you may get rid of most of the seeds. But don't count on it.

The weed-and-feed combinations mentioned earlier, if applied early enough, are good for both feeding the lawn and killing the crabgrass sprouts. Normally you'd give this treatment late in April. If you are putting in a new lawn, you can buy a mixture containing both fertilizer and crabgrass killer which can be applied the same day you sow the grass seed.

Finally, you'll find crabgrass killers on your dealer's shelf for use after the plants have started to grow. Good advice: get after crabgrass as soon as you can. It grows very fast in the late

HOW TO CONTROL COMMON LAWN WEEDS

WEED	BEST TIME TO TREAT	CONTROL	EFFECT
Bermudagrass	Spring or summer	DowPon; Basfapon (dalapon); Roundup (glyphosate)	Good
Bindweed, field	Spring, fall	2,4-D	Good
Chickweed, common	Spring, fall	Dicamba; Sencor; MCPP; Banvel; Casoron G-4	Good
Chickweed, mouse-eared	Spring, fall	Dicamba; MCPP	Good
Crabgrass	Winter, spring, summer	See separate crabgrass section	Fair to good
Dandelion	Spring and fall	2,4-D; Dicamba	Good
Garlic, wild	Late fall, early spring	2,4-D; MCPP	Good
Goosegrass	Spring, early summer	2,4-D; DSMA; CMA; MAMA; MSMA	Poor
Ground-ivy	Spring, fall	Dicamba	Good
Henbit	Spring, summer	Dicamba, Casoron, G-4	Good
Knotweed	Late winter, early spring	2,4-D; Banvel, Dicamba	Good
Nimblewill	Spring	Zytron (repeated treatments); Roundup	Fair
Plantain, Buckhorn	Spring	2,4-D, Dicamba	Good
Plantain, rugel	Spring	2,4-D, Dicamba	Good
Quackgrass	Spring, summer, fall	Dalapon (kills all plants)	Fair
Sorrel, red	Spring	Dicamba	Fair
Woodsorrel, yellow	Spring	MCPP	Good

HOW TO CONTROL COMMON LAWN DISEASES

DISEASE	SYMPTOMS	CONTROL
Helminthosporium leaf spot	Kentucky bluegrass susceptible. Reddish-brown spots appear on leaves, which shrivel, and plant discolors and rots.	Acti-dione-thiram, Captan, Dyrene, Fore, Ortho Lawn and Turf Fungicide, PMA
Dollar spot	Affects many species, but particularly destructive to bentgrasses. Appears during cool, wet weather. Silver-dollar-size spots appear on lawn, black at first, then brown, then white. Grass dies.	Cadmium-containing fungicides, Dyrene, Ortho Lawn and Turf Fungicide, Tersan OM
Brown patch	Attacks virtually all species. Prevalent in warm humid areas. Irregular circular spots from few inches to several feet in diameter appear and turn brown. If weather stays hot and humid, grass dies but leaves remain erect.	Mercury-containing fungicides, Dyrene, Fore, Ortho Lawn and Turf Fungicide, Tersan OM
Rust	Attacks many grasses, but particularly destructive to Kentucky bluegrass. Usually occurs late in summer. Yellow-orange powdery spots appear on leaves. If cloth is rubbed across leaf, spores will leave a yellowish or orange stain.	Acti-dione-thiram, zineb
Snow mold	Affects many grasses, but particularly bentgrasses. Appears on grass which is growing while still covered with snow. White cottony growth appears on leaves.	Dyrene, mercury-containing fungicides, Ortho Lawn and Turf Fungicide, Thiram
Curvularia fading-out	Attacks many southern grasses when humidity is high. Damage severe on grass that has been covered by water. Older leaves die, but tips of new growth remain green.	Acti-dione-thiram, Captan, Dyrene, Ortho Lawn and Turf Fungicide, PMA, Thiram
Gray leaf spot	Attacks St. Augustine grass. Small gray circular or elliptical spots appear on leaves. May spread to kill large areas of turf.	Acti-dione-thiram, Captan, Dyrene, Ortho Lawn and Turf Fungicide, PMA, Thiram

FERTILIZER

FERTILIZER	FERTILIZER NEEDED TO SPREAD 1 POUND OF NITROGEN OVER 1000 SQ. FT. AREA
5-10-5	20 Pounds
4-12-4	25 Pounds
5-10-10	20 Pounds
10-10-10	10 Pounds
8-8-8	13 Pounds
10-6-4	10 Pounds
8-6-4	13 Pounds
4-8-4	25 Pounds
6-12-4	17 Pounds
Processed sewage sludge	17 Pounds
Ammonium nitrate	4 Pounds
Ammonium sulfate	5 Pounds
Nitrate of soda	7 Pounds
Steamed bonemeal	50 Pounds
Cottonseed meal	17 Pounds
Peanut hull meal	50 Pounds
Cocoa shell meal	50 Pounds
Dried cattle manure	50 Pounds
Dried sheep manure	70 Pounds
Sewage sludge	50 Pounds
Tobacco stems	50 Pounds
Urea	3 Pounds
Processed tankage	13 Pounds
Soybean meal	17 Pounds
Urea-form	3 Pounds

spring, and the bigger it gets, the harder it is to kill. Most crabgrass killers of this type require two applications, 7 to 10 days apart.

watering know-how

How the lawn is watered is a lot more important than most homeowners realize. The reason is simple: Roots, including grass roots, always go where the water is. If you water frequently but only to a depth of an inch or two, then your grass roots will grow in that moist inch or two.

Good grass roots should go deep—six inches or more. When you water lightly, you not only keep them near the surface, but you also provide a soggy surface soil in which weeds thrive.

The right way to water your lawn is to soak it so that the soil is wet to a depth of at least six inches—and even deeper if possible. This means at least two hours of sprinkling with the average sprinkler, and perhaps more. (Test your sprinkler by placing some coffee cans around the yard while it sprinkles. Note how long it takes two inches of water to collect in each can. That's about how long the sprinkler should run to properly soak your lawn.)

After the lawn has been soaked, leave it alone for a week. Let it dry out, then soak it the same way. If there is rain between your soakings, take this into account. You can test the moisture of the ground by pushing a screwdriver into it. If it goes down easily to a depth of six inches, the ground is wet. The harder it is to push in the screwdriver, the drier the soil.

Many sprinklers will cause the water to run into the street before it has had a chance to soak into the ground. They either apply the water too fast or the soil absorbs it slowly. If this is your problem—then divide your watering time. Run the sprinkler for half an hour, wait an hour, and run it again.

Keep in mind that all soils are different, so you must judge your own yard. Sandy soils take water fast, and clay soils absorb slowly. Spend a little time determining just how to get water into the top six inches of your lawn without wasting it. It will pay off in a healthier stand of grass.

Final watering hint: when you walk across your grass and leave footprints, water is needed. Grass which has enough moisture bounces back so your footprints don't show.

mow, mow, mow your grass

It has been said, that improper mowing has ruined more good lawns than any other single thing. Maybe so. It is certain that bad mowing can throw your grass into shock, even if it doesn't actually ruin the lawn.

There are three ways to give your lawn a bad time with a mower: First, cut it too short. Second, let it grow too long before cutting. And third, cut it with a dull blade, which tears rather than cuts.

The height of the cut depends, of course, on the type of grass. Bermuda, zoysia and bent grasses must be cut very short to keep the thatch from building up. But bluegrasses should be left fairly long—longer than most people believe. Two inches is a good minimum.

The reason is that the leaf of the bluegrass produces the food on which growth and root development depend. If you cut too much of the green blade, you cut down on the plant's ability to develop food. In addition, bluegrass likes a cool soil, and longer leaves shade the soil and help keep it cool. This is the main reason why it is good to allow bluegrass to grow even longer in very hot weather.

How often to cut? When the grass is about 1/3 taller than its regular height. This may mean frequent cutting during strong growth periods, but there is a good reason. When you allow the grass to grow too tall, then cut it short, you expose stems which have been shaded to sunburn, and cut away too much of the green leaf. The lawn takes on a scalded look and may take a long time to recover from the shock.

Dull, knicked mower blades flail and slash at

GOOD LAWNKEEPING

KEEPING THE EDGE NEAT can be a problem. One way to reduce tedious hand trimming is to install a mowing strip at least 6 in. wide around flower beds. You can use brick, small concrete blocks, and even railroad ties.

THE AREA AROUND A TREE can be hard to mow and usually is shaded so grass doesn't grow well. Remove the grass and cover the area with wood chips or pebbles. Another method is a good ground cover and edging.

SMALL GRASSY AREAS are troublesome to mow and to keep neat looking. Best way is to remove the grass and install attractive landscaping additions such as raised flower beds or small walking areas of brick or patio stone.

COVER STEEP SLOPES with ground cover. Slopes are difficult to mow and present watering and erosion problems. Use English ivy, which holds the soil well, or myrtle or pachysandra. Flower plantings won't help here.

the tender grass blades, ripping them instead of cutting. The result is frayed ends which turn brown, and additional shock to the plants. Use a file to sharpen the blade, disconnecting the mower's spark plug before you begin. (You run a risk of starting the engine by turning the blade if you don't take this precaution.)

Additional mowing hints: Pick up the sticks and stones in the yard before you begin to mow. Don't try to cut wet grass, but wait until it has dried. Use a bag to collect clippings as you mow. Accumulated clippings can create a thick thatch which smothers the grass roots and which harbors insects and disease. And finally, always clean the mower blades when you finish.

how to rejuvenate your lawn

If your yard looks as if it were covered with a green shag rug, you still may be able to pump some life into it. If about half of the area is still covered with good perennial grasses, there is hope. Plan to begin the rejuvenation in the middle of August. Here are the steps to follow:

1. Apply 2, 4-D according to the directions on the can to kill the broadleaf weeds. Read the herbicide labels to get the best one for your problem. If crabgrass is evident, be sure the label specifies that the herbicide kills crabgrass too.
2. If no lime has been applied for four years, apply dolomitic agricultural limestone at the rate of 50 to 75 lbs. per 1000 sq. ft.
3. Apply fertilizer. Use the fertilizer formula to be sure you apply 1 lb. of nitrogen per 1000 sq. ft.
4. Mow closely. Rake the bare areas to loosen the soil.
5. Seed perennial bluegrass/fescue mixture into the bare areas (in the north), or plant stolons of grasses (in the south). Use 1-2 lbs. of seed per 1000 sq. ft.
6. Water the seeded or planted areas lightly. Keep soil moist until seed germinates and seedlings are established.
7. Continue to mow whenever the older grass needs it.
8. Early in the spring, apply a pre-emergent crabgrass killer and give the lawn its first feeding. By June, you should see a considerable improvement, and by the end of the summer, a thick turf should have developed.

How and when to de-thatch your lawn

Thatch and soil compaction may be smothering the grass in your lawn, preventing air, water and fertilizer from getting through to the roots. The best cure for the problem is mechanical de-thatching and aerating. You can rent the equipment to do the job

By LEN HILTS

SEE ALSO

Gardening . . . Grass . . . Hand mowers . . . Landscaping . . . Mowers . . . Paths, garden . . . Patios . . . Playgrounds . . . Putting greens . . . Retaining walls . . . Swings . . . Transplanting . . . Trees

IS YOUR LAWN in trouble in spite of the good care you've been giving it? Does it seem to be thinning out instead of growing thick and lush? Have you been plagued with lawn insects or had severe outbreaks of diseases such as striped smut, leaf spot and dollar patch?

If you have been doing everything you should—weeding, feeding and watering—but nothing seems to bring your green carpet up to the level of your neighbors', there is a pretty good chance that your grass is choking to death.

There are two chief causes for this choking: a build-up of thatch deposits on the soil at the base of the grass plants; and dense, overcompacted soil. These two conditions prevent air, water and nutrients from getting to the grass roots, and as a result, the grass is slowly choking and starving.

Fortunately, both conditions can be cured and your lawn restored to its original healthy condition.

Thatch. Stick your fingers down into the grass and scratch around. If you have thatch build-up, you can feel it. Thatch is the accumulation of dead grass, old clippings, leaves and other undecomposed organic matter. Thatch accumulates over a period of time, and as it builds up, it forms an almost impenetrable matlike layer over the soil. Air, water and fertilizer can't get through it efficiently. Root development is discouraged and the grass leaves become thin and scraggly. Tough weeds, which can thrive in almost any condition, take this opportunity to overpower the weak grass.

The thatch makes an ideal breeding ground for lawn insects, and many types of fungal spores thrive in it. The total result, after the thatch has become well established, is weak, thin grass, rapid increase of weeds, diseased patches, and insect damage.

The major cause of thatch formation is grass clippings which you neglect to collect as you mow. If your lawn is in good balance, it can take a limited amount of clippings, which decompose on the ground and help in the formation of new soil. But if your soil is too acid, this decomposition may slow down, since composting requires an alkaline soil. In addition, some chemicals, notably pesticides, may reduce the rate of decomposition by destroying the microorganisms which carry out the composting process.

THE TYPICAL de-thatching rotor has 52 blades. These are individually removable so you can adjust the machine for light or medium combing. Ask your rental agent if adjustments are permitted.

THIS VERTICAL-CUTTING mower cuts out dead plant matter with eight oil-tempered spring-steel blades.

YOU MAY FIND machines like this one, equipped with interchangeable reels. You can install the tine, the knife or the flail, depending on the type of problem.

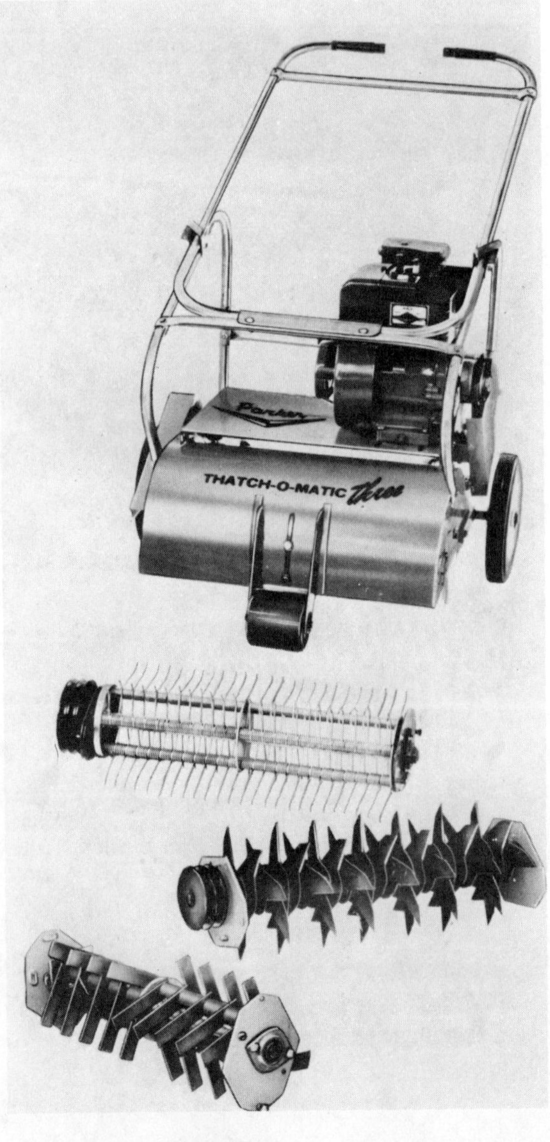

Soil compaction. Good soil is spongy. It breathes through a network of pores and capillaries. It accepts water readily and air can get through it. When good soil is severely compacted, its breathing network is crushed and shut off. Then more water runs off the surface than is absorbed into the soil, and little or no air gets in. Fertilizers applied to the surface never get to the grass roots.

The major cause of compaction is heavy traffic. Play areas and footpaths in the lawn usually are compacted. If you have observed such places, you know that they soon lose their grass covering, and new grass seed sown on the surface of such compacted places germinates, then quickly dies.

Earthworms, ants and other insects bore through the soil and play an important role in aerating it. They help to keep it loose and spongy. When you apply chemicals which kill them, you encourage compaction.

Compaction can take place all over the lawn area. The soil may not become so dense as to kill the grass, but dense enough to cut the penetration of air and water by a half. The result is weak, sickly grass.

Compaction, too, can be cured. Best of all, you can cure it without digging up the lawn and starting over.

How can you tell when your lawn soil has become compacted? Make the screwdriver test. Try to insert the blade of a long screwdriver into the soil. If the soil is in good shape, you should be able to push the blade down into the soil about 4 in. without much trouble. If you really have to push, then the chances are your lawn needs aerifying.

Pull the blade out of the ground carefully, pulling straight up, trying not to dislodge any of the soil deposits on it. Now look at the deposits. The lower part of the blade should have soil, but just above the soil, you may see a peat-like layer. This is thatch. If the layer of thatch is more than ½-in. thick, then you have a thatch problem as well as a compaction problem.

The solutions to both problems. You can rent de-thatching machines by the day to remove the thatch on your lawn. And you also can rent aerifying machines which cut tiny plugs from the lawn surface and give the soil a chance to breathe once again.

De-thatching machines. Sometimes called a vertical mower, the average de-thatching machine is powered by a gasoline engine and is slightly larger than a rotary mower. Most de-

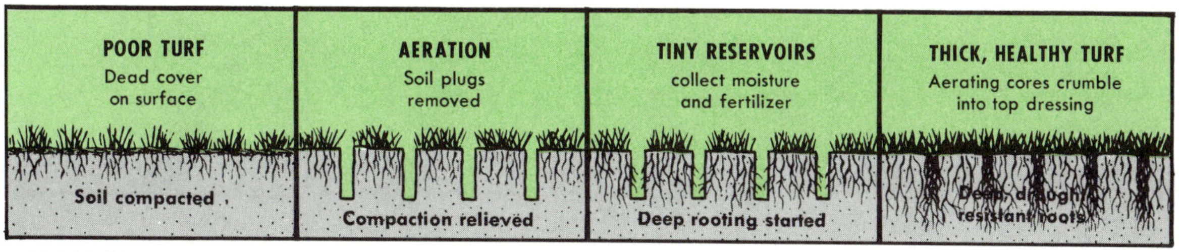

THE ACTION which takes place in the soil after aeration is shown in these drawings. Plugs average 2½-in. in depth.

thatchers have rotating reels designed to pull out the thatch and deposit it on the surface of the lawn—where you can collect it and haul it away.

There are three basic types of reels employed in de-thatching. Each type has a specific use:

Blade or flail type. This machine has a reel with 30 to 60 steel blades about ⅛ x 1 x 4 in. in size, either rigidly attached to the reel or free swinging. As the reel turns, the blades pass vertically through the living grass and cut into the thatch below, lifting it out. At the same time, the blades make narrow slits in the soil, providing some aeration and making a good bed for new grass seed.

The blade/flail type of de-thatcher is well-suited to bluegrass lawns. One version permits the removal of some of the blades to provide the best thinning and slicing action for lawns of southern bentgrass.

Tine type. The reel on this machine has 100 or so thin, wire-like flexible tines in place of flails and was designed specifically for use on bluegrass lawns. The tines provide a combing action and lift the thatch out with a minimal removal of living grass.

Knife type. This reel has from 25 to 50 tiny knives which remove some living grass as well as loose thatch. This unit is particularly effective on Bermuda, zoysia and centipede grasses commonly found in the southern sector of the United States. It helps in controlling the growth of such weeds as wild fescue, crabgrass and nimblewill.

You can expect to de-thatch about 5000 square feet of lawn an hour, and the average lawn will yield as much as 20 to 30 bushels of thatch per 1000 square feet. The best way to remove the thatch once the machine has deposited it on top of the grass is to rent a power sweeper for the purpose. You'll find hand raking pretty hard.

The thatch can be packed into plastic bags for disposal or you can use it in a compost heap. Mix in some black soil and some compost activator, which you can buy at the garden store, and later you will have a supply of black dirt for your lawn and garden.

Aeration machines. An aerating machine cuts small plugs, about 2½ in. deep, from the surface of the lawn, thus opening up pore spaces for penetration of air, water and fertilizer. Water getting into the holes helps the surrounding soil to expand and loosen up. Fertilizer goes straight to the grass roots and encourages good, quick growth.

One type of aerator has hollow tines which cut plugs on 5-in. centers. During operation, a plug of soil is forced into the central core of the tine.

Another type employs open, half-rounded spoons which scoop out a core of soil to give the surrounding earth room to expand. The action provides a loosening effect without disturbing the grass.

You can sweep the cores which are deposited on the grass to remove them, but experts recommend that you leave them where they fall. The action of rain will cause them to crumble and fall back to the surface as loose top soil.

You may find machines with solid tines or spikes instead of hollow tines or spoons. These poke holes in the earth's surface to permit water to enter the soil. They prevent runoff. But they also actually increase compaction as they punch their holes, and so should not be used on the average lawn with a compaction problem.

The best times for de-thatching and aerifying are when the grass is growing vigorously—in the spring and fall. The fall is probably the best for aerifying. Nature does her own aerifying in the early spring through the action of alternate freezing and thawing of the surface soil.

Don't wait until too late in the fall to aerify. It is best to do it before mid-October. The reason is that the holes remain open for a while. If they don't fill, and the winter proves to be dry and lacking in snow, wind action can have a severe drying effect.

De-thatching is best in the spring, when the grass is growing most vigorously. The lawn has a month or so of good growing to recover from the shock of the treatment and reestablish itself before the slow-growing summer months.

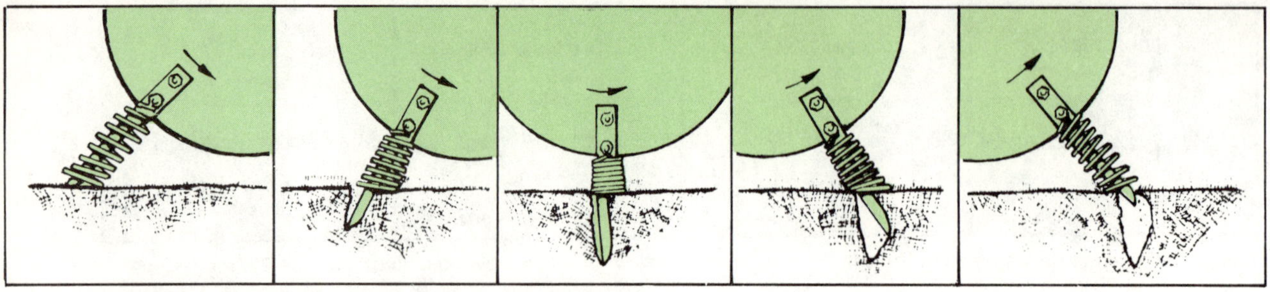

AS THE AERIFYING MACHINE rolls, its multiple spoons scoop out cores of soil, leaving holes every 5 inches or so.

How to prevent thatch buildup. The best way to prevent the buildup of thatch is to minimize the clippings you allow to stay on the lawn as you mow. Cut your grass often enough so that each clipping is short. If you allow the grass to grow too long, the long clippings are too much for the decomposing process and thatch begins to form. When the grass is long, use your grass catcher and collect the clippings as you go.

You can also prevent the build-up of thatch by vigorously hand raking the lawn every spring and fall. This is effective only when there is little buildup already present. Once the thatch has become established, the only effective way to deal with it is with a de-thatching machine.

Some experts recommend that de-thatching and aerating be done once a year—but not at the same time. The ideal annual program calls for de-thatching in the spring and aerating in the fall. However, most homeowners aren't eager to incorporate this much work into their outdoor maintenace schedule and could work on a de-thatch-this-year aerate-next-year schedule. This system will work best if care is taken to remove clippings during mowing.

Care after treatment. Following aeration or the removal of thatch, water the lawn thoroughly to stimulate recovery growth. If the lawn is in need of fertilizer, this is a good time to do it. Apply the fertilizer, then water the lawn to release the nutrients to the roots.

If the lawn has thinned out because of thatch or compaction, it may need reseeding. Both machines do an excellent job of preparing the lawn for seed, so this is a fine time to scatter new seed. You'll have to be sure the soil is kept moist during the germination period. Spring and fall rains may do the job for you, but if they don't, you'll have to use the sprinkler.

The new seedling grass is shaded by the old grass, and so will thrive as long as there is sufficient moisture, but will shrivel quickly if the top ½-in. of soil dries out completely.

Special problems. Bermuda and zoysia grasses are slower to decompose than other types, and as a result, lawns consisting of them are more likely to have thatch problems. De-thatching these lawns at least once a year may be necessary.

If you have a sandy soil, very little aeration is necessary, and an aeration machine won't help. If your grass isn't healthy, you can assume that lack of air isn't the cause.

When installing a new lawn, starting with bare ground, you do a lot to prevent compaction in later years. For one thing, mix plenty of sand into the top four to six inches as you prepare the ground for seed. This will help keep the topsoil loose.

For another, if the soil has a lot of clay in its composition, you can mix gypsum into it to prevent compacting. Take a sample of your soil to your garden store, or to your county agent. Talk to the county agent or someone at the store who knows soil, and work out a formula of materials you can add to condition the soil. These may include sand, gypsum, peat or lime, depending on the composition of the soil.

A LEFTOVER LENGTH of threaded rod can be used as a round rasp in a pinch. The sharp edges of a newly threaded rod, such as Redi-bolt sold in hardware stores, will cut soft wood almost as well as a regular coarse file. To avoid a punctured palm, fit one end with a handle. I force-fitted an old doorknob over the rod.—*Ken Patterson, Regina, Sask.*

FOR READY ACCESS to my jigsaw blades, I fashioned a convenient holder. I drilled three holes in a scrap block of wood, which I then fastened to the saw arm with large rubber bands. Now, when I change blades, the replacement is always at my fingertips.—*Ned Somner, Houston.*

KEEPING A PENCIL on a clipboard is a challenge that's inspired many. Here's an idea that's proven successful. Simply fasten a fuse clip to one edge of the board with a 6-32 machine screw and nut. The pencil can then be held snugly, yet is easily removable.—*Marshall Lincoln, Wickenburg, AZ.*

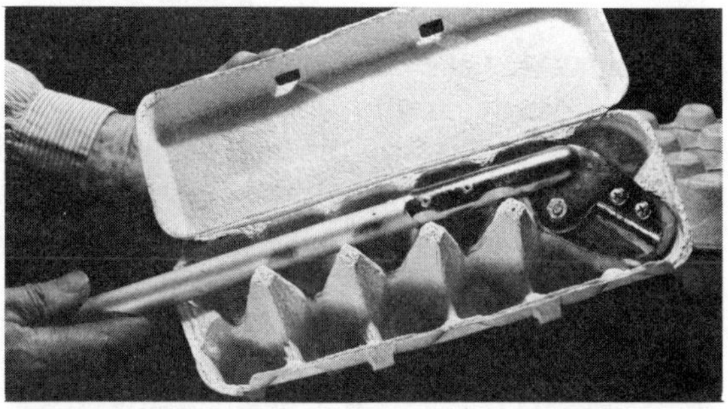

A SHIELD for garden tools, hooks and other items can be made from press-fiber or plastic-foam egg boxes. These covers will prevent accidental contact with sharp edges and points and protect the tool from rust. To provide space for the head of the pruning tool shown, one cone in the box was trimmed off.—*Walter E. Burton, Akron, OH.*

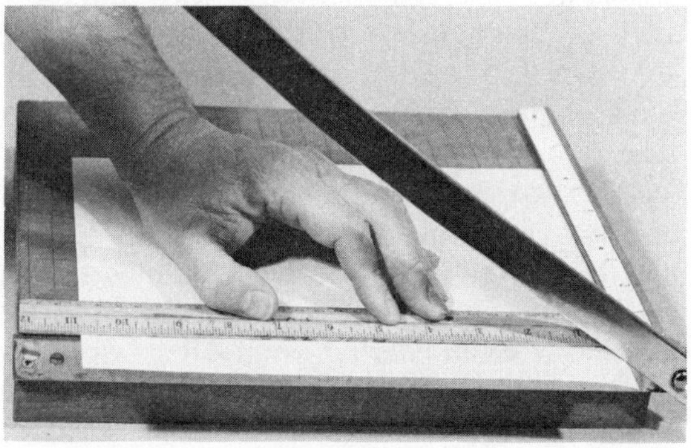

WHEN YOU'RE TRIMMING thin stock—such as pictures cut from a magazine—the paper will frequently crease and shift as the knife blade starts its shearing action. By keeping a 12-in. or longer wood rule at the paper cutter, you will always have a handy paper holder that spans the paper to hold it securely while you cut.—*Ken Patterson, Regina, Sask.*

A lazy Susan table server

By ROSARIO CAPOTOSTO

■ YOU DON'T NEED a lathe to make this handsome lazy Susan table server. You can buy the 12 little gallery spindles already turned at many lumberyards.

The circular base is cut from a glued-up square of cherry ¾ x 18 x 18 in. You make it by cutting four triangular segments from a 10-in. board with the miter gauge set at 45° and flipping the board for each pass. The butting edges of the four segments are shaped with a glue-joint cutter, or drilled for dowels. The glued-up square will have lateral-running grain of interesting symmetry and good workability when you're ready to shape it. Note the use of C-clamps and bar clamps to hold the work while glue dries (photos on opposite page).

The stock for the upper ring is glued-up the same way, but to economize on lumber, the segments need not be full triangles; they may be truncated. Cut them from a 6-in. board to the same measurements you used for the base. When the four are joined, you will have an 18-in. square with a square opening in the center. When sabre-sawing the ring, you'll have to insert a piece of scrap stock across the center of the opening to provide a surface for the saw's pivot point. This can be toenailed in place. Be sure to saw the outer circle of the ring first. Use a router or shaper to mold the edges.

Alignment of the spindle holes will be easy if you tape the ring to the base and drill the holes from the bottom side of the base and partly into the underside of the ring. Make an identifying mark on both pieces so they can later be matched as they were when drilled.

A worthwhile tip: Sand the parts and apply the finish before assembling your server for a top-notch job. A coat of sanding sealer followed with stain and a final coat or two of clear satin finish such as Wood-glo will give you a smooth handsome finish that will last for many years.

To complete the project, you'll need a 4-in. lazy Susan bearing. Attach this to a piece of wood scrap ½ x 9 x 9 in. Drill a 1-in.-dia. screw access hole in this subbase, attach the bearing and then screw the unit to the circular base. You can obtain the Wood-glo finish, as well as the 4-in. lazy Susan bearing, from Albert Constantine & Son, Inc., 2050 Eastchester Ave., Bronx, NY 10461.

SEE ALSO
Bookracks . . . Centerpieces . . .
Gifts, Christmas . . . Kitchen accessories . . .
Plexiglass projects . . . Servers . . . Trays, folding

FOUR TRIANGULAR segments for circular base are ready for jointing butted edges prior to gluing.

C-CLAMPS ARE USED at corners; bar clamp applies pressure to the center area of glued-up work.

OUTER CUT of ring is made first to preserve support for the saw's pivot when making inside cut.

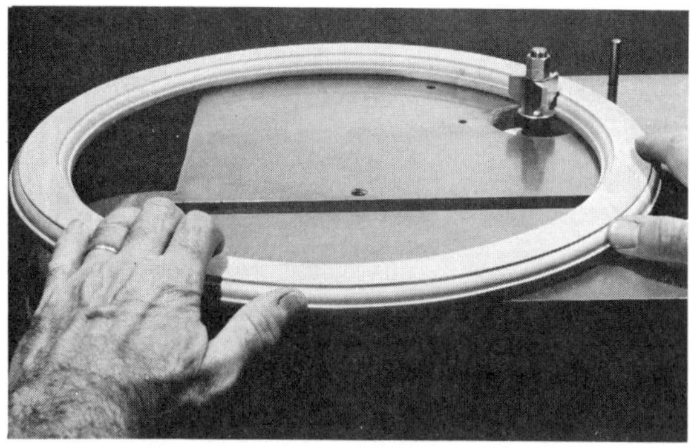

COLLAR CONTROLS depth of cut when you shape edges with a shaper; you can also use a router.

PILOT HOLES for spindles are drilled in base and ring at the same time to assure perfect alignment.

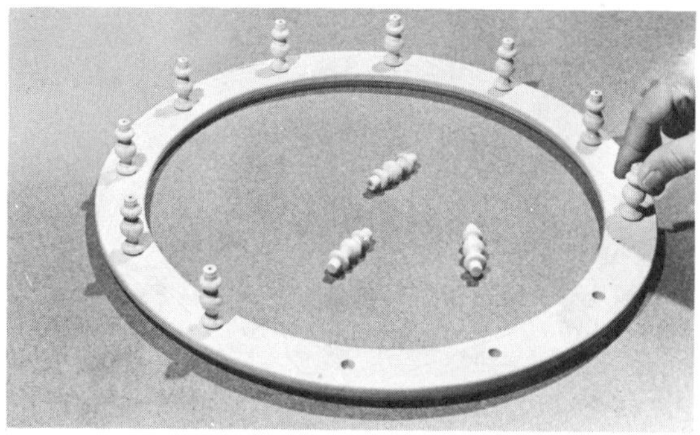

READY-MADE spindles fit ⅜-in. holes. They are not glued until finishing has been completed.

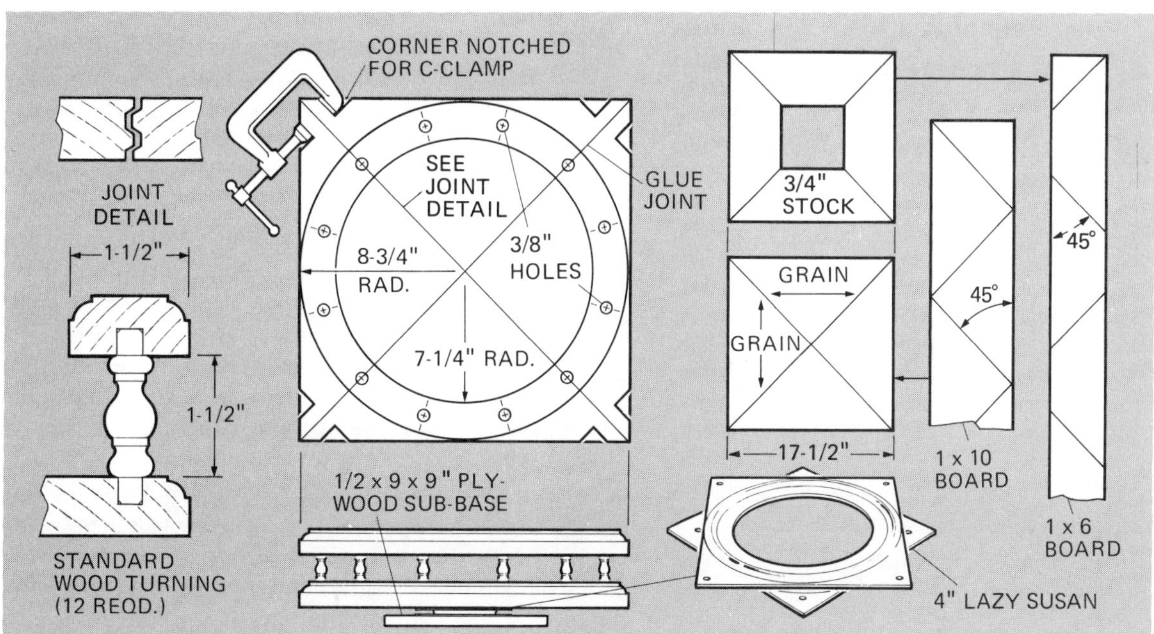

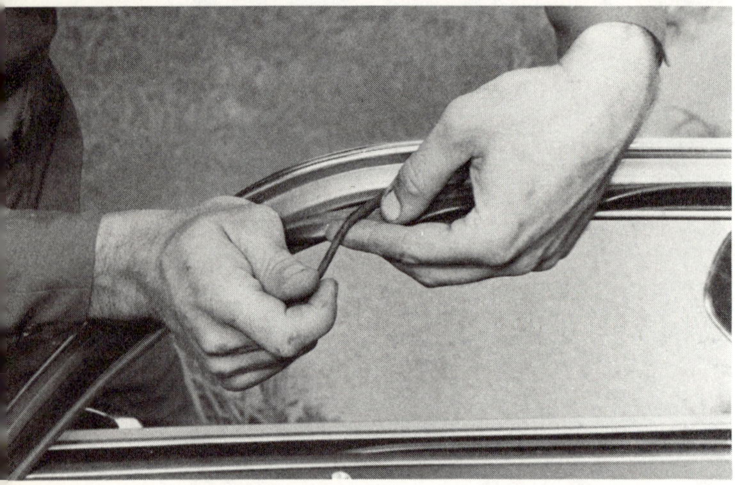

SHIM UP weatherstripping by pulling the seal away from the frame and inserting roll-type caulking.

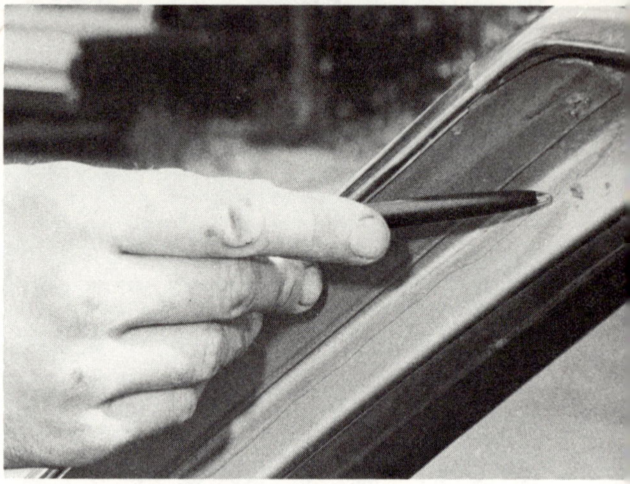

SMALL CONSTRUCTION flaws such as solder lumps can generate annoying noise around windows.

How to stop wind noise and water leaks

By MORT SCHULTZ

Here are professional tips on how to keep wind and weather—and their noise—outside your car where they belong. The gaps can be elusive, until you know the tricks of locating them

YOU NEEDN'T endure irritating wind noise while you're driving. Nor must you risk getting wet because of a hard-to-find leak—one that takes effect only when it's raining. Use the pros' techniques to find and fix these problems. It need not be difficult.

There are two kinds of wind noise: that caused by air leaks and that by turbulence.

Air leaks occur when weatherstripping around doors and windows wears out, wasn't installed properly to begin with or doesn't seal for some other reason. Turbulence—the interruption of airflow around the outside of a car—is caused by the shape of the body, or a protruding or loose part.

You can often trace an air leak with the car parked in your driveway. Troubleshooting noise caused by turbulence usually requires a road test.

Noise caused by an air leak occurs frequently when air leaks *out of* rather than into a car, because air pressure becomes greater inside the car than outside. This happens when you drive with doors and windows closed, and air vents open, or the heater or airconditioner turned on.

Higher in-the-car air pressure forces the top edges of door glass outward. If glass loses contact with weatherstripping, the air leak that results will produce an annoying noise.

Air leaks that cause noise are normally confined to the upper part of a car to about a foot below the bottom of windows. Leaks lower down cause drafts, and may let dust and water into the car, but they seldom produce noise.

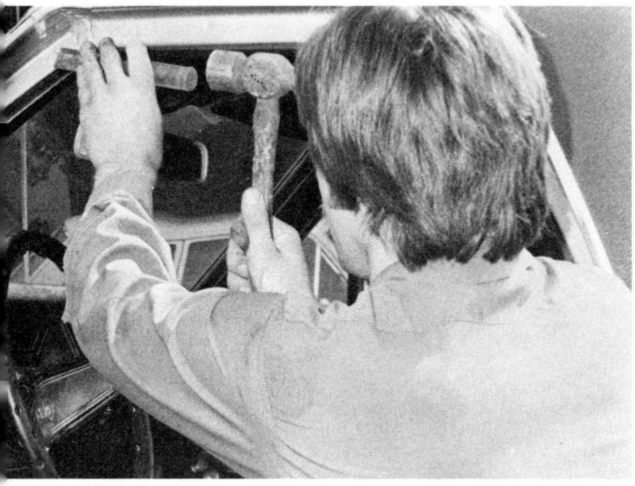

HIGH SPOTS or solder lumps can be chipped off with hammer and chisel if they're used carefully.

A HOSE USED as a stethoscope can detect air leaks when the car's interior is pressurized.

To troubleshoot a noise created by an air leak, proceed as follows:

Examine all weatherstripping for worn-out spots, tears and looseness. Reglue loose weatherstripping, using rubber cement. Worn-out weatherstripping can often be salvaged by inserting some roll-type caulking beneath the worn spot. If weatherstripping is torn or badly damaged, replace it.

Inspect each door for holes in the sheet-metal joints and for rusted-out spots. Remove rust and seal holes with auto-body caulking compound.

The bottom of each door has drain holes that allow water getting inside the door to run out. This prevents rusting. Door drain holes must *not* be sealed. In fact, you should make sure they are free. Use an awl, icepick or some such tool to clean them out.

Examine door-opening surfaces for solder lumps and other uneven spots that are preventing full contact of weatherstripping with the door frame. Solder lumps should be filed off or cut off with a hammer and metal chisel. Weatherstripping must have an even surface against which to seat firmly if air leaks and the noise they produce are to be prevented.

The least irregularity could have produced an air leak, yet escaped detection thus far. So roll up all windows and shut fresh-air inlets. The inside of the car must be completely closed off.

Start the engine and set heater or air-conditioner controls to admit air into the car. Set the blower at top speed.

Get out of the car. Check that doors and windows are tightly shut, and allow pressure to build up inside several minutes.

Take a length of hose, hold one end to your ear and pass the other end slowly around the edges of the doors and glass. Even the hiss of a small air leak will be audible.

The hose method of finding a leak is almost as reliable as modern electronic air-leak detectors used by some auto body and glass shops. The usual version has two components.

One is a signal generator that is placed inside the closed car. The other is a detecting unit held outside the car to pick up the generated tone signal. The signal can't be heard unless it is "leaking" from the car.

If you took your car to a shop that uses an electronic leak detector, the manager might not charge you for finding the leak. However, he would expect to make repairs, and they aren't free. Managers of other shops tell us that they charge about $10 for tracing air leaks.

Up to now, we've been dealing with noise made as air inside the car leaks out. But outside air can leak in, as well, creating noise.

To determine if a leak exists because of a bad weather seal around the door, place a strip of paper between the weatherstripping and door frame. Pull the paper out. If it comes easily, without resistance, the weatherstripping should be shimmed or replaced. Check all around every door. If weatherstripping doesn't seem worn or loose, the door may be misaligned and require

CLOSING THE DOOR on a strip of wrapping paper checks tightness of weatherstripping's grip.

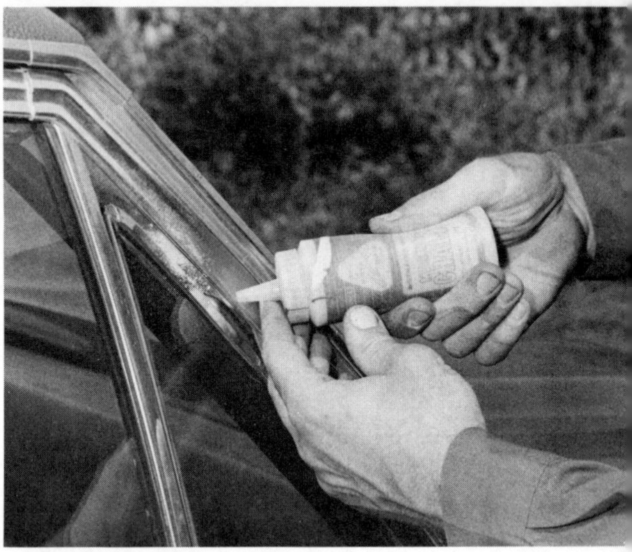

A SQUEEZE BOTTLE of marking chalk helps to check windows' seal; try to puff it through any gaps.

tightening of hinges, repositioning of the striker or some other adjustment.

Air can also leak into a car from around windows. Close each window tightly and blow tracing powder or chalk in along the edges. Check for traces of powder or chalk on the inner side of the window. If dust shows up on the inside, the window seal may have to be replaced or the window may have to be readjusted.

tracing noise created by turbulence

You won't be able to get rid of all noise made by turbulence. There will always be some because of the design of the car.

A perfectly streamlined car wouldn't create turbulence. But it wouldn't provide much room for comfort either.

So, although some turbulence noise will be heard, you don't have to stand for noise produced by a loose or protruding part. But you have to find it. Here's how:

For your road test, select a route in an open, low-traffic area which will allow you to drive at cruising speed and to pull safely off the road to make adjustments. Equip yourself with a roll of masking tape and strips of automotive caulking. Close all windows and doors tightly. Make sure the blower is off, fresh air vents are closed, and heater and airconditioner controls are off.

Drive at the speed at which the noise annoys you. If the noise seems to be outside the car, it is being caused by turbulence. If the noise sounds to be in the car, you may have an air leak that was unnoticed during the driveway test.

Using masking tape, cover each part of the car's body that may create turbulence and noise. Molding strips are prime candidates. Cover a small section at a time. When the noise disappears during a particular phase of the road test, it means you have found the offending area.

Quite often, noise created by turbulence occurs when wind rushes under a strip of molding. This can be corrected by removing the molding strip, filling the space with automotive caulking and replacing the strip.

Another part creating noise is the weatherstrip around the outside of vent windows, especially at the lower front corner. The weatherstrip here may be distorted and pulled away from the body. Called a pucker, this could have been caused by overtravel of the vent. If weatherstrip is rubber, get rid of distortion by softening it with a heat source, such as a propane torch. When the material becomes pliable, smooth out the pucker and work the weatherstrip into shape as it cools. The distorted spot may need a few heat applications before it is finally smooth.

Another source of turbulence noise is roof railings. These, too, should be taped one small section at a time until the road test demonstrates that the noise disappears, revealing the offending section. If rails are rusted or have pulled away from the body of the car, they should be repaired if noise is to be eliminated.

SPECIAL, LOW-COST tool helps remove windshield molding without cracking the costly glass.

RUBBER SEALING strip may pucker at the corners, causing a leak. Heat and smooth it carefully.

tracing water leaks

There are several spots through which water can leak into a car, but the front and rear windshields are always prime candidates. Concentrate on the front one if water has appeared in the front of the car. Test the rear windshield if water has leaked into the trunk.

Tape a garden hose, minus a nozzle, to the top of the car and place a can in front of the snout. See that water spreads over the entire windshield.

Keep water flowing for at least 30 minutes; it may take this long for water to show up inside the car. Now and then, rock the car from side to side. Water occasionally accumulates in a seam along the windshield and will leak into the car only when the car corners.

Resealing a front or rear windshield is no easy task. You shouldn't apply sealing compound right over molding. It often won't provide an adequate seal, and if the windshield ever does have to be removed, you're more likely to break the glass.

Molding should come off, but don't use a screwdriver or some other common tool. You could crack the glass. Instead, get a windshield clip tool. One style is for Chryslers; another for other domestics. They're inexpensive. Slip the tool beneath the molding and slide it along until it touches each molding clip (see photo above, right). Twist the tool to pop the molding loose from the clips.

Buy new molding clips (same kind as the old clips) from an auto glass dealer and insert them into place along the glass. Now, apply a liberal bead of windshield sealer around the entire circumference of the windshield. Reattach the molding by pressing it onto clips.

If a water leak up front isn't uncovered by hosing down the front windshield, apply a heavy flow of water from a hose (no nozzle) for several minutes on each spot up front that may be leaking. These include every bolt and seam along the firewall, drip rails, and the A-post (the part of the body on each side of the windshield).

Have someone in the car yell when water begins to leak. When this leak is revealed, seal the weak area with silicone rubber caulk.

If water is leaking into the trunk by some other way than through the rear windshield, the location of the leak can be found by having someone crawl into the compartment with a flashlight. Close the lid and play a heavy stream of water from a hose (no nozzle) along each part through which water can leak—including the trunk-lid seam, stop- and backup-light seams, and rear body seams. Be sure to concentrate a heavy flow of water on one section at a time for a long enough period. When your friend in the trunk sees water starting to drip in, he can yell or tap on the lid to tell you to open up.

A leaking trunk lid can often be repaired by prying off the gasket, repositioning it and gluing it back into place.

A dozen ways to attach legs

By W. CLYDE LAMMEY

Whether you're building new furniture or restoring the old, there's no substitute for sturdy legs to carry the load

YOUR CHOICE of methods for attaching legs depends on the piece of furniture and its style. If you're building a simple modern chest or slab table, you can get by with purchased legs that screw into their own mounting plates. But if you're reproducing or refurbishing a period piece, you'll most likely have to go to hand joinery.

The dozen methods sketched on these pages cover most means of attaching legs to rails and aprons or flat undersides. Say you want to build a workbench that won't jiggle or "walk" when you plane stock or do some hammering. For this, use the butt joint with a drawbolt to join the legs to the rails of the frame. You'll get a job that will take the roughest usage—even without bracing or gluing.

In making a cabinet or table with turned legs, use rails-to-legs joints with mitered, wedged or draw-pinned tenons.

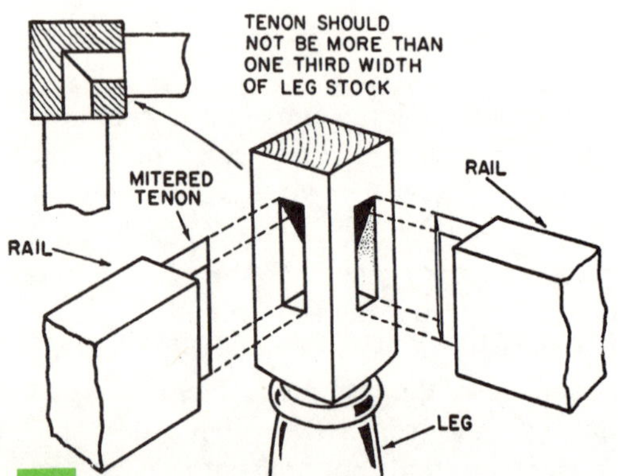

1 MORTISE-AND-TENON JOINT WITH MITERED TENONS

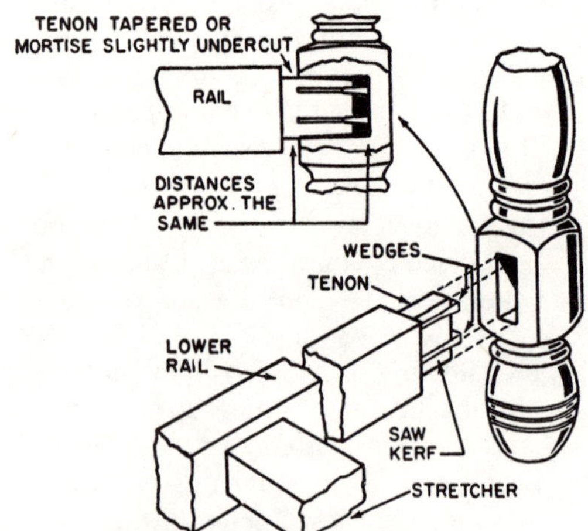

2 MORTISE-AND-TENON JOINT WITH WEDGED TENON

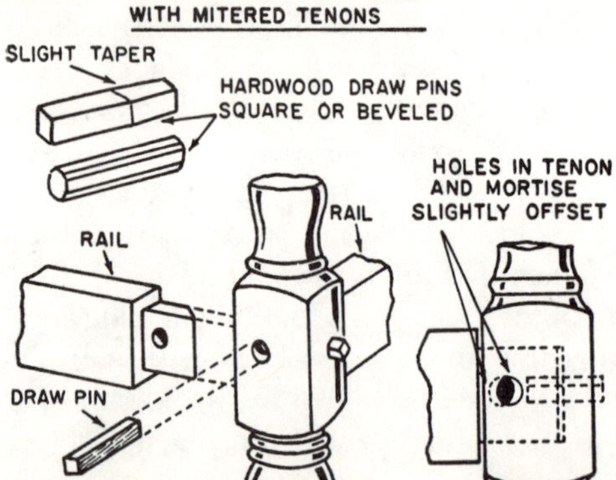

3 MORTISE-AND-TENON JOINT DRAW-PINNED

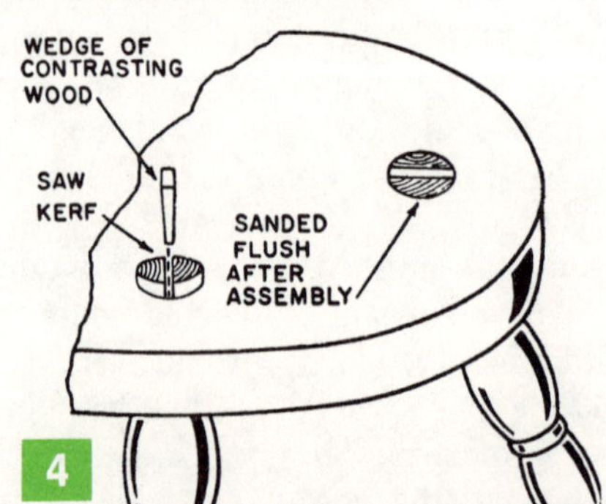

4 SPLINED OR OPEN WEDGED, TENON EXPOSED FOR ORNAMENTATION

SEE ALSO
Adhesives . . . Bolts . . . Chairs . . .
Children's furniture . . . Clamps . . . Joinery . . .
Miter joints . . . Sanding . . . Screws

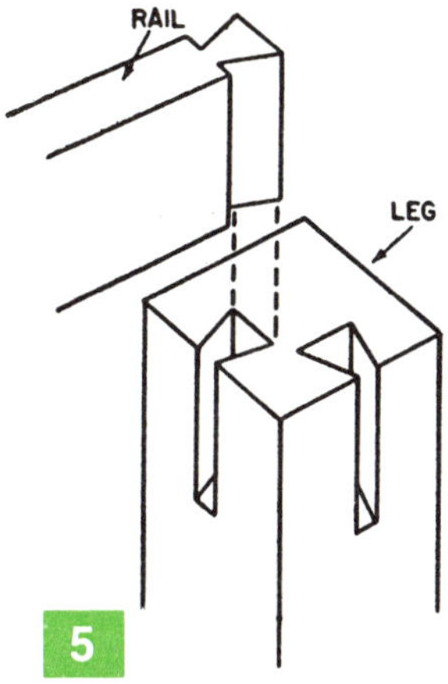

5

DOVETAIL MORTISE AND TENON
RAIL-TO-STILE, OR RAIL-TO-LEG JOINERY

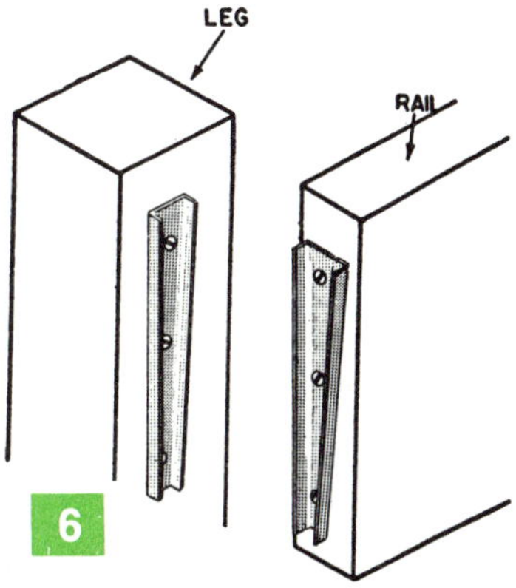

6

TAPERED METAL WEDGES
FOR KNOCK DOWN RAIL-TO-
LEG JOINERY

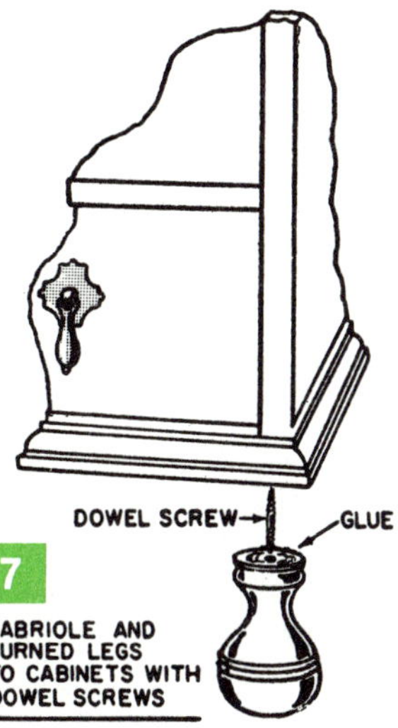

7

CABRIOLE AND
TURNED LEGS
TO CABINETS WITH
DOWEL SCREWS

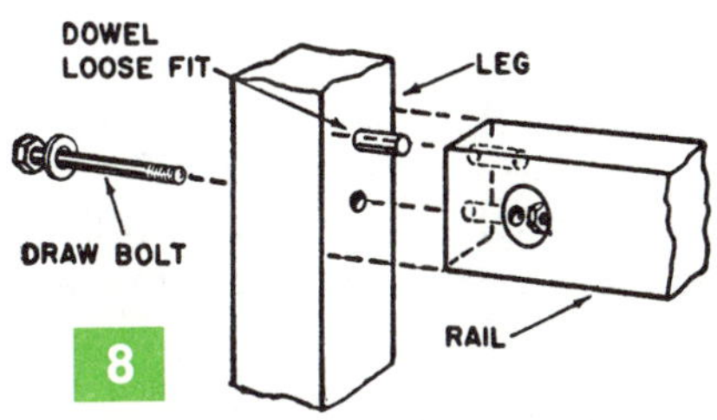

8

BUTT JOINT WITH DRAW BOLT, FOR
WORKBENCH FRAMING, SIMILAR CONST.

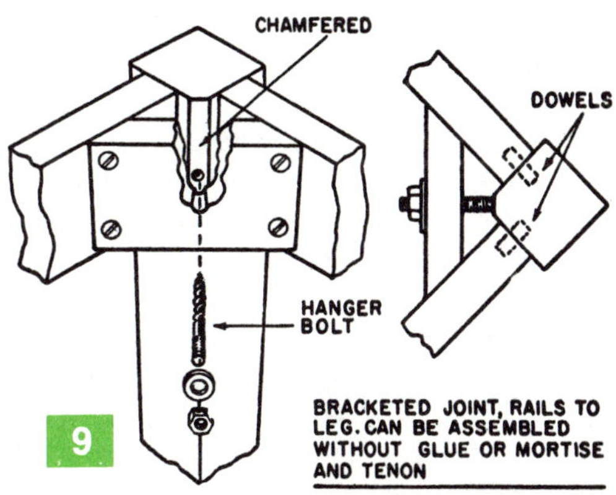

9

BRACKETED JOINT, RAILS TO
LEG. CAN BE ASSEMBLED
WITHOUT GLUE OR MORTISE
AND TENON

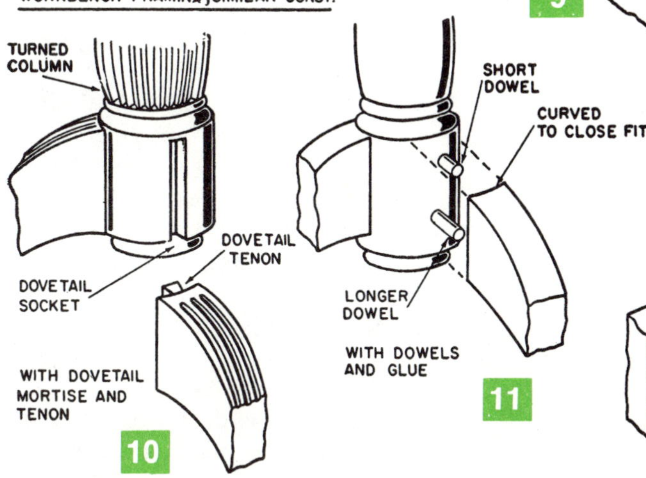

10

11

JOINING CURVED LEGS OR FEET TO
SINGLE COLUMN-TWO WAYS

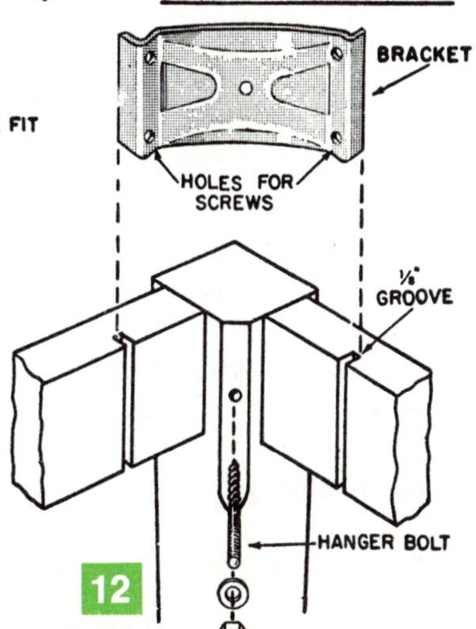

12

Two letter racks to organize your mail

Organize, and you won't lose those monthly bills in the stack on your dining-room table

COLONIAL

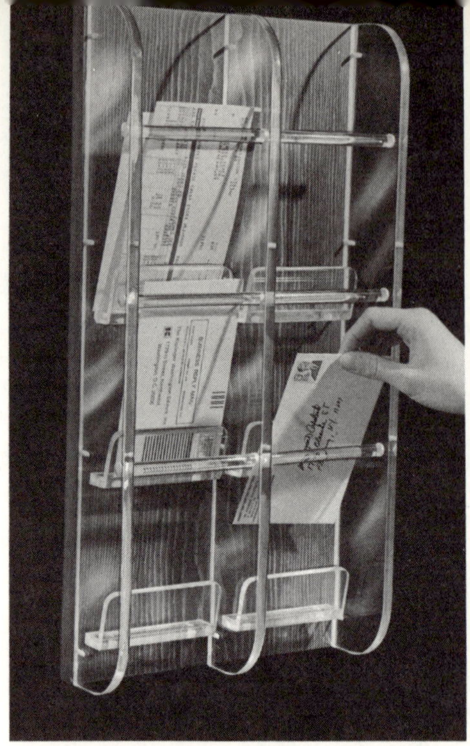

CONTEMPORARY

■ IF YOUR INCOMING mail gets tossed on the nearest counter or table when you walk in the door, build one of our handsome letter organizers. It will put an end to the clutter, confusion and annoyance of mislaid letters. The contemporary-styled organizer is made with clear-acrylic sheet dividers and retainers and a pine backboard. The colonial-styled unit is made entirely of clear pine.

MAKING THE COLONIAL ORGANIZER

Start by cutting board A (see plans, page 1713) from a piece of 1x12 clear pine and all other parts from ½-in. stock. Use a jig, coping or bandsaw with narrow blade to make the scroll cut at top. The shaped sides (D) can be ganged together and cut and sanded in a single operation. The same goes for the compartment fronts (B).

All edges are rounded with a rounding-over router bit. The small pieces are best handled on a router accessory table, which lets the router function as a shaper. Parts are simply passed against the cutter. Lacking the table, clamp workpieces to your workbench and use the router in the usual manner.

Assembling compartment members to center board (E) is tricky because nails can't be driven through from both sides. However, protruding nails can be used to assure alignment for gluing. Clip heads from nails and bore pilot holes for nails on inner edges (those that abut E) of six compartment fronts (B). Push nails into holes with points protruding about ¼ in. Tack-nail side pieces (D) to the compartment sections. Then press parts together against center dividing strip (E). Do this step on a flat surface.

Since the shape of this rack is too confining to permit successful application of stain, it is important to stain *before* assembly. While the unit is temporarily assembled with nails, mark outlines of all butt joints with a pencil. Then disassemble. Apply masking tape to all outlined surfaces. This keeps stain from areas to be glued.

After staining all parts except the outsides of the side members (D), remove the tape and reassemble the rack with glue. Outsides are stained later because they must be sanded flush with the back after gluing. Apply a varnish spray coat to completed assembly.

THE CONTEMPORARY ORGANIZER

Start by cutting the verticals (A,B) using a fine-tooth plywood blade (see drawing above). Gang the three pieces together with masking tape and cut the round corners at the same time using a bandsaw, if available, or cut the corners individually with a sabre or coping saw. Be *certain* to leave the protective masking paper intact during all machining and finishing operations.

Use a scraper or sharp chisel with a pulling

SEE ALSO

Bookracks . . . Bridge sets . . . Comb boxes . . . Desk accessories . . . Desks . . . Gifts, Christmas . . . Kitchen accessories . . . Magazine holders . . . Trays, folding . . . Weekend projects

SCROLL patterns on colonial-style organizer can be cut with jigsaw, bandsaw with narrow blade, or coping saw.

TO SAVE time, side members (D) are taped together before cutting scroll. Use a sharp blade and slow feed.

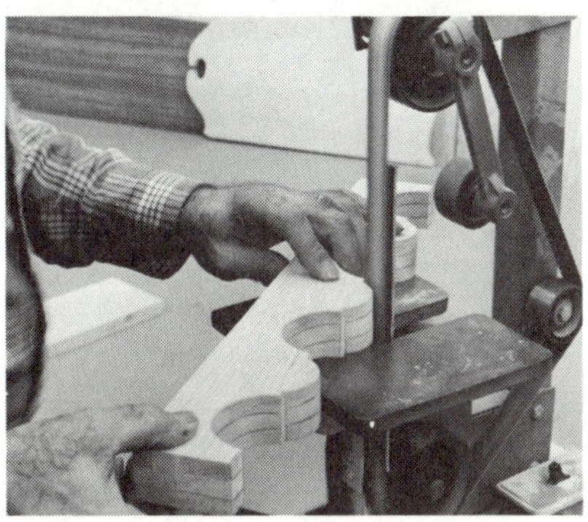

SAND convex curves with sander/grinder. Use drum sander, drill, or drill press to smooth concave curves.

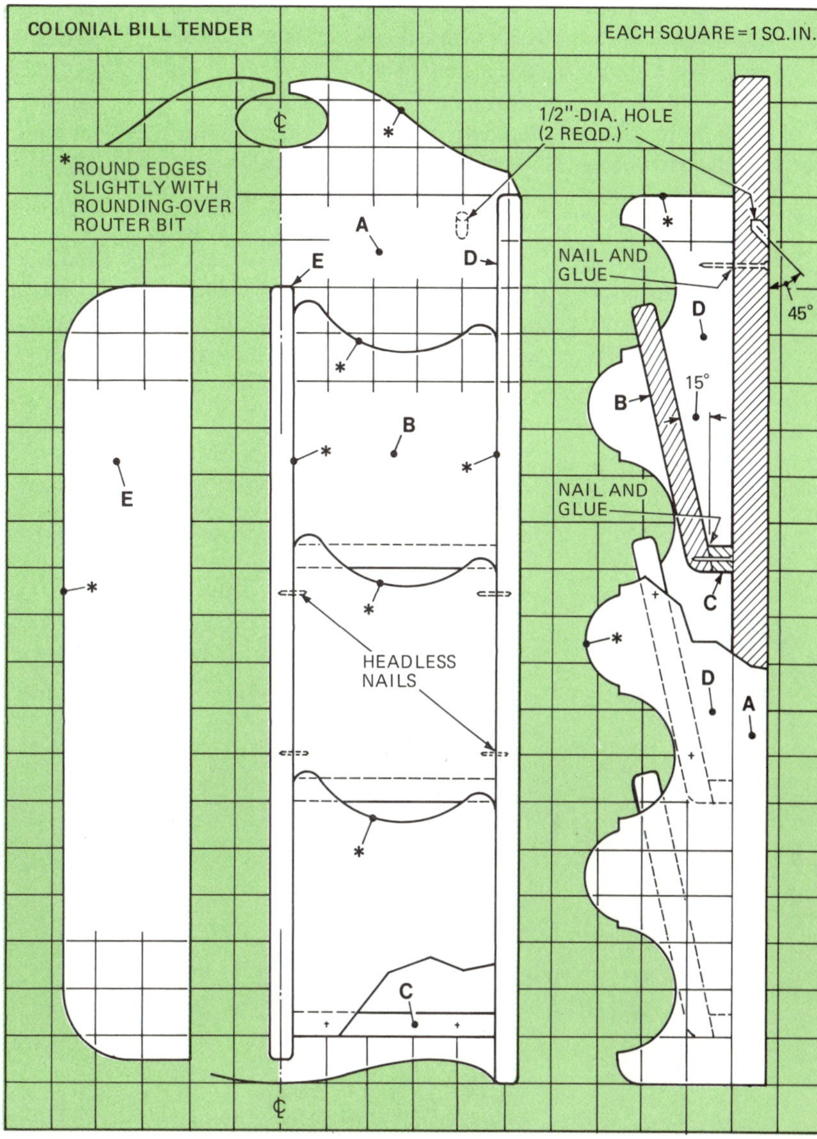

MATERIALS LIST—COLONIAL LOCATER

Key	Pcs.	Size and description
A	1	¾ × 10½" clear pine
B	6	½ × 4½ × 5¾" clear pine
C	6	½ × ⅝ × 4½" clear pine
D	2	½ × 3¼ × 19" clear pine
E	1	½ × 2¾ × 16½" clear pine

Misc: White glue, nails to suit.

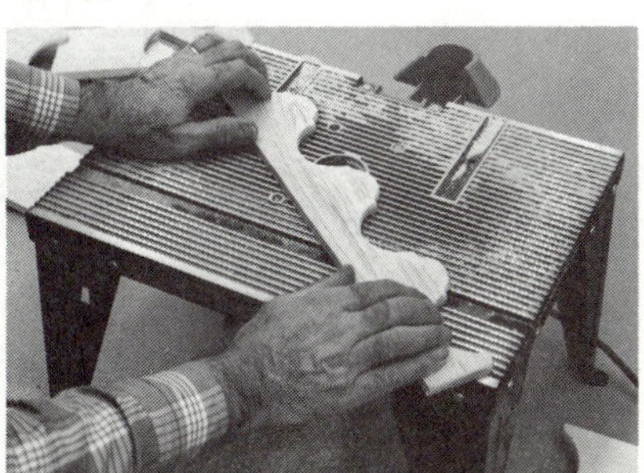

ROUTER table simplifies rounding-over the edges; use a piloted bit to make a pass on both sides of the work.

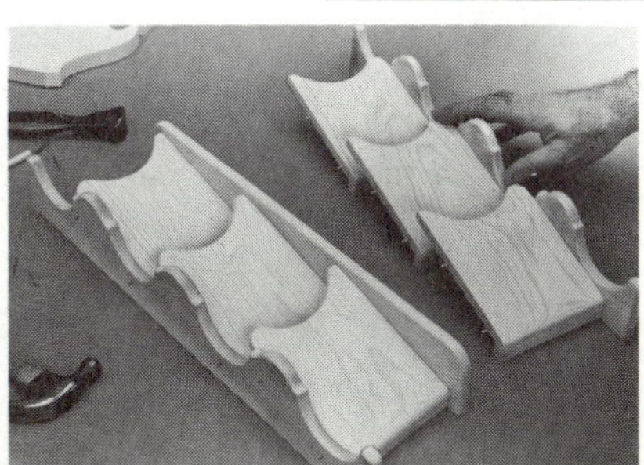

BEFORE gluing, use protruding-nail trick to align halves of organizer with central divider (see text).

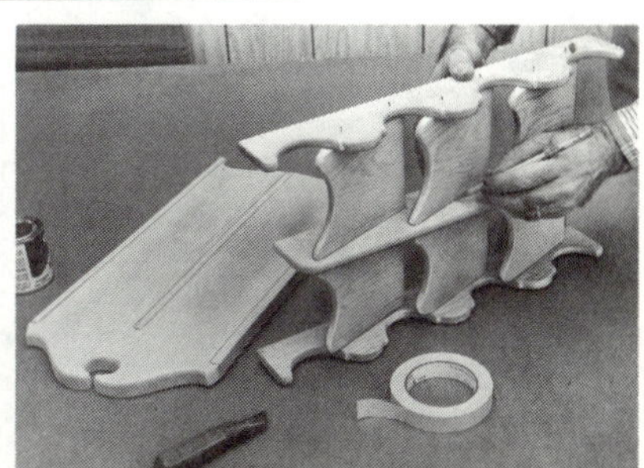

TRACE JOINT locations and mask them with tape. Apply stain to pieces. When they are dry, reassemble with glue.

stroke to smooth out all saw marks. Follow up by sanding all edges with silicon carbide paper, working up from 220 to 600 grit.

Next, bore all holes and tap where necessary. Be particularly careful when drilling blind holes in (B) pieces. Since masking paper conceals view, make test borings in scrap to get it right. Cut shelf pieces with appropriate bevels. Then cement front pieces (D) to bases (E) with solvent cement.

The solvent works by capillary action, which requires that surfaces to be joined be in close contact. To obtain the necessary smooth, flat surface on the beveled edges of the fronts, do this: After smoothing edges with a chisel or scraper, lay a sheet of abrasive paper face up on a flat surface. Stroke workpiece firmly back and forth, making sure not to rock it. Work with progressively finer grits of silicon carbide paper. After sanding the beveled edges of the fronts, do the same to the beveled edges of base pieces. Sand remainder after cementing.

Remove the protective masking paper before cementing. Use masking tape to hold parts together. A fine-nozzle, squeeze-bottle cement ap-

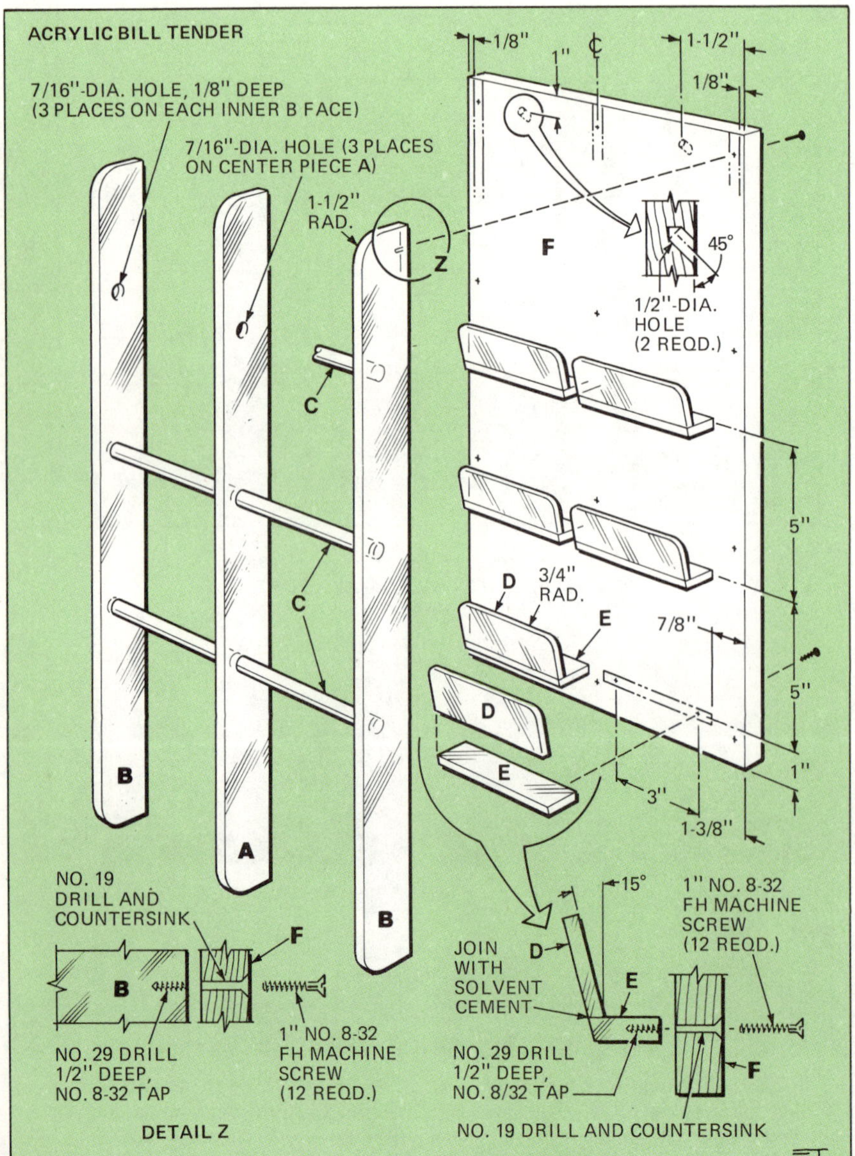

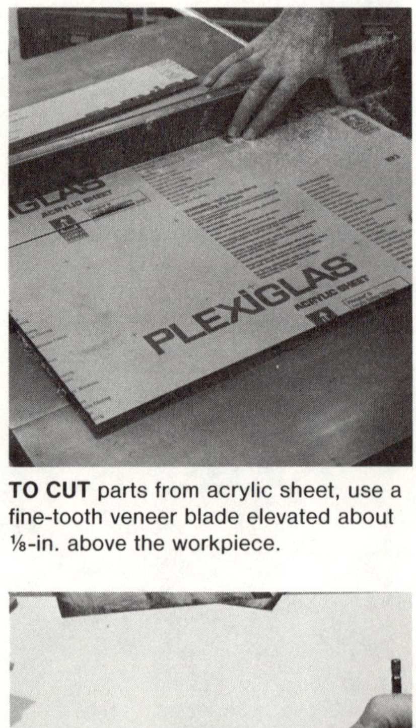

TO CUT parts from acrylic sheet, use a fine-tooth veneer blade elevated about ⅛-in. above the workpiece.

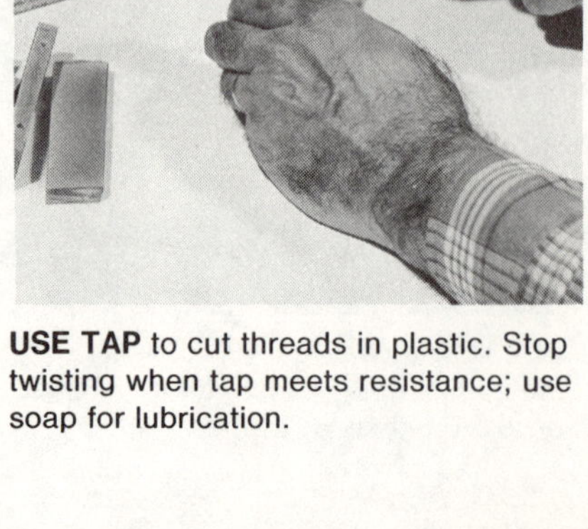

USE TAP to cut threads in plastic. Stop twisting when tap meets resistance; use soap for lubrication.

plicator, available where you buy the acrylic, is used to apply cement. Lay assemblies down so the joint is horizontal. Apply a thin line of cement on joint line. If pieces are in good contact, cement will be sucked in and quickly weld the joint. Don't touch parts for five minutes.

Sand all the flat edges of the shelves and slightly round the front bottom corners. Also cut and sand the rounds on the upper corners.

All edges which do not contact wood backboard are polished to a high gloss by buffing with polishing compound such as Du Pont Auto-Polishing compound or the Plexiglas brand. Use a buffing wheel, or a soft cloth shoeshine fashion.

If the screws meet resistance during assembly, rub a bit of soap on them. Attach two of the uprights; then insert the ⅜-in. rods before adding the third upright. The backboard is given a finish of walnut stain and satin topcoat varnish. (Do this before attaching the acrylic parts.) Plexiglas or similar acrylic sheet and rod are available at some home centers and at plastics supply houses. Look in Yellow Pages under "Plastics-Sheets & Rods."

MATERIALS LIST—MODERN LOCATER

Key	Pcs.	Size and description
A	1	⅜ × 3× 21" clear acrylic plastic
B	2	⅜ × 3 × 21" clear acrylic plastic
C	3	⅜"-dia. x 9¾" clear acrylic plastic
D	6	¼ × 1½ × 4" clear acrylic plastic
E	6	⅜ × 1⅛ × 4" clear acrylic plastic
F	1	¾ × 10½ × 21" clear pine

Misc: Solvent cement, screws to suit.

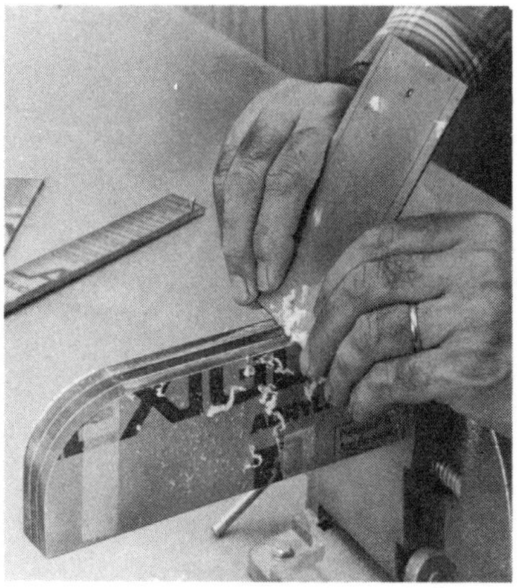

USE A cabinet scraper or sharp chisel to remove saw ripples. Upright dividers are ganged to save time.

FOR CLEAN holes, run drill press at high speed. Set depth so bit stops 1/16 in. from bottom of B pieces.

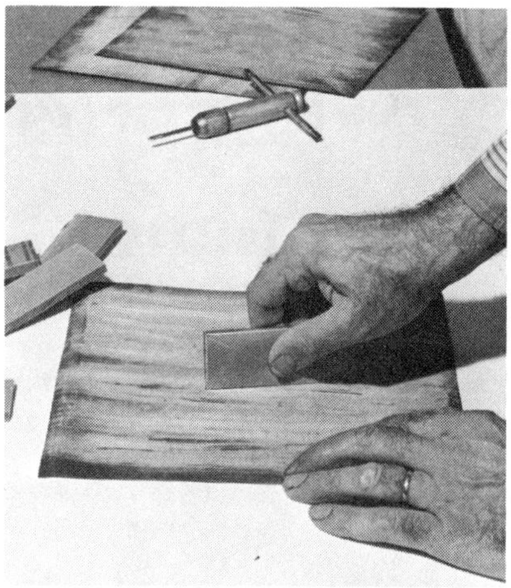

RUB EDGES of parts to be glued against abrasive sheet to obtain a perfect flat.

REMOVE protective masking paper, tape parts together and apply solvent—with the joint line horizontal.

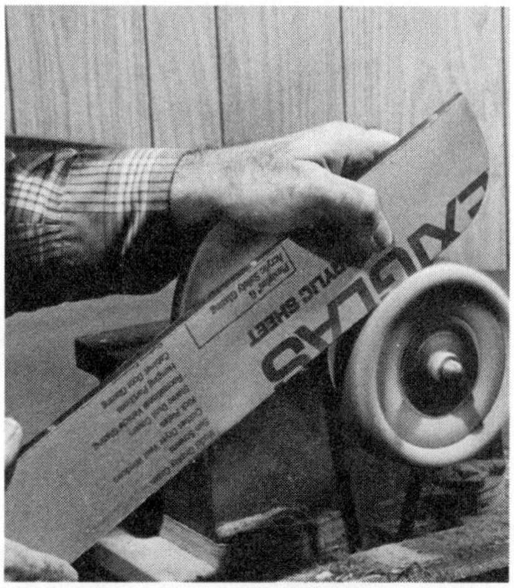

AFTER SANDING edges with 600-grit paper, polish on buffing wheel charged with auto-polishing compound.

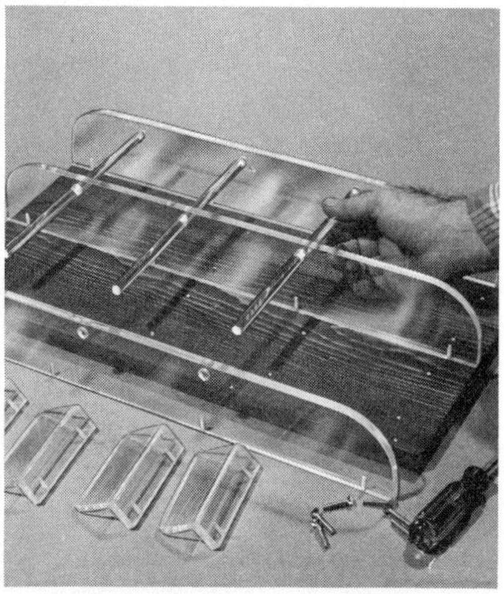

INSERT retaining rods (C) before screwing on last divider. Pine backboard should be finished first.

WELLCRAFT 24-ft. Nova: I, II or III.

SCATCRAFT also has PFD for skier.

MONARK 14 needs I, II, III or IV.

STARCRAFT 15 uses types I to IV.

SLYVAN 28 has I, II or III plus IV.

DUO SPRITE, like all sailboats and powerless craft, now needs PFDs.

What preserver should you choose?

By GEORGE DANIELS

IF YOU OWN A BOAT, or even plan to rent or ride in one, you need to be aware of federal regulations. The Boating Safety law now makes it necessary for *every* boat to carry approved life preservers for every passenger. Though the law applies only to federal waterways (and that includes most of the boating waters in the country), nearly all states have passed similar statutes to cover any ponds that have been left out. It makes sense. Sometimes a little rowboat on a river can turn over more easily than a large power craft out on open seas. Now the rules specify preserver types for every kind of boat. It's getting more difficult to drown.

Approved life preservers are called personal flotation devices (PFDs) by the Coast Guard. They are divided into five categories—according to the amount of buoyancy and performance you can expect from them. Which PFDs you must use depends on the length and type of your boat.

Now the law requires a PFD (personal flotation device) whenever you're in any boat—and sometimes when you're not! Different types are required for different boats

SEE ALSO

Accident prevention, water . . . Boating, safety . . . Canoes . . . Kayaks . . . Sailboats . . . Skin diving . . . Sports, water

Old Preservers = New Types

Old Preservers	New Types
160.002, 160.003, 160.004, 160.005	Type I
160.009 ring buoy	Type IV
160.047 vest	Type II
160.048, 160.049 cushions	Type IV
160.050 ring buoy	Type IV
150.053 work vest	Type V
160.055 preserver	Type I
160.060 vest	Type II
160.064 special devices—	

Devices worn may equal Type II or Type III. Type III is marked "may not turn unconscious wearer." Grasped device equals IV.

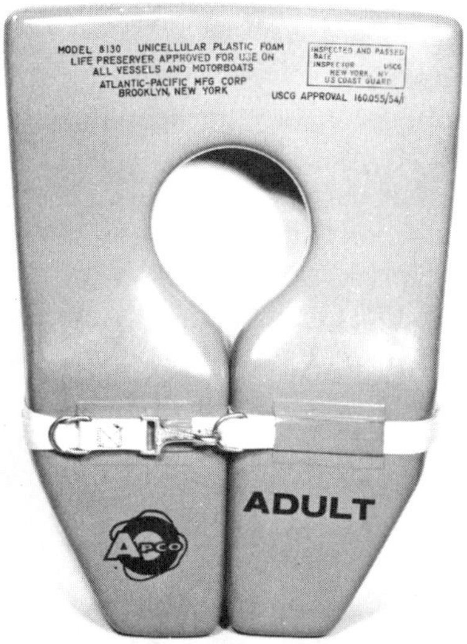

TYPE I—These personal-flotation devices may be bulky to wear but are designed to turn an unconscious person face upward in the water. The 20 pounds of buoyancy will float the wearer in a vertical or a slightly backward position. This is the PFD recommended for extended rought-water use offshore.

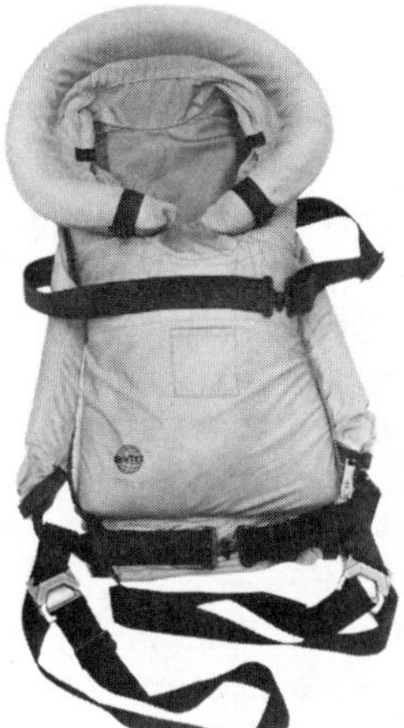

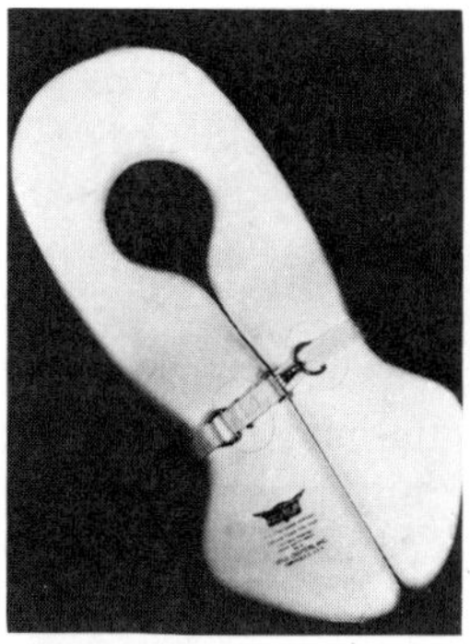

TYPE II—Less buoyancy (15½ lbs.) but more freedom of action are found in these PFD designs. Wearer is turned face up if unconscious; models with collar help hold head up. Racing jackets, like those by Gentex, left, may have leg straps to prevent ride-up, give driver added protection.

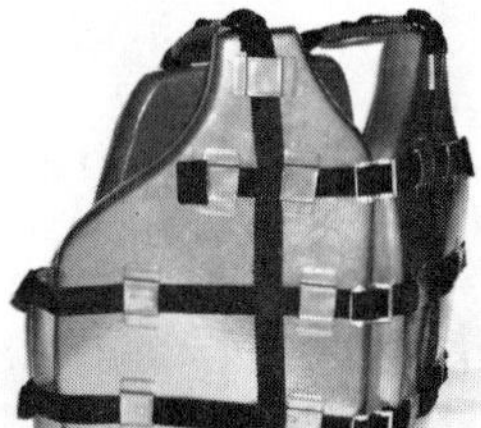

TYPE III—Suitable for more sheltered waters where man overboard may be picked up quickly, these PFDs are for conscious wearers, sailors, even ski jumpers with model above. Stearns makes models at left. Sears, others have similar PFDs.

SPECIAL-PURPOSE PFDs are permitted for white-water events in canoes and kayaks. Extralight air-cell vests like Flotherchoc models above from Old Town Canoes use sealed polyvinyl sacs for flotation.

Type I personal flotation device is designed to turn an unconscious person from face downward in the water to vertical or slightly backward position. As it must have more than a 20-lb. buoyancy, it is the type for rough water, but it is not very comfortable to wear.

Type II provides the unconscious person with the same position change, but may have as little as 15½-lb. buoyancy, permitting a more comfortable design suited to average boating conditions.

Type III, with at least 15½-lb. buoyancy, is designed to keep a conscious person in a vertical or slightly backward position. As less position-turning is necessary, this one can be designed for still less bulk and more freedom of action. You can wear it for boating activities likely to result in frequent dunkings, as in windy weather while sailboarding.

Type IV, with at least 16½-lb. buoyancy, is designed to be thrown to a person in the water and to be grasped, not worn. Buoyant cushions and ring life buoys are both in this class.

Type V is the special purpose PFD category for specific and restricted uses. The only preserver of this type now approved is a "work vest" used around merchant ships. Other Type V PFDs may come later.

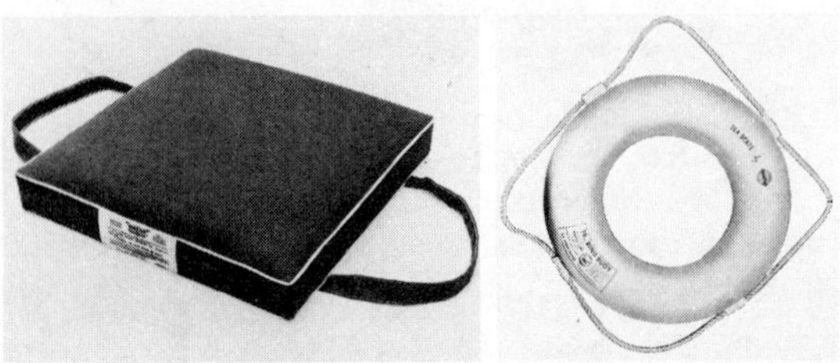

TYPE IV—Intended for throwing to a man overboard, these preservers can count as the required PFDs aboard craft under 16 feet in length. Larger boats must carry at least one Type IV ring or cushion.

You can continue to use your present Coast Guard-approved life preservers, as long as they are serviceable, if they are the type permitted for your boat. Check our Old-New chart on page 1834 to compare preserver numbers with type classes. All PFDs must be immediately accessible and of the proper size for the wearer. Small youngsters will need child-sized PFDs.

Boats under 16 feet long, including canoes and kayaks, must carry at least one PFD of Type I, II, III or IV for each person aboard. You can choose any regular type or its equivalent under the old number system.

Boats over 16 feet must carry a Type I, II or III (not IV) for each person aboard, except for canoes or kayaks where a Type IV is permitted for each person.

All boats, however, must carry at least one Type IV for man overboard emergencies. If this is a permitted type for your boat and you carry one for each person aboard, that's all you need. If your boat is over 16 feet and is required to carry one of the other types for each person, the Type IV must be carried as an extra. The only time you would not be required to carry a Type IV is when you're out alone and have one of the other required PFDs, or if all aboard are wearing such PFDs. The easy answer: Carry an approved buoyant cushion along.

An exception is made for white-water canoes and kayaks enclosed by a deck and spray skirt. Since some regular PFDs might be difficult to wear while paddling, you're permitted to wear a vest-type life presever that contains permanently inflated air sacs. The sacs must be made of not less than 12-mil polyvinyl chloride film. If you weigh more than 90 pounds, the rules require at least 150 sacs and 13-lb. buoyancy. If you're under 90, it's 120 sacs or more and 8½-lb. buoyancy. Canoe and sport suppliers carry these special vests.

If your boat is less than 16 feet, you can get by with Type IV buoyant cushions, but they are difficult to wear in the water and now is a good time to get approved vests or jackets while keeping the cushions as extras.

So long as you carry the required type and number of PFDs for all aboard—even for water skiers being towed behind—passengers may wear any other flotation devices, approved or otherwise, or none at all. And if you fall overboard, just yell for a Type IV.

Make a table lifter for your drill press

Save your back from the strain associated with raising and lowering the heavy table on your drill press by constructing this table lifter and allowing it to do most of the work

By HAROLD T. KENNEDY

ADJUSTING THE TABLE HEIGHT on your drill press can be a real test of strength. A heavy cast table can weigh a considerable amount and the awkward movement often required to lift it can cause serious back strain and in some cases even a hernia. Inertia and the sheer weight of the table (with everything that might be resting on it) can be a considerable lifting force. Add to this the friction of the table against the drill press column and the lifting force can be well over 55 lbs.

The simple lifting device described here can change all that. Whether you have to lift it once or make repeated moves, this table lifter can change those 55 lbs. to a mere 10. The cost? Probably a fraction of the cost of a doctor visit to look into that sore back!

The lifter is quite simple to construct. It consists of a lever, collar clamp and a link that connects the two.

The collar clamp can be made right in your shop. Or, if you want, you can order it from

SEE ALSO

Angles, drilling . . . Drill press techniques . . .
Motors, shop . . . Power-tool maintenance . . .
Power-tool stands . . . Safety, workshop . . .
Shop techniques . . . Shop tools . . .
Workbenches . . . Workshops

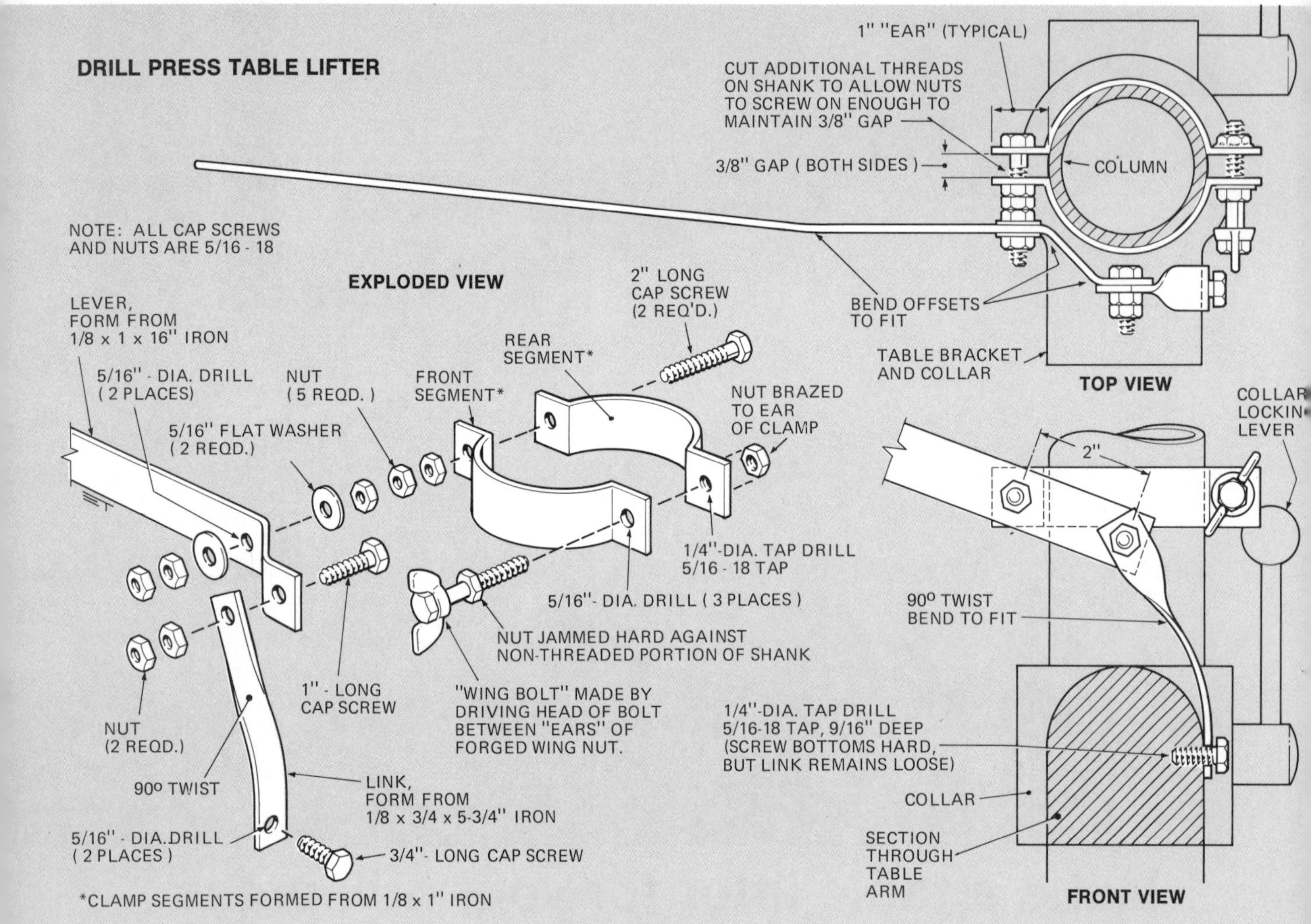

BEND YOUR own column clamp for the drill press lifter by making and using this form. It is made from a couple scraps of 2x4. A semicircular block is cut out of one piece of 2x4 and an arc cut out from the other (see text). The blanks are then placed in this form and the form placed in a vise. Applying pressure to the vise provides the bending force.

Sears. It's a standard 2¾-in.-dia. clamp that fits most drill presses. To order from Sears, specify part No. 9-2438, model No. 2450. The cost is reasonable.

You will need two 6-in. long blanks if you plan to make your own clamp. They should be suitable to use on a 2¾-in. column. Begin making the clamp by bending the ends of the two blanks 90° to form 1-in.-long "ears." Next, use a compass to draw an arc with a 1½-in. radius on a 6-in. length of 2x4. The centerpoint for the arc should be located 5/16-in. beyond the edge of the 2x4. Carefully cut along the line of the arc with a jigsaw and remove the piece of waste stock.

You will need a second piece of 2x4 to form the male part of the bending form. In this piece, cut out a semicircular block with a 1⅜-in. radius to produce a curved tool for forcing the iron strips into the first notch. Keep the center-point of this arc at least ⅛ in. from the 2x4's edge.

Place the male and female mold around the blanks and put into a hefty bench vise. As you begin to apply pressure to the vise the necessary bending force will be exerted to make the clamp fit the correct shape. A column with a diameter more than 2¾-in. diameter calls for proportionately longer blanks and a larger jig for forming clamps. Cut the notch with a radius equal to the column radius plus ⅛ in. Make the radius of the corresponding block equal to the column's. Maintain a ⅜-in. gap between the ears of the assembled clamp to allow for final tightening.

drilling holes for cap screws

Now, in the center of each clamp segment ear (except one), drill 5/16-in. holes to accept two 2-in. long cap screws. In the remaining ear, drill and tap for a 5/16-18 hole. This threaded hole goes to the right rear when the clamp is in position (see plans) and accommodates the right-hand, clamp-tightening bolt. A nut, brazed to the right-rear clamp ear may be used to reinforce or supplant the threaded hole.

Using a forged wingnut will make hand-tightening possible. To do this, slip the forged wingnut for a ⅜-in. bolt up to the head of the right-hand bolt, and drive the head tightly between the wings. Run a hex nut hard against the end of the threading. This is used to provide clearance for adjusting the wingbolt.

ALL OF THE NECESSARY parts to make the lifter are shown here before assembly.

LOCKED NUTS (two nuts jammed and tightened securely) are used at several places. They help prevent loosening at pivotal connections.

WINGBOLT DRAWS clamp segments together to keep the table from dropping when collar locking lever is loosened.

determining fulcrum point

The fulcrum hole is located on the lever about 3 in. from the end and 2½ in. (center to center) from the connecting-link bolt hole. The lever must be made so it won't strike the drill press column. This is accomplished by forming an offset bend in the lever.

The link can be made from scrap ⅛x1-in. iron. It can alternately be made from the ⅛x¾-in. iron specified in the plans. Twist this link 90° and bend it as needed to secure it to the side of the table arm.

To attach the link to the table, it is first necessary to find the exact "balance point" on the table arm. This point is located where the effort to lift the table seems the least.

When you have located the "balance point," drill and tap for a 5/16-18x9/16-in. hole to receive the ¾-in. long capscrew. Be sure the link will fit loosely on the tightened bolt.

adding extra washers

After the lifter is all together you may discover that there is some wobble at the connections. To eliminate this you can add a few extra washers to obtain the specified gaps. We had to place one under the head of the left-hand clamp bolt as a spacer. Its purpose there was to help produce the required ⅜-in. gap between the segment ears. If friction is a problem, you can oil movable joints and the wingbolt.

To operate the lifter, tighten the table clamp and release the collar by loosening the wingbolt. Slide the collar up the column as far as it will go, then retighten the wingbolt. Release the table clamp screw and press down on the main lever to lift the table. For a lift over 3 in., repeat this same procedure.

When it comes time to lower the table, simply follow the reverse of the raising procedure. The handle may tend to cut into your hand while you are operating the lifter. For a more comfortable grip, slip a short segment of rubber or plastic hose over the handle.

a backup safety clamp

A second column clamp, similar to the one described, installed below the drill press table, will prevent it from dropping accidently to the floor or bench. The second clamp limits the table's fall if both lifter clamp and collar lock are loosened at the same time. Even if you do not install the lifter described here, this backup safety clamp is a smart precaution.

Build an inexpensive lightbox

By CLARENCE E. BANISTER

This low-cost lightbox does triple duty. It can be used for tracing or drawing, or as an illuminator for viewing and sorting slides

CRAFTSMEN, draftsmen or youngsters will find a lightbox to be the handiest thing ever for tracing and drawing. And photographers won't find a better slide viewer for the money.

Actually, it's more than a lightbox; it's also a portable drawing table in that it has a tilting top, built-in measuring rules along three edges and a 24-in. T-square. Two 15-w. fluorescent fixtures, plus two 40-w. showcase lamps, provide even lighting over the entire frosted-glass top.

SEE ALSO

Coffee tables . . . Cutting boards . . . Darkrooms . . . Illuminators, slide-copy . . . Photography . . . Prints, photo . . . Projector stands . . . Slides, photo . . . Theaters, home

The unit consists of three separate assemblies: a base, box and cover. The base consists of two bandsawed hardwood side members, which are joined front and back with two 1 x 23½-in. dowels shouldered at the ends to glue in ½-in. holes. A 1 x 2¼ x 23½-in. stretcher across the back (part X) is notched at the ends to receive the side members and also provide tilting clearance for the lampbox. The locking bracket for the tilting box is later attached to this stretcher. Holes are made in the base members for a ½ x 23-in. metal shaft which passes through the lampbox to pivot it to the base. The shaft is drilled for two 1-in. No. 6 screws which anchor the shaft to the inside of the lampbox and keep it from shifting sideways. A 1⅛-in. washer cut from ⅛-in. hardboard is placed on the shaft between lampbox and base members.

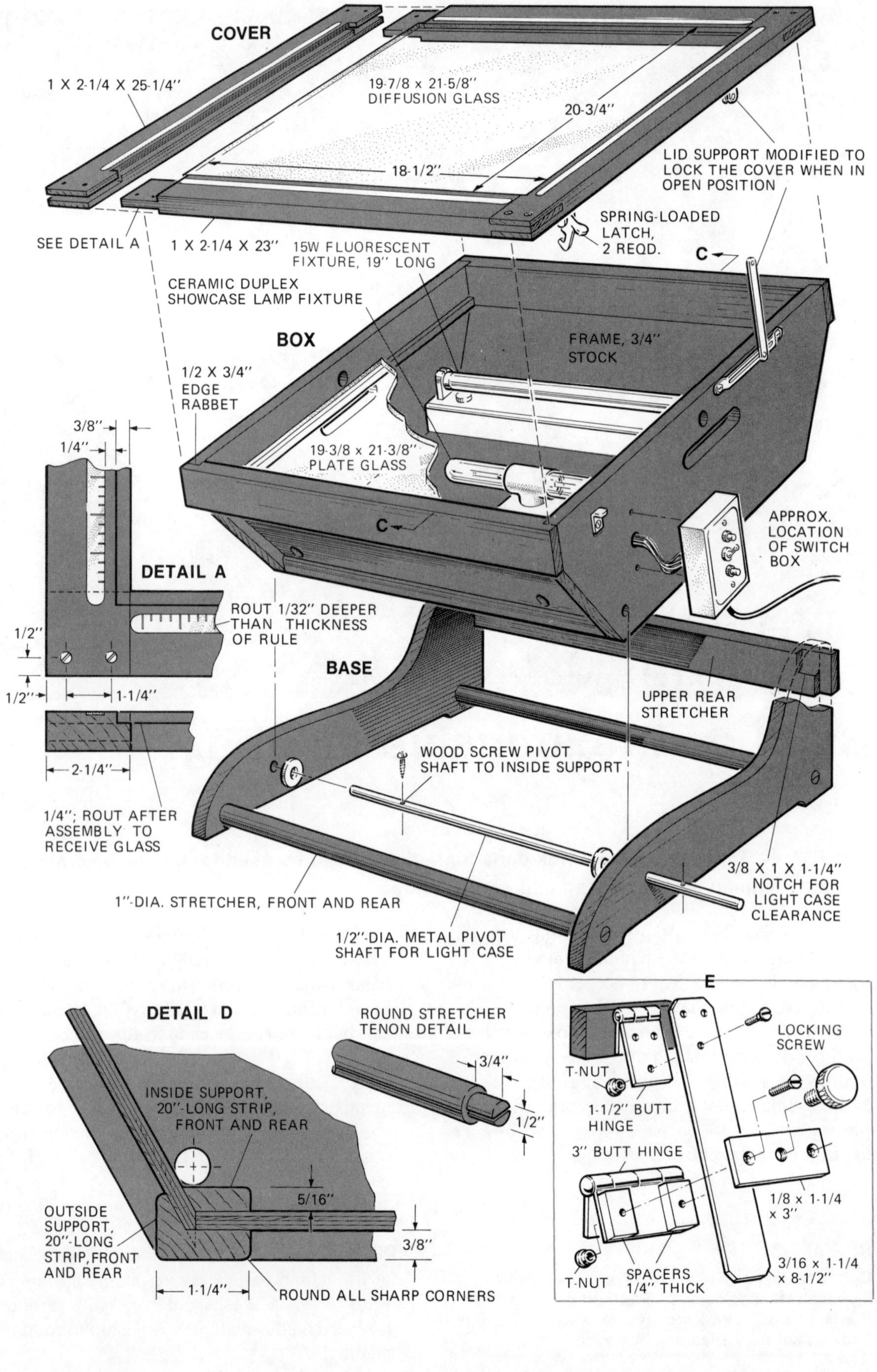
COVER
1 X 2-1/4 X 25-1/4"
19-7/8 x 21-5/8"
DIFFUSION GLASS
20-3/4"
18-1/2"
LID SUPPORT MODIFIED TO
LOCK THE COVER WHEN IN
OPEN POSITION
SEE DETAIL A
1 X 2-1/4 X 23"
15W FLUORESCENT
FIXTURE, 19" LONG
SPRING-LOADED
LATCH,
2 REQD.
C
CERAMIC DUPLEX
SHOWCASE LAMP FIXTURE
BOX
FRAME, 3/4"
STOCK
1/2 X 3/4"
EDGE
RABBET
3/8"
1/4"
19-3/8 x 21-3/8"
PLATE GLASS
C
APPROX.
LOCATION
OF SWITCH
BOX
DETAIL A
ROUT 1/32" DEEPER
THAN THICKNESS
OF RULE
1/2"
1/2"
1-1/4"
BASE
UPPER REAR
STRETCHER
2-1/4"
WOOD SCREW PIVOT
SHAFT TO INSIDE SUPPORT
1/4"; ROUT AFTER
ASSEMBLY TO
RECEIVE GLASS
3/8 X 1 X 1-1/4"
NOTCH FOR
LIGHT CASE
CLEARANCE
1"-DIA. STRETCHER, FRONT AND REAR
1/2"-DIA. METAL PIVOT
SHAFT FOR LIGHT CASE
DETAIL D
ROUND STRETCHER
TENON DETAIL
3/4"
1/2"
INSIDE SUPPORT,
20"-LONG STRIP,
FRONT AND REAR
5/16"
OUTSIDE
SUPPORT,
20"-LONG
STRIP, FRONT
AND REAR
3/8"
1-1/4"
ROUND ALL SHARP CORNERS
E
LOCKING
SCREW
T-NUT
1-1/2" BUTT
HINGE
3" BUTT HINGE
1/8 x 1-1/4
x 3"
3/16 x 1-1/4
x 8-1/2"
T-NUT
SPACERS
1/4" THICK

THE BIG VIEWING SURFACE holds over 100 slides at a time. Fluorescent lamps provide illumination.

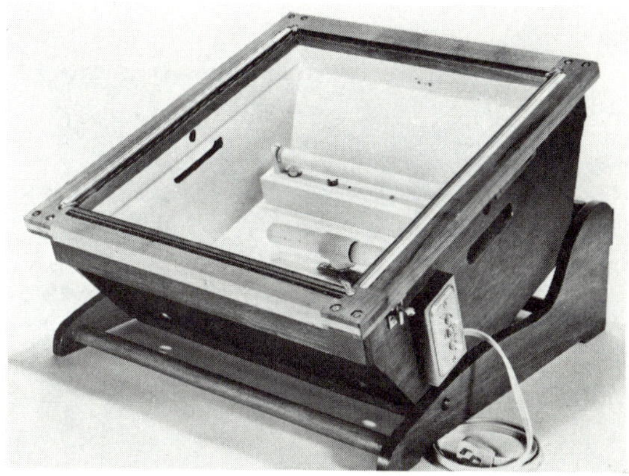

THE LAMPBOX INTERIOR is painted white, first with undercoater, then with two coats of enamel.

The two sides of the lampbox are cut from 3/4-in. plywood. A 1/4 x 1/4-in. groove is routed in the inside faces 3/8-in. in from the edges to house the 1/4-in. plywood panels which form the bottom, front and back members. The lower edges of the front and back panels are beveled 30° to butt against square edges of the bottom panel. Notice that the two sides of the box have air holes in them and hand holes. Study detail D to see how the beveled joint is sandwiched front and back, between two cleats. Two 1 x 2 1/4 x 21 1/2-in. stretchers, notched at the ends, brace the box at the top, front and back. Shallow grooves cut in the lower edges of these stretchers let in the front and back panels. There are air holes in these pieces, two in front and two in the back. The plate-glass top rests on 3/8 x 3/8-in. cleats nailed and glued to the ends 1 1/2 in. down.

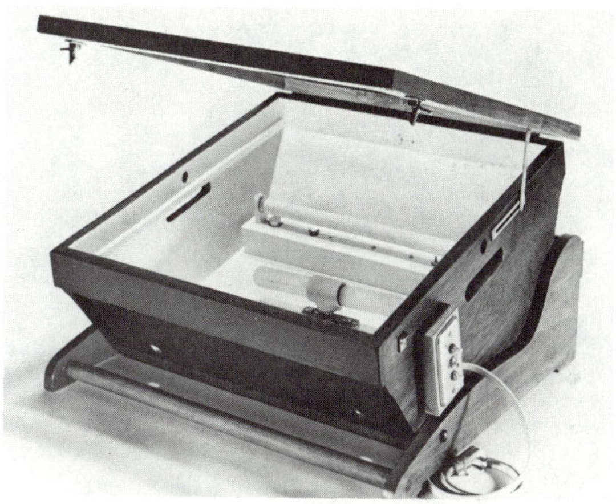

THE COVER is fitted with a desk-lid support, which has been modified to lock in an open position.

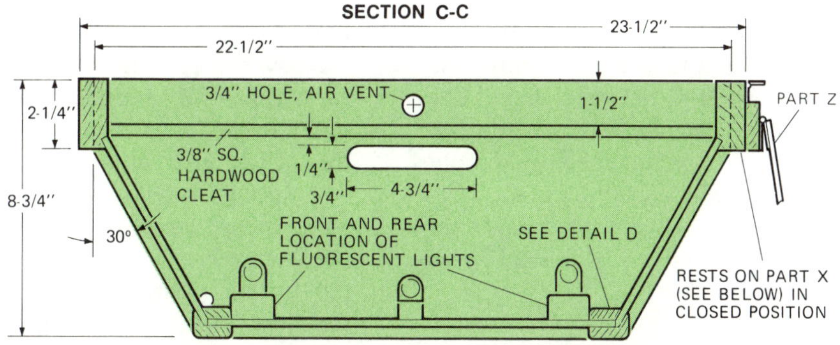

NOTE: END PANELS 1/4 X 8 X 20-1/2"
LOWER EDGES BEVELED 30°
BOTTOM PANEL 15-1/4 X 20-1/4", EDGES 90°

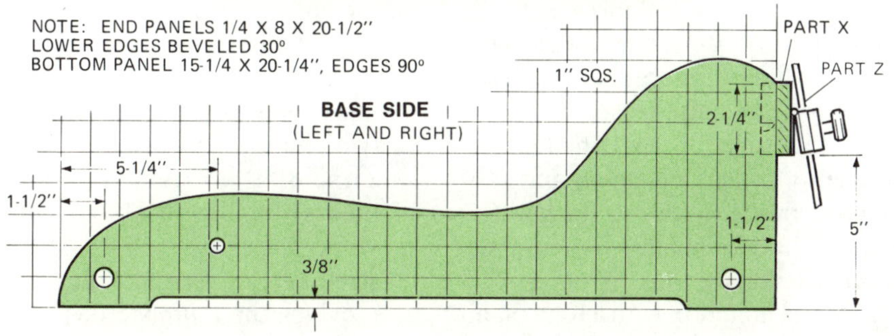

A BRACKET lets you tilt the glass top when the box is used as a tracing table. A knob locks it securely.

A PLYWOOD TEMPLATE, tacked to the faces of the lampbox sides, guides router in running ¼-in. grooves.

A PLUG CUTTER forms the tenons on the ends of the dowel stretchers. A bench saw cuts the shoulders.

A DADO HEAD is used to run ¼-in. grooves in the front and back rails. The arbor is tilted 30°.

Section C-C shows the position of the two fluorescent fixtures, and the two showcase lamps which are centered between them. The lamps are wired to toggle and pushbutton switches mounted in a box attached to the right side of the lampbox. The switch box is a wire-mold type, 1 in. thick. I center-drilled the cover with a ½-in. drill and cut the additional holes with hole cutters.

Pushbuttons control the fluorescents, the toggle the showcase lamps. Both fluorescents are used for normal density, only one for extreme transparency. All of the lamps are used when the slide or negative is extremely dense.

The cover is a four-sided frame joined at corners with an open mortise and tenon and rabbeted like a picture frame to receive flush a 19⅜ x 21⅜-in. piece of ¼-in. plate glass. A turnbutton at each corner holds the glass in place. The cover is hinged to the lampbox with a long piano hinge, and a lid support, modified to suit, locks the cover open when necessary. If you use the same type of lid support as I did, you can file a notch in the lower edge of the slotted track and the lid will lock automatically.

A spring-loaded elbow catch holds the cover shut, and a strip of cloth adhesive tape stuck to the front edge of the diffusion glass provides a tab for removing the glass. The self-sticking tape-line rules, which are added to three sides of the cover, are recessed and cemented in routed grooves as shown in detail A.

The hinged bracket for holding the lightbox at the desired angle is shown in detail E. Pivoted by two hinges, it consists of a sliding flat strip (part Z) held by a locking thumbscrew. The 1½-in. butt is attached to a block glued to the lampbox while the 3-in. butt is attached to the base stretcher. A tapped hole through a crossplate receives the thumbscrew.

Noisy condominium

I live in a condominium and noises are my problem. I like my neighbors and don't wish to offend them. Is there any practical way I can dampen the ordinary sounds of living that come through the wall between us? Also, my living-room window fronts on a parking space. How do I go about soundproofing it?—P.L., Fla.

Much depends on room arrangement, room size, window size, noise volume at a given time, whether you are a late riser, and so on. You refer to "ordinary" sounds, so I assume the decibels are relatively low, perhaps rising to higher levels mornings and evenings.

You can achieve a measure of peace and quiet, but only at some sacrifice of convenience and living space, by hanging lined, full-length draperies or tapestries from ceiling to floor along the separating wall. They will act like soundproofing "curtains" in a conventional soundproofed wall. Hang the same fabric on a traverse rod at the window to soften the racket from the parking area.

For maximum effect, use a heavy, lined fabric and hang them with ample folds. Window drapery should extend about a foot beyond the trim at top and sides and within 1½ inches of the floor. Hanging of such draperies will have the general effect of reducing room size, even though they harmonize with your furnishings.

Borers in fireplace wood?

I'm told I'll bring wood borers and other insects into the house with fireplace wood. Will the borers find their way into my furniture?—F.D., Pa.

It's not impossible, but very unlikely. Stack the wood some distance from the house and cover it with a plastic sheet to keep it dry. It's a good idea to raise the bottom tier of logs clear of the ground. Bring in only enough wood for the evening fire.

Drippy chimney flue

I've installed gas logs in my fireplace. After an hour or two of operation, I notice water dripping, apparently from the chimney. Where does it come from?—R. Munroe, Cleveland.

Water vapor is a product of combustion of concentrated fuel, such as natural gas. It condenses in the chimney flue and accounts for the dripping. There's little you can do about it, but turning down the flame will reduce the amount of vapor produced. If your flue is tile-lined, the drippings should cause little damage, except over a long period of time.

Septic tank and detergents

I have a septic tank and have been told that household wastes that include detergents will affect its operation. What must I do to maintain efficiency? What chemicals are to be used and in what amount? Or must we stop using detergents completely?—H.H., Kans.

Ordinarily, present-day detergents in an average household do not measurably affect operation of a properly installed septic tank of ample capacity. Chemical compounds are available (you should be able to obtain them locally) that are designed to speed disposal action in septic tanks. They should be used judiciously, according to instructions given. Be careful not to introduce an undue amount of kitchen fat into the disposal system; in time, this may cause trouble. Dispose of the fat in a separate container that goes with the garbage.

What's 'whitewood'?

Recently I've looked at some unpainted furniture with the idea of finishing several pieces by myself. My dealer refers to the wood as "whitewood." What's he talking about, and what wood do I get if I buy it?—K.G., Ill.

As a rule, you'll get either selected white pine or what is known to the trade as yellow poplar. However, the more expensive pieces of unfinished furniture are often made from a hardwood, with birch being probably the most common used. In general, the dealers use the term "whitewood" to describe their unfinished furniture, while the manufacturers and cabinetmakers are more likely to use the phrase "in the white."

Drawer trouble

Two drawers in one of my chests—not old—stick when only part way open. I can't pull either one all the way out. I tried rubbing bar soap on the exposed sides, but it doesn't help. What do I do now?—Mrs. Don Kerney, Lincoln, Neb.

Don't use soap—it just makes matters worse. The drawer sides have absorbed moisture and swelled, and soap will attract more moisture. Instead, put a 25 or 40-watt bulb inside the drawer, using an extension cord and placing the bulb in a chinaware dish—or use a trouble lamp with a basket guard. Keep close watch that nothing overheats. Heat from the bulb will dry the wood and in time permit you to open the drawer. Then remove the soap and spray lower edges of the sides with one of the silicone sprays available in aerosol cans.

Simple kitchen lights you can make

Carefully selected and located, lighting can transform an ordinary working area into a striking picture. And custom-built fixtures you design and construct yourself will pinpoint what you choose—dramatically

SEE ALSO

Electrical wiring . . . Extension cord reels . . . Fluorescent lamps . . . Home improvement . . . Lamps . . . Testers, continuity . . . Wiring, electrical

SURPRISINGLY SIMPLE homemade lighting fixtures can make a dull, drab kitchen suddenly come alive. Soft lighting under cabinets will emphasize colorful counter surfaces. Carefully spaced "spots" will capture the beauty of the cabinetry. And light spilling out from behind valance boards and cascading over draperies will add a strikingly dramatic effect.

When adding over-sink and under-cabinet

SHADOW-FREE LIGHT over countertops and sink helps to take eyestrain out of food preparation, while the overhead lighting prominently illuminates appliances, enriches the natural wood.

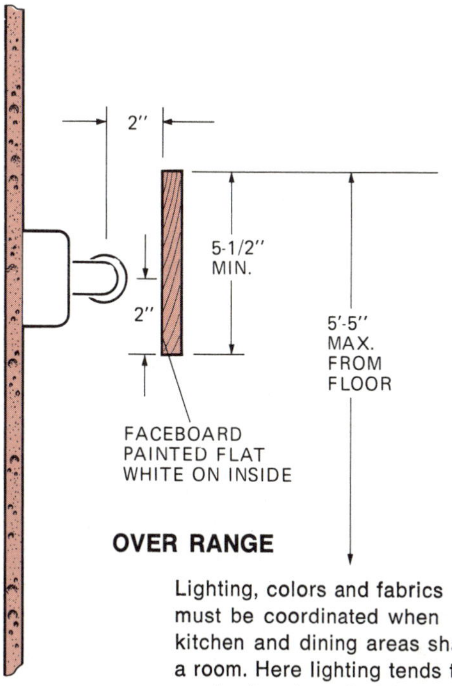

OVER RANGE

Lighting, colors and fabrics must be coordinated when kitchen and dining areas share a room. Here lighting tends to emphasize the colorful countertops, the wood tones and drapes

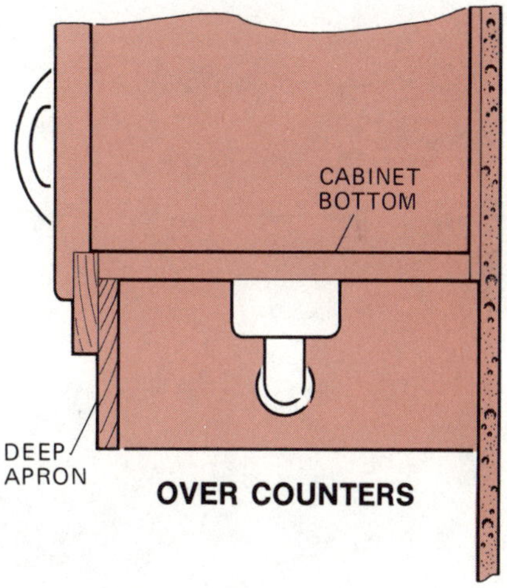

OVER COUNTERS

lights, your biggest job will be running wires to them. This will be easier in a ranch house where wiring can be brought down from attic junction boxes; more difficult in a two-story house. Sometimes the cable can be brought up from a basement junction box by snaking it through a hole in the kitchen floor, between a base cabinet and the wall.

You may have to remove a wall cabinet temporarily to bring cable out through a hole behind it. Or you may have to cut a 1-in.-wide slot in the plaster behind a cabinet to permit fishing the cable from one point to another. And, when you're up against a hidden obstruction with no way to bypass or bridge it, you may have to cut through an exposed portion of a wall, which can be patched later.

In working out individual wiring problems, you

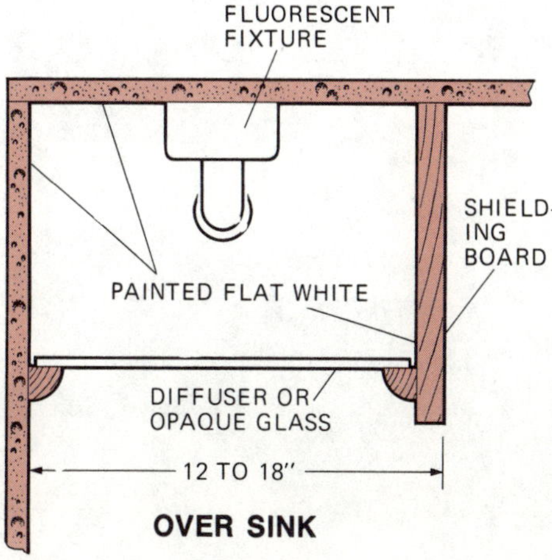

OVER SINK

must keep in mind that over-sink and under-cabinet lights must be controlled by conveniently located switches which, in turn, must be connected to nearby outlets or junction boxes in basement or attic.

Romex or BX (armored) cable is generally required wherever wiring is to be concealed inside walls (some areas require that such wiring be run through conduit) and such installations must conform to your local electrical code.

Adding a fluorescent lamp over a sink often requires nothing more than fitting a faceboard across the front between cabinets. Angle brackets can be used on the inside to fasten it in place, and it can be finished to match the wood cabinets; it can be made plain or scalloped. A diffusing glass or grid, resting loosely on strips of quarter-round molding, hides the lamp from view, yet makes lamp replacement an easy task.

Lamps under cabinets are shielded from view by a faceboard attached to the fronts. Use Deluxe Warm White lamps here; wattage depends on the total countertop area. Lamps over draperies are shielded so light spills out top and bottom. In all cases, the rear side of faceboards should be painted flat white.

Attractive modern downlight fixtures are simple to make by placing boxlike assemblies over ceiling-mounted junction boxes fitted with porcelain sockets.

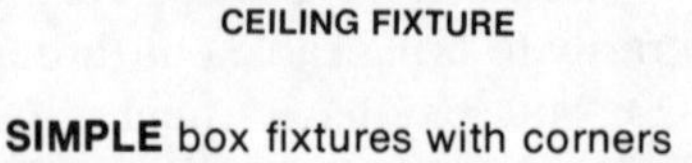

SIMPLE box fixtures with corners mitered are made to slip over wood sleeves attached to ceiling.

MOST HOME HANDYMEN have a favorite way to hold a paint can when working on an extension ladder. But I've yet to see a simpler setup than the "hook" use. I tighten a C-clamp anywhere on the ladder and hang the pail on the threaded portion.—*Jackson Hand, Westport, CT.*

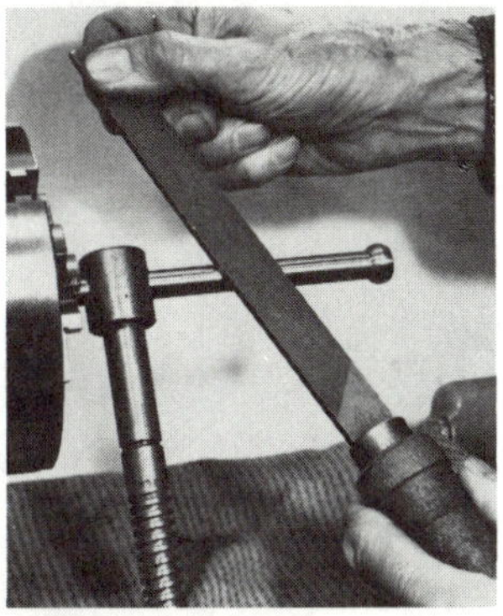

TO UNFREEZE a vise handle quickly use your lathe. Clamp one end of the handle in the chuck with the ball end inside to clear jaws and, with screw resting on a protective cloth, slide a file along the handle as it turns. Reverse the handle to file the other half.—*B.W. Ervin, Kent, OH.*

WHEN SOLDERED to a suitable wall bracket, a funnel makes a novel dispenser for a ball of twine that unwinds from the center. The twine is pulled through the spout. If you sharpen one bracket arm, you will also have a handy built-in twine cutter.—*Walter E. Burton, Akron, OH.*

WHEN THE METAL STRAINER BASKET for my swimming pool rusted out, I made a serviceable and noncorrodible one from a heavy plastic pail. I picked one that would fit the skimmer hole, cut it down to match the old basket, drilled countless $^1/_{16}$-in. holes in the bottom and sides and finally attached a handle with pop rivets.—*John R. Orend, Orlando, FL.*

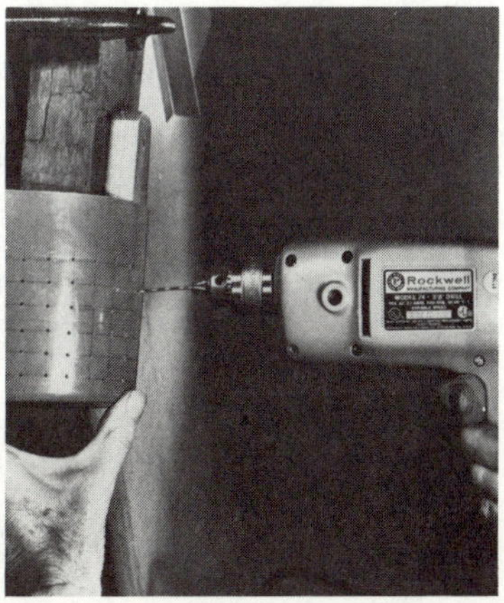

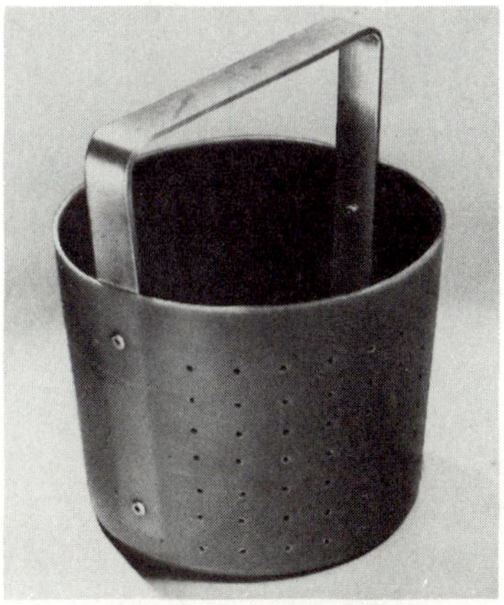

How to install a fast-set door lock

LOCATE THE HOLES FOR THE LOCKSET

The job starts by lining up the template (packed with the lockset or on inside of the box) with the door edge as in the drawing at left. Standard doorknob distance from floor is 36 to 38 in. Tape the template so it cannot shift, then drill ¼-in. pilot holes in door face and edge. Remove template and, using a hole saw to suit diameter of the lock you've bought, bore the large hole through door.

The best hole-saw technique is to drill halfway through from each side; while holding the drill at right angles—in both planes—to the door surface. Then, using a spade bit of a diameter to suit the latch mechanism, drill a hole in the edge for the latch.

To keep the door from moving while drilling, you simply wedge a pair of undercourse shingles under the door.

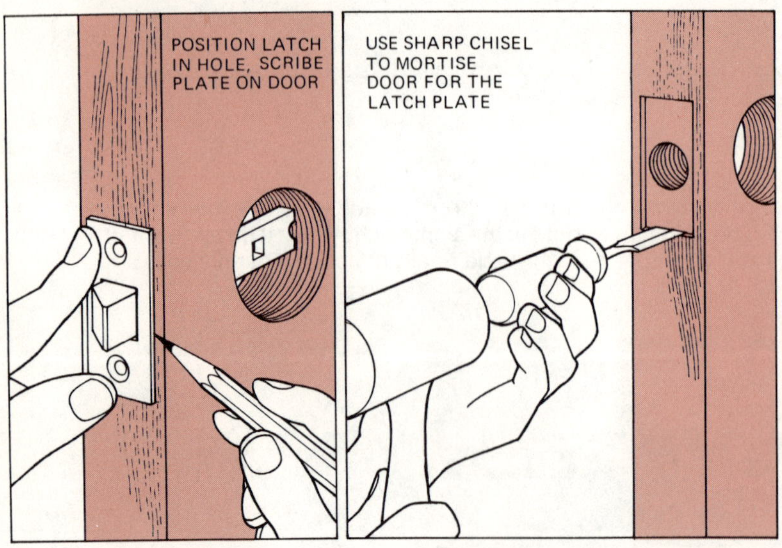

MORTISE FOR LATCH

Test-fit the latch mechanism in the hole you have just bored in the door edge; it should slide in and out freely without binding. Insert the latch in the door, firmly hold the plate against door edge and draw a pencil line around the plate. With a utility knife, score this pencil line. (This acts as a safety guide when mortising with a chisel.) Finally, using a ¾-in. chisel, remove the waste inside the mortise. *Caution:* When approaching the correct depth, avoid a too-deep mortise by stopping occasionally to check the mortise depth by inserting the latch.

SEE ALSO

Burglar proofing . . . Doors . . . Entryways . . . Home improvement . . . Lubrication, home . . . Security, home . . . Sliding glass doors . . . Winterizing, homes

INSTALL LATCH MECHANISM

Latch plate must be absolutely flush with the door edge: If it's too deep the door may not stay closed; if not deep enough the plate or screwheads may keep the door from closing. When plate is flush with the edge, permanently install it with screws provided.

Push plate fully into mortise and, with an awl, make pilot holes for the screws. Install the flathead screws, turning them fully home. If the latch plate has a sloped surface, the slope should be toward direction of door closing. For smooth lockset operation, bar extending into the door must be at right angle to door edge.

EXTERIOR TRIM GOES IN NEXT

Next, install the exterior trim (knob with the tie rods) through appropriate holes in the latch. Tie rods should slide freely, not bind against latch or door. Important: If installing a lockset with a key, place lock so the keyhole is at bottom of the knob (in 6:00 o'clock position). This is particularly important in installations where the lock is exposed to the weather. Correct installation allows moisture to escape, instead of trapping it and damaging the lockset. Never insert the key into the lockset before the installation is complete; you could disturb the tumblers.

continued

FINISH LOCKSET INSTALLATION

Install interior mounting trim plate (rosette) over spindle and tie rods. On the lockset shown (there are several types of fast-set locks), the rosette is then rotated until holes in the rosette are centered over the tie rods. Hold both plates with one hand, insert lockset holding screws and catch the threads in the tie rods. Here, because the doorknob is usually partly in the way, it is best to use a slender-shank screwdriver to turn home the screws. Screws should be tightened until snug; not tightened with brute force, nor should they be so loose that the lock operates sloppily.

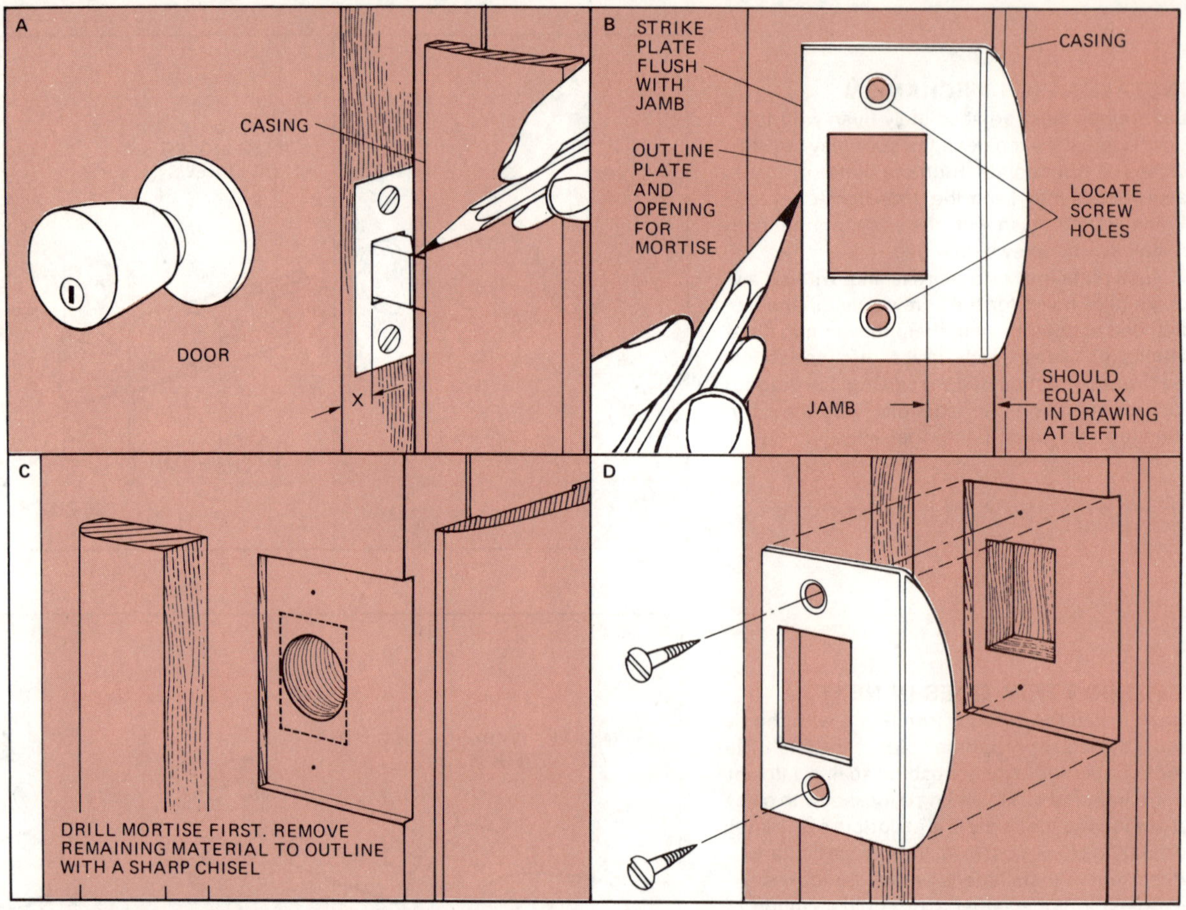

LOCATE STRIKER PLATE ON DOOR JAMB

To locate the exact position of the striker plate on the door jamb, close the door until the striker barely touches the jamb (drawing A above). Mark top and bottom of the striker on the jamb and open the door. Using a combination or try square, transfer these marks to face of the jamb—these are the horizontal marks that the opening in the striker plate must be located on.

Next, measure the distance from face of the door to the flat side of the striker in latch mechanism (dimension X in drawing A). The striker plate can then be precisely located as shown in drawing B. Horizontal edges of striker-plate opening are positioned on marks scribed on jamb earlier; vertical edge (of opening) nearest door is set back from edge of jamb to equal dimension X.

When satisfied that the striker-plate position is accurate, use a pencil to scribe lines for the plate mortise cut. Score the outline with a utility knife and chisel the mortise. After mortising the jamb so the striker-plate face is flush with the jamb, hold the plate in position in the mortise and mark for the striker mortise (dotted rectangle in drawing C) and screw pilot holes. Using an appropriate-size spade bit (usually ¾ in. dia.), bore a hole in center of the mortise area (indicated by circle in drawing C). It is not necessary to drill completely through the jamb; just drill deep enough to fully accept striker. In most cases the bored hole will give satisfactory results, but for looks it is best to clean out this rectangle to the necessary depth using a chisel.

On many locksets, the edge of the striker plate toward the door is curved to such a degree that it will be necessary to remove additional material from the edge of the jamb near the door and, in some cases, the edge of the casing. You can do this with a chisel or pocketknife. Finally, position the plate and permanently install it using flathead screws provided. Open and close the door several times to check installation—be sure to stand on the hinge-pin side of the door in case the lock malfunctions.

Frost-clogged chimney

I'm building my small home and living in the basement. I have an oilburning space heater vented to a temporary "block" chimney capped with a clay chimney pot. In cold weather the flue fills with frost which gradually builds up until the burner goes out, often with a loud "bang." In warmer weather the frost melts and runs into the basement through the smokepipe opening. What causes this? What's the remedy?—N.Y., Minn.

One of the products of combustion of concentrated fuels is water vapor. When the burner is operating you will see what appears to be "smoke" issuing from the chimney pot. But this is not smoke; it's water vapor. When the temperature is much below freezing this tends to collect in the flue as frost. This builds up to narrow the flue opening and eventually causes the burner to "plop" out. You are fortunate the burner has not "exploded" and caused you more trouble. Probably you have the pipe damper—on some installations this is an atmospheric damper—very nearly closed, thus releasing minimum heat to the smokepipe and flue.

Usually you can prevent this buildup by opening the turn damper half way, or a trifle more, to release more heat to the flue and prevent frost from forming. If the damper is of the atmospheric type, set it to remain more nearly closed, which will have essentially the same effect. A little experimenting will determine the best setting for either damper.

Garage floor sweats

My attached garage floor sweats in winter, spring and fall whenever the temperature rises from a lower reading. There are small children in the neighborhood and I keep the door closed. Why does the concrete floor sweat? Is there any remedy?—L.R., Mich.

Condensate forms because the floor surface is at a lower temperature than the air with which it is in contact—the reason that beads of moisture form on a tumbler containing cold water on a warm summer day. For the simplest remedy, keep the doors open until the temperature equalizes and the water on the floor evaporates. In your case, raise the large door a foot or so and block it so it can't be fully opened; crack the other door, if any, a few inches and block it likewise. Do this each time the temperature rises appreciably.

You could also install louvers in the lower door panels. Remove the lower panels in each door and substitute framed louvers made in your home shop or custom-made at a local millwork plant. These provide constant air circulation.

To paint or not

I'm having a house built next spring and two of my friends, one a farmer, say to let the wood siding weather without painting. Their arguments are quite convincing and I'm confused. Can you set me right?—M.K., Ark.

In general, it can be said that paint on exteriors has both a protective and aesthetic value. Weathered siding may be attractive to some but to many such a home is just an eyesore in the community. Even though it may remain structurally sound over the years an unpainted structure usually acquires a neglected, untended look not pleasing to the eye. For this reason alone I would paint the new house. Using paint, you can change the color at repainting time to suit your fancy and also gain the weather-protective values of a paint coating.

Truing a whetstone

I have an old whetstone that has become cupped by long use. How does one flatten the worn surface and make it usable again?—Leroy Hoadley, Dallas.

This is one of those things easier said than done. Rubbing the stone against another of coarser grade only improves the first by damaging the second. Rubbing the stone against concrete is better. But if you have a table saw and a worn disposable blade, turn the blade to run backward, with just a fraction of an inch of tooth projecting above the tabletop, and pass the higher portions of the stone over the blade. This will cut away the high spots quite effectively. Be sure to wear safety goggles.

Termites or rot?

Wooden beams and supporting posts in the basement of my old home—which I've recently bought—are a brownish color and the surface of the wood seems soft and crumbly. Is this certain evidence that termites are at work?—Edward Van Vellen, Reading, Pa.

Rather, I think it's evidence of what is known as "dry rot," caused by a fungus that attacks the cellular structure of the wood. "Wet rot" might be the better term, as this fungus is activated by moisture. You can't undo the damage, but you can at least slow deterioration by providing better ventilation and coating wood surfaces with a preservative containing pentachlorophenol. This is sold as liquid, and where immersing the wood is not practical, as in your case, it should be brushed on in two or more heavy coats. *Caution:* Protect eyes and skin when you work with pentachlorophenol.

How to cut and stack firewood

■ A GLOWING FIRE in a fireplace is a welcome sight expecially if fueled with relatively low-cost wood you've cut yourself. Wood is a heat source that helps reduce your fuel bill while it creates a warm glow in your home.

CUT-OFF PART of log hangs outside the sawbuck.

A CHAIN SAW MAKES LOG-CUTTING GO FASTER AND EASIER

FUEL YOUR saw at a distance from work area so spills won't be a danger.

START CUT with saw bumper against log, bar tilted upward. Open throttle . . .

. . . then touch chain to log. Keep bumper in contact with log.

IF YOU MUST cut within the sawbuck, lay 2x4 under the log to support it.

ANTIKICKBACK on this bar tip prevents accidents if object is touched.

WHEN USING cradles, release throttle as soon as chain cuts through log.

SEE ALSO

Boxes, chain-saw . . . Chain saws . . .
Crosscut saws . . . Fireplaces . . .
Firewood . . . Sawbucks . . .

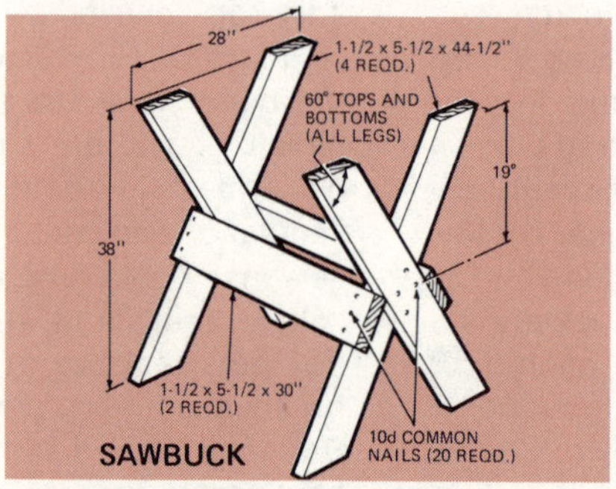

YOU SHOULD have a sturdy sawbuck to cut logs safely and efficiently.

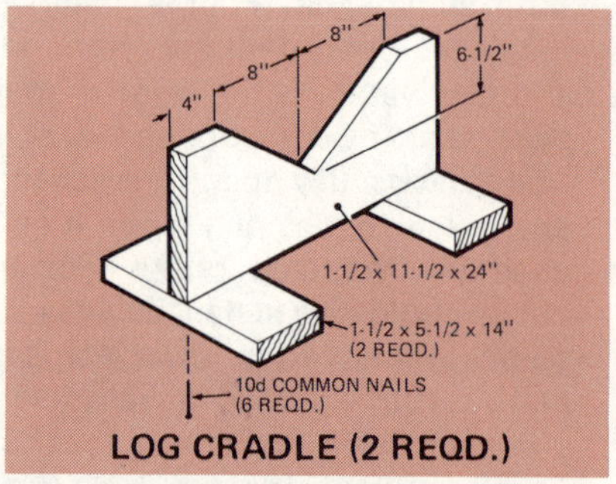

A PAIR OF log cradles is helpful for cutting logs too heavy to lift.

FIRST FELLING CUT DETERMINES THE DIRECTION

CUT A NOTCH ⅓ trunk diameter. Make lower cut first. Back cut is 2 in. above.

CUT THE BACK cut 2 in. short of notch; then push wedge in the backcut.

SPLIT LOGS TO SIZE BEFORE YOU STACK THEM

SPLIT SMALL LOGS with an ax. Keep your legs out of the line of swing.

USE A splitting wedge and sledge to halve large logs. Wear goggles.

ONE-HAND sledge (maul) is easy to use when splitting log into quarters.

The best firewood is hardwood such as hickory, locust, maple, oak or beech. It burns slower and with fewer sparks than softwood from such needle-bearing trees as pine, fir or spruce. Softwood also leaves flammable substances (pitch) on chimney walls. But fast-burning softwood *sticks* are great for kindling.

where to get firewood

If you're resourceful, there are several ways to gather a season's supply of free firewood. Thinning out an overwooded site on your property will give you firewood, as well as reduce competition for soil nutrients among the remaining trees. Also, when you prune add the cut branches to your woodpile.

An occasional trip to the town dump will pay off with discarded tree trunks and limbs. Other potential sources are curbs and sidewalks after a storm. Scout your area after heavy storms and you'll be well paid for your time and effort.

On the far extreme from free wood is cut wood you can purchase from several sources. Often you can find good firewood bargains at tree service companies. They usually make available their accumulations of tree trunks and limbs at reasonable prices.

The most direct approach to purchasing firewood is to go directly to a firewood dealer. He

PROPER STACKING SHORTENS THE AIR-DRYING PROCESS

TO STACK LOGS, lay down 2x4s. Pile log pairs alternating at right angle.

EASILY-MADE tent keeps rain off wood, yet allows good air circulation.

STRIKE two pieces together. A thud says wood's moist; clear sound means it's dry.

sells logs by the cord—a pile measuring 4x4x8 ft. The cost of a cord of wood varies with the locale and species, but for hardwood in an average suburban area today it's $60 to $100. Sound expensive? During the height of the fuel shortage several years ago the average was even higher.

The least expensive way to purchase firewood is to cut it yourself. National, state, county and city forests often section off portions of forest or mark trees that can be cut. You can usually cut them for free or a minimal charge. Besides cutting equipment, you'll need a truck to carry the wood.

cutting firewood

The tools that you'll need to cut and split firewood most efficiently include a chain saw, ax, small and large sledgehammers and splitting wedge. Goggles and gloves are safety musts. You'll also want a sturdy sawbuck and perhaps a pair of ground level cradles for heavy logs.

Cut the logs to a length that will fit your fireplace easily. Small logs of a few inches diameter don't have to be split to be stored for drying. Logs of about 4 in. diameter should be split in half with one good ax blow. Split, then quarter, larger-diameter logs using small and large sledgehammers as well as the splitting wedge.

proper stacking

Although bad fireplace design can cause poorly burning fires, just as frequently a cause of an unevenly burning fire is green wood that has neither been dried nor properly seasoned.

Wet wood doesn't burn as well as dry wood; the entrapped water cools the fire and prevents complete combustion. Wet wood is difficult to ignite, it will go out more quickly and it's more likely to smoke than dry wood. Splitting large logs after they've been cut helps assure proper seasoning by exposing as much log surface as possible to the air to accelerate drying time.

Even then the air-drying process takes at least six months if it's done properly. This entails stacking the wood as shown so the air can circulate readily throughout the pile.

First lay two lengths of 2x4 on the ground for a base. Then place two logs spaced about 18 in. apart across them. Next, place two logs equally spaced and at a right angle to the first two. Continue building upward, alternating the position of log pairs until the pile becomes shaky. Then begin building a similar pile next to the first one. If the logs are about 24 in. long, you can easily stack from 75 to 80 split logs per 8-ft. base. After the logs have dried, they can be restacked close together to conserve storage space.

shelter the piles

The drying process will take longer if the logs aren't protected from rain and snow. You can make a shelter for the piles by ripping 2x4s down the center and lashing them together tepee-style with the bottom ends set 10 in. in the earth. Then tack a plastic sheet over the top as shown in the photo.

To check the wood for dryness strike two logs together. A dull thud indicates moisture. A sharp ringing sound tells you that the wood is dry and ready to be burned.

Build a charming colonial lowboy

By ROBERT J. LOVELING

■ PERFECT IN SIZE for the small dining room, this charming Colonial lowboy provides a handy place to keep your china, stemware, silver and linens, and a plate groove lets you display your choice pieces.

Made entirely of pine and finished with knotty-pine stain and lacquer, it involves two separate assemblies: the main cabinet and the upper drawer unit. The front facing for the cabinet is made first, butting and doweling the members, after which the rest of the cabinet is made to fit it, as shown in the pull-apart drawing. Screws driven through the top attach the upper drawer unit. All are in counter-bored holes and pegged.

SEE ALSO

Chests . . . Cupboards, china . . . Dining tables . . . Drawers . . . Dry sinks . . . Gossip benches . . . Servers

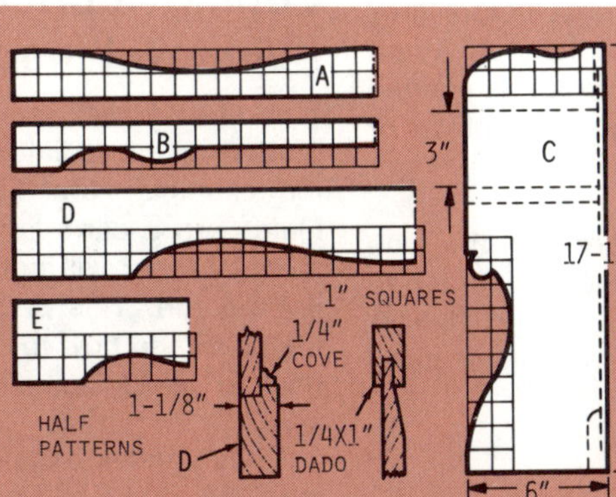

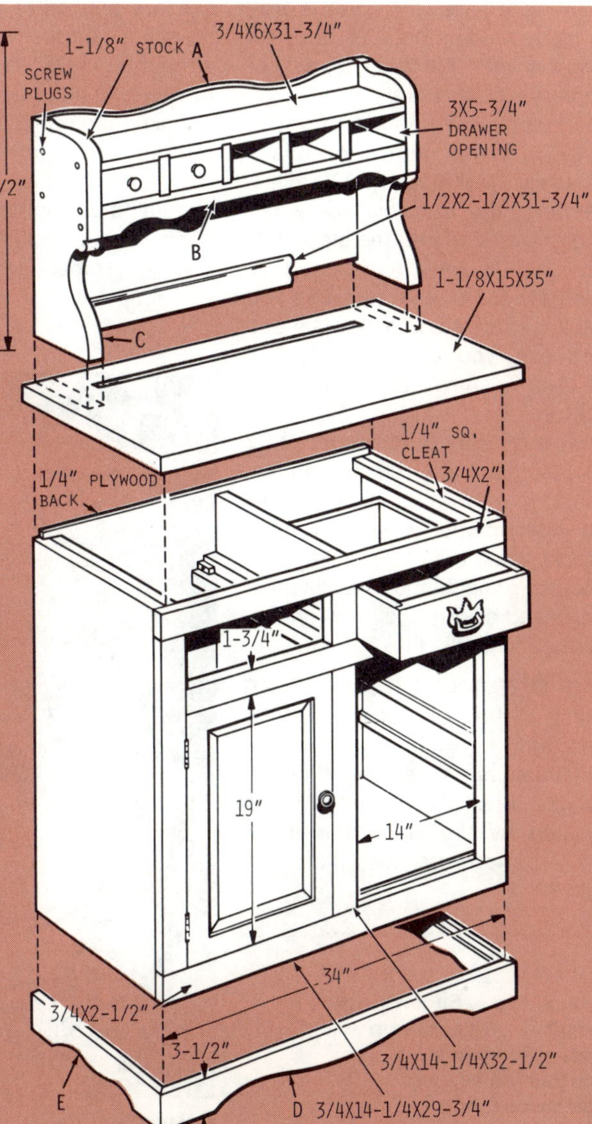

How to lubricate your car

■ AS ONE AUTOMOBILE model year has followed another, new cars have needed less servicing than their predecessors. Remember the 2000-mile motor-oil change recommended for, among others, the 1955 Ford? Now, many models go 10,000 or six months between oil changes, whichever interval comes first.

Sparkplugs are another example. Until 1975, it was normal to replace plugs every 10,000 or 12,000 miles. Since then, the catalytic converter, unleaded gasoline and the electronic ignition system have lengthened intervals between engine tune-ups and sparkplug changes. In a new General Motors car, you can drive 22,500 miles before new sparkplugs are called for.

However, despite these and other advances, car care remains an important part of owning a new, as well as an older, model. Failure to maintain a car leads to

- Recurring mechanical headaches.
- Increased cost of fuel and repairs.
- Reduced vehicle life.

More often isn't too often

Those who are conscientious about caring for their cars often ask: "In maintaining a vehicle, should I follow the interval recommendations suggested by the manufacturer, or should I perform services more frequently?"

SEE ALSO
Brakes, auto . . . Engines, auto . . .
Motor oil . . . Noises, auto . . .
Noises, auto engine . . .
Power-train noise, auto . . .
Transmissions, auto . . .
Tune-up, auto

The more frequently you do certain services, the greater your chance of averting trouble. This does not mean you have to replace sparkplugs, air-cleaner filter, drive belts, shock absorbers and other parts before they have outlived their usefulness. A part should be replaced on an as-needed basis when an operational problem or an inspection tells you it is no longer performing properly.

There are other services that you should do on a mileage or time-period basis. These include oil and oil-filter changes, other fluid changes (automatic transmission, for example) and lubrication. They contribute to longer car life if done more frequently than the manufacturer recommends.

EQUIPMENT you need for changing oil and filter. Get the right oil.

Engine lubrication and fluid-level inspection

The engine and some associated parts (brakes, radiator, transmission, for example) are fluid reservoirs. Fluids are a car's lifeblood. Without them, the car will not run or should not be run. This section discusses motor oil and how to change it; then, how to check some important fluid levels.

Oil lubricates engine components, reducing friction between moving parts and minimizing wear. Oil also cleans the engine, helps cool it, protects it against rust, and seals the cylinders. Most engines, depending on size, take a maximum of four to six quarts of oil.

Oil is stored in the oil sump (also called oil-pan or crankcase), which is a storage pan attached to the bottom of the engine. An oil pump siphons the oil through a pickup and filtering screen in the sump, and pumps it into the oil filter.

The oil filter does the job of removing dirt particles held in suspension by oil. Eventually, the filter becomes loaded with contaminating matter. Thus, it has to be replaced.

Manufacturers insist that an oil filter need not be replaced every time oil is replaced. "Every other oil change is sufficient," they contend.

However, there are some who don't see the logic of contaminating four to five quarts of fresh oil with the one quart of dirty oil remaining in the oil filter.

Pressure forces the oil from the oil filter into the engine and through galleries and passages to main bearings, connecting-rod bearings, camshaft bearings, rocker arms and other parts. In the process, the oil picks up and retains particles, and the oil additives and detergents begin wearing out. To avert engine damage that may be caused by a buildup of sludge formed by dirt-laden oil, oil should be changed before a critical point is reached.

Manufacturer-recommended oil-change intervals reflect this critical point. If the car is driven under "severe" conditions, manufacturers suggest cutting the recommended interval in half. Severe conditions include using the car mainly for stop-and-go driving, pulling a trailer or driving in desert areas.

Owners manuals provide manufacturer-suggested intervals. They also give the viscosity and type oil the manufacturer feels is best for your individual driving conditions. However, additional information regarding oil may be useful.

What viscosity numbers mean

Numbers you find on cans of oil—such as SAE 10W-50, SAE 30—are viscosity (or weight) numbers, which indicate the thickness of the oil. The higher the number, the thicker the oil.

SAE stands for Society of Automotive Engineers, which established the grading system, and W means the oil is intended for use in cold weather. The W designation is particularly important to keep in mind when temperatures drop to 32° F. or below. Above that level, oil having a viscosity number without W works satisfactorily.

When you start an engine in cold weather, oil with a low viscosity number (for example, SAE-10W, SAE 5W-30, SAE 20W-40) flows readily, reducing friction that might otherwise make starting difficult. Oils with high viscosity numbers (SAE 30 or 40) become thick in cold weather and usually make it harder to start your engine.

However, there is a drawback to using oil with a low viscosity number. As the engine gets hot, oil gets thinner. An oil with low viscosity to begin with may not give the engine the protection it needs.

Since more than one grade of oil is usable over any one temperature range, you have to decide which is best.

One of the most important points to consider in selecting the right viscosity of oil for your car is the type of driving you do. For instance, 10W oil may be ideal if you live in a cold part of the country and drive under ideal conditions. But if you make long trips and carry heavy loads in the car, you will need the cold-starting advantages of a 10W oil plus a higher viscosity oil to protect engine parts. You would, therefore, select a 10W-30, 10W-40, or 10W-50 oil.

Another factor to think about in choosing oil is whether to buy a multigrade or single-grade product. Single-grade oil is less expensive, but there are other considerations.

Multigrade vs. single-grade oil

Multigrade oils are those that have two numbers, such as SAE 5W-30, SAE 10W-30, SAE 20W-50. Multigrade oil allows engine starting in cold weather while providing the protection of high-viscosity oil when the engine is hot. Its biggest advantage is that you don't have to change oil as the seasons change.

Multigrade oils contain special additives called polymers. As engine heat rises, the polymers change the character of the oil to prevent oil from thinning too much. Such oils are convenient, too, but no multigrade has quite as much high-temperature viscosity as the corresponding single grade. For instance, 10W-40 oil isn't as thick in a hot engine as a single-grade 40,

"You get a little better protection at high temperatures with a single-grade oil," Shell Oil Co. states. However, to take advantage of this protection, the oil generally has to be changed from one grade to another as the seasons change. An exception to this involves use of SAE 20W-20 oil.

Incidentally, if your car is burning oil, you can cut consumption until you are able to repair the engine by using a high viscosity single-grade oil.

What API letters mean

The American Petroleum Institute (API) tests motor oil for its ability to prevent wear, rust, corrosion, sludge and contamination. The oil is then classified. Letters designating the API recommended oil for your car should appear on the can of oil you buy. Classifications (see below) should be observed in selecting the right oil for an engine, since the right oil helps prolong engine life.

API OIL CLASSIFICATION SYSTEM

Letter Designation	Description	For Use In (model year)
SA	Straight mineral oil.	Not recommended.
SB	Straight mineral oil with anti-oxidant and antiscuff properties.	Not recommended.
SC	Meets automobile manufacturers' warranty requirements.	1967 and prior years.
SD	Meets automobile manufacturers' warranty requirements.	1970 and prior years.
SE	Meets automobile manufacturers' warranty requirements.	1980 and prior years.

How to change oil and filter

Note: Do this after the engine has been run and is warm. The engine should be turned off.

1. Place a waste pan under the crankcase drain plug. The car wheels may remain on the floor or the front may be raised. Engage the parking brake, place the automatic transmission in PARK or the manual transmission in gear, and place chocks around the rear wheels to keep the car from moving.

2. Loosen the crankcase drain plug. You can probably use an ad-

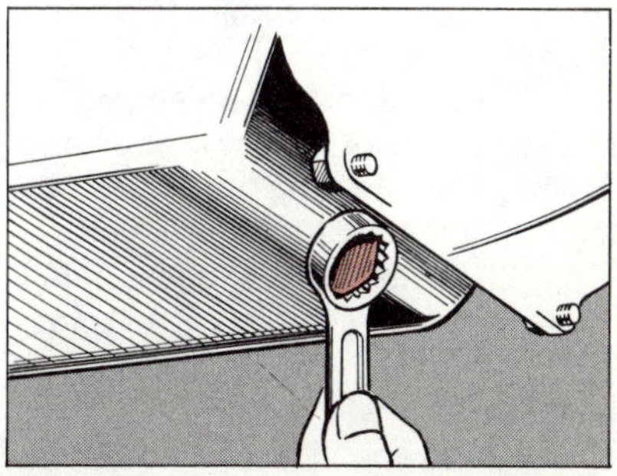

WITH ENGINE warm, remove the oilpan plug and let the old oil drain out.

justable open-end or box wrench. Then, unscrew the plug by hand.

If the drain plug is countersunk, get a special drain-plug wrench of the correct size. Trying to loosen the plug with a conventional wrench may ruin the plug or damage the oilpan.

3. Wait for the crankcase to empty. This usually takes about three minutes, but don't be hasty. The more dirty oil you allow to drain, the less dirty oil remains in the engine.

4. Screw the drain plug carefully back into the oilpan and tighten it by hand. Then, with a torque wrench, tighten the plug to 20 foot-pounds. If you don't have a torque wrench,

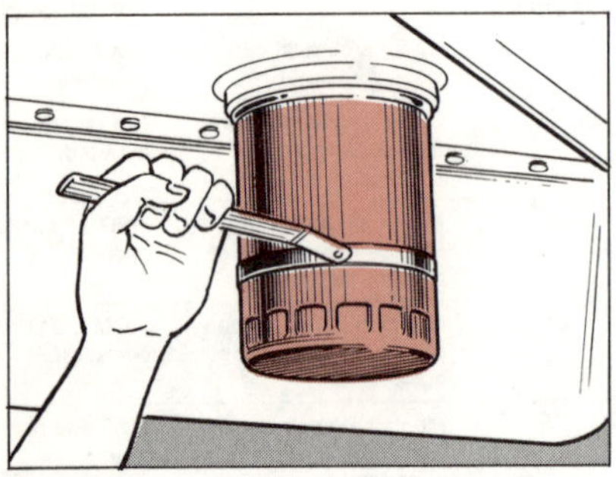

REMOVE OIL FILTER. It should come off easily; if not, refer to text.

tighten the plug snugly with the conventional (special) wrench, but do not overtighten it since you may distort the oilpan.

5. Place a waste pan under the oil filter, and use an oil-filter wrench to turn the filter counterclockwise. If the filter is frozen in place, hammer a chisel through the filter canister and smack the chisel handle with a mallet. This will loosen the filter. Remove and discard the old filter.

6. Clean the filter seating surface on the engine. Make sure none of the old gasket material stays stuck to the surface. Use a putty knife to scrape off gasket material.

7. Spread some clean engine oil on the gasket of the new filter and on the filter seating surface. This helps seal the filter to the surface.

8. Hand-tighten the filter, being careful not to cross or strip threads. Tighten the filter until the gasket just touches the seating surface. Then, hand-tighten the filter an additional one-half to three-quarter turn. Do not use a wrench; it may distort the filter.

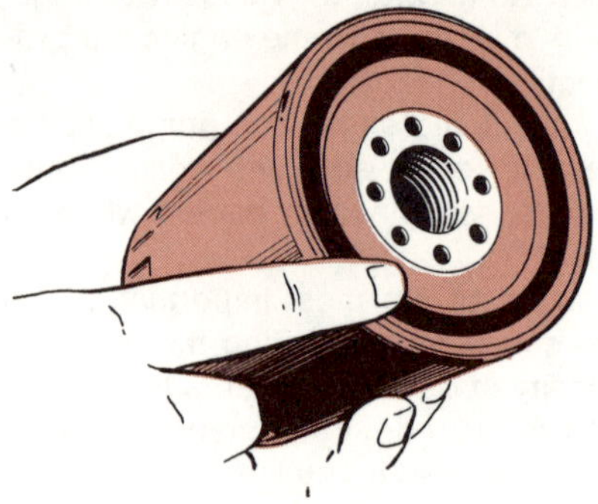

BEFORE installing new filter, spread oil over gasket to help seal filter.

9. Fill the crankcase through the oil filler to the capacity called for in the owner's or service manual. Check the dip-stick oil level to see that oil is at the full mark.

10. Start the engine and run it at fast idle for a minute or two. Turn off the engine and check for leaks at the crankcase drain plug and oil filter. If there is a leak, tighten the plug or filter a bit more. If the leak persists, the component is damaged.

Fluid level inspection

Inspect fluid levels after changing oil. The following outlines how to check the brake master cylinder, automatic transmission and cooling system, but don't forget the battery, differential, power-steering reservoir and other fluid components your car may have.

Brake master cylinder. Release the clip or bolt holding the master cylinder cover, and lift off the cover. The brake fluid level should be ¼- to ½-inch below the top of the cylinder.

If fluid is needed, draw it from a fresh container of the type of brake fluid specified by the manufacturer. Do not use brake fluid that has been

THIS IS a typical lubrication guide that you will find in service manuals.

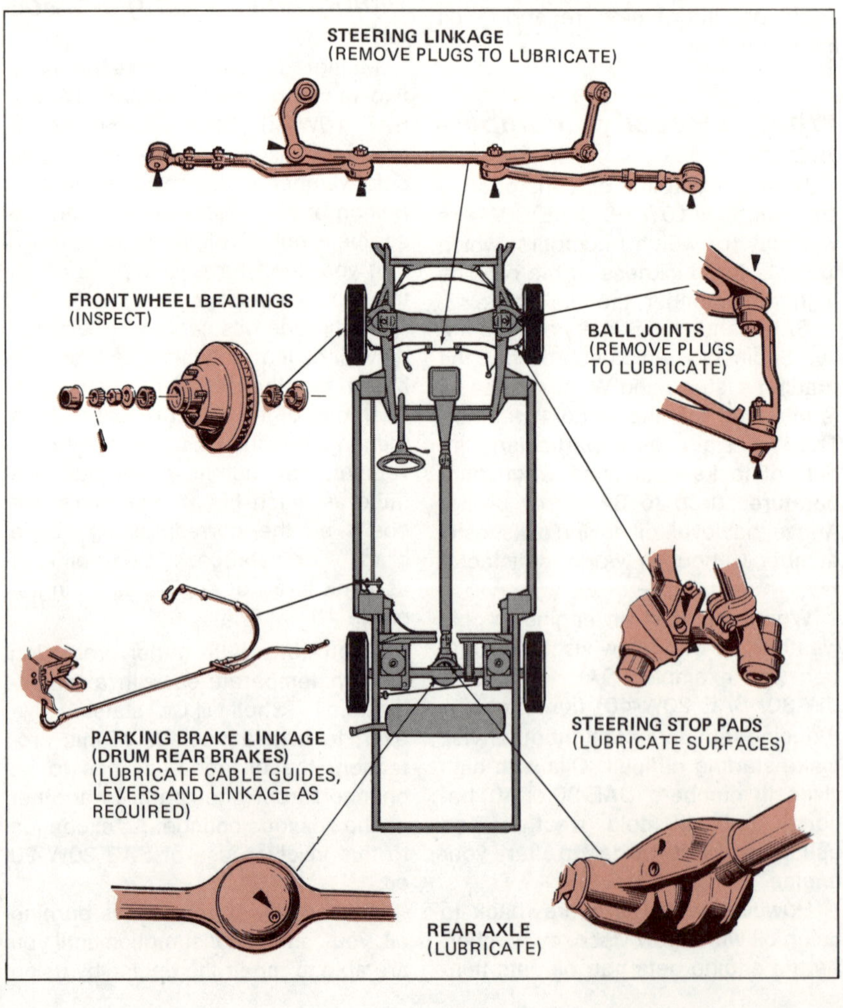

stored in a can which has been opened. Fluid may be contaminated. Be careful not to get dirt in the master cylinder.

Automatic transmission. Each manufacturer recommends a somewhat different procedure:

1. American Motors. Warm up engine and transmission (10-mile drive or longer); idle the engine; place the transmission selector in NEUTRAL; check the level.

2. Chrysler. Warm up engine and transmission (10-mile drive or longer); idle the engine; move shift lever slowly through each gear position; pausing at each until the gear engages; move the shift lever back to NEUTRAL; check the level.

3. Ford. Warm up engine and transmission (10-mile drive or longer); idle the engine; move shift lever slowly through each gear position, pausing at each until the gear engages; move the shift lever back to PARK; check the level.

4. General Motors. The engine and transmission may be cold, warm or hot (see below); idle the engine; place the shift lever in PARK; check the level.

For all makes of cars, withdraw the dipstick and wipe it with a clean rag. (If you can't locate the dipstick, consult the owner or service manual.) Reinsert the stick, seat it fully, withdraw again and read the level. In all cases except GM, the level should fall between the FULL and ADD marks. Do *not* add fluid unless the level is below the ADD mark.

With a GM car, touch the fluid with clean fingers. If fluid is cool, the level should be ⅛- to ⅜-inch below the ADD mark; if fluid is warm, the level should be close to the ADD mark; if the fluid is hot (uncomfortable to the touch), the level should fall between the ADD and FULL marks.

To add fluid in all cases, insert a clean funnel in the dipstick tube and pour in the type of fluid recommended by the manufacturer in the owner or service manual. Automatic transmission fluid that is suitable for one car may not be suitable for another.

Do not allow fluid level to go above the FULL mark. Excessive fluid in the transmission may create an aerating condition, causing gear slippage.

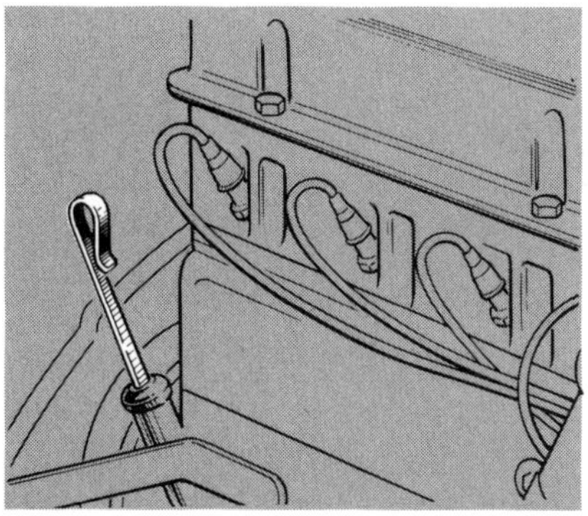

IN rear-wheel-drive cars, the automatic transmission dipstick is located at the rear of the engine. In the front-wheel-drive models, it's placed up front.

Cooling system. Most new cars have coolant recovery systems. Coolant level is checked by looking through the clear-plastic coolant recovery tank. Many tanks have two level marks—COLD and HOT. If the level is below the mark for the engine temperature when you check the coolant, add coolant to the coolant recovery tank.

If an engine is not equipped with a coolant recovery system, check the coolant level by removing the radiator cap when the engine is cold. The coolant should be 1½ to 3 inches below the top of the filler neck.

Chassis and body lubrication

Refer to the lubrication chart for your car, which you may find in the service manual. If you cannot find it you can do without it by checking pivot points for grease fittings and using the list below for greasing other parts.

How to lube chassis ball joints

1. Grease fittings (often called zerk fittings) allow you to attach a grease gun to pump grease into ball joints, which are load-carrying, and into swivel points on a car's chassis. Some ball joints have been made with rubber plugs instead of grease fittings. These plugs should be removed, discarded and replaced with fittings.

2. Wipe the grease fitting clean; otherwise, you may pump dirt into a suspension or steering ball joint. Dirt increases wear and causes premature failure.

3. Attach a hand grease gun filled with chassis grease to the fitting.

4. If you are lubricating a Chrysler or General Motors car, pump the handle of the grease gun slowly until grease oozes from the bleed hole in the base of the ball joint seal or until the seal swells.

5. If you are lubricating an American Motors or Ford car, pump the handle of the grease gun slowly until the ball-joint boot starts to swell. You can see or feel the swelling.

6. If grease oozes out more than slightly between the tip of the grease gun and zerk fitting, replace the fitting, which is probably clogged.

Greasing other parts

There are many parts of a car that should receive grease to prevent squeaking, corrosion and premature wear. Points common to all cars that should be lubricated when the chassis is greased, and the lubrication to use, are the following:

☐ Hood-latch mechanism and hinges—light oil or white lithium grease.
☐ Door lock rotor and strike plate—light oil or white lithium grease.
☐ Door hinge pins—light oil.
☐ Lock cylinders—powdered graphite.
☐ Weather strips and window channels—silicone spray.
☐ Seat tracks—CRC, WD 40 or white lithium grease.
☐ Rubber bushings (stabilizer bar, shock absorbers, springs)—rubber lubricant.
☐ Parking-brake cable—CRC, WD 40 or white lithium grease.

Depending upon the model, the following parts may require lubrication:

☐ Transmission shift-linkage pivot points.
☐ Steering stop plate.
☐ Clutch-release idler lever.
☐ Clutch-linkage pivot points.
☐ Clutch-fork joint and cross shaft.
☐ Gear-shift control mechanism.
☐ Kickdown-linkage pivot points.

A 'well-oiled' home runs smoother

By STEVEN J. HOWARD

The right lube in the right place can spare you costly repairs. Here's how to set up a semiannual lubrication program to keep your house running smoothly

KEEP METAL PARTS, such as the rod in a door closer, lubricated with general-purpose white lubricant.

■ BY SPENDING a few minutes twice a year lubricating things around your house that swing, slide and turn, you can save yourself both money and aggravation. Experts in home maintenance claim that for every billion dollars that Americans spend annually for home appliances, an additional $200 million is spent on repairs required because of inadequate lubrication. That's a staggering amount for fixing things that would not need fixing if a little oil and grease were applied at the right time.

But appliances aren't the only household items that require lubrication. Just about everything around your home that moves will perform better and last longer if it's properly lubricated regularly.

For example, let's look at the number of objects in a supposedly *nonhardware* room (living room) which require periodic attention. Door jambs should get an occasional spray of silicone grease, hinge pins a dab of general-purpose white grease to eliminate squeaks. And windows need care; a small amount of silicone applied to double-hung sash channels assures freer and easier up-and-down sliding. And, while at the window, put a drop or two of white grease on the sash lock. If you have casement windows, a dose of household oil in the cranking device keeps the mechanism from failing.

SEE ALSO

Attic ventilators . . . Doors . . . Drapery rods . . . Drawers . . . Furnaces . . . Garage doors . . . Hinges . . . Locks, door . . . Sliding glass doors . . . Storm doors and windows . . . Windows

Don't neglect drapery traverse rods. They'll operate better and won't bind if kept lubricated with paraffin. Check rolling furniture, such as serving carts, regularly and keep them operating smoothly by oiling the wheel hubs. Even zippers on seat covers (especially the machine-washable type) will open and close more readily if you coat them periodically with silicone. All in all, this is quite a list for a nonhardware room.

Since many items around the home need lube maintenance, a helter-skelter, disorganized approach to lubricating will not give satisfactory results. Your best bet is to draw up a plan—a master lubrication chart. The chart should list what needs to be lubricated, how often, and with what.

To insure a good plan, follow several general rules:

• *Never overlubricate.* It's wrong to think that because a little lubricant is good, a lot of it is better. Overlubrication—like underlubrication—can ruin a piece of equipment. For items that require a liquid lubricant, one to three drops is usually all that's needed. When using a silicone, apply light film.

• *Follow directions.* Always add a manufacturer's lubricating instructions to your master plan. If you've misplaced the maintenance manual for any part of your equipment, write the manufacturer for a replacement copy.

• *Use the right lube.* Until a few years ago, a lightweight all-purpose household oil was used for just about all home-lube tasks. It's still im-

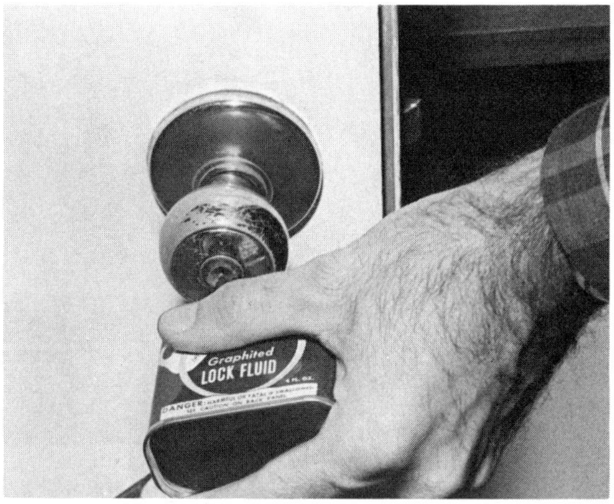

USE GRAPHITE OIL to keep door locks in good working order. Rule of thumb: A little dab will do it.

portant but, for certain chores there are other agents that do a better job. The chart on page 1872 will serve as an aid here.

• *Practice preventive maintenance.* Lubrication before the fact can prevent squeaks, rattles, binds and failures. Thus, if a part calls for lubricating twice a year, *do it twice a year,* although everything appears to be running smoothly.

• *Always clean before lubricating.* Alcohol, kerosene and plain detergent and water all make good cleaners, depending upon the part being washed. Use them whenever possible, but always make sure the surface is dry before applying the lubrication.

Basically, there are five household lubricants you should have on hand. Each is available in hardware stores in some type of handy-to-use applicator such as a puff-type dispenser, squeeze-type tube or can, or an aerosol spray can. The lubes to stock are:

BUY HEAVY OIL (SAE 20) to keep your large equipment, such as an attic fan motor, running noiselessly.

GET RID OF SQUEAKS that annoy you every time a door swings. Put a couple of drops of oil on the pins.

1. Lightweight household oil for light machinery such as small electric fans, blenders and automatic can openers.

2. Heavy household oil (SAE 20) for larger machinery—sump pumps, large ventilation fans, oil burners, warm-air furnace blowers and dishwashers.

3. Silicone lubricant in stick or spray form for use on all metal and wooden sliding surfaces.

4. General-purpose white lubricant for all metal parts that move against other metal parts—hinges and latches in the house, on cabinets and appliances.

5. Weather-resistant combination graphite-and-oil lubricant for exterior locks and equipment.

The chart lists a variety of household items that need lubrication; it can serve as the basis for your household lubrication plan. To the list, add equipment, appliances and the like whose lubri-

OVEN DOORS will swing easier if you coat them semiannually with a general-purpose white lubricant.

cation is dictated by manufacturer's instructions.

Be observant as you go from room to room in search of equipment that requires lubrication. In the kitchen, in addition to appliances, kitchen-cabinet hardware needs lubrication. Swing faucets and water taps could do with an occasional shot of graphite-oil. In bathrooms, lubricate sliding shower doors, medicine cabinets and sink and toilet hardware. This will give you an idea of what to look for in each room. As you come across additional items, add them to your master lube chart.

DON'T OVERLOOK nonmetal surfaces such as a sliding-door track in furniture. Here, use a silicone spray.

MASTER HOME LUBRICATION CHART

ITEM	LUBRICANT	WHERE TO APPLY	WHEN	AMOUNT
Window cranks	Lightweight household oil	At handle spindle	Semiannually	One drop
Casement and jalousie channels	General-purpose white lubricant	Along channels	Semiannually	Light covering film. Work window to spread lubricant
Overhead-type garage door	Graphite-oil	Along tracks, at pulleys and locks	Semiannually	One to three drops, then activate parts
Storm-door snubber	General-purpose white lubricant and lightweight household oil	On sliding surface and in snubber	Semiannually	One drop grease on sliding surface; two drops oil in snubber
Furnace blowers	Heavy household oil	In lube cups. Prepacked types need no lube	Twice during season	As per maker, usually two to three drops
Plumbing fixtures	Graphite-oil	At moving surface	Semiannually	One drop
Sliding shower and medicine cabinet doors	General-purpose white lubricant	In channels	Semiannually	One to two drops. Slide door to spread lube
Light machinery (including small appliances)	Lightweight household oil	Per manufacturer's instructions	Semiannually	Per maker, usually one to three drops
Heavy machinery (including large appliances)	Heavy household oil	Per manufacturer's instructions	Semiannually	Per maker, usually one to three drops
Locks	Graphite-oil	Open latch and apply lubricant through keyhole	Semiannually	Two drops. Work into crevices by inserting key
Drawers and sliding furniture doors	Silicone	On tracks, drawer or door rails	Semiannually	Light covering coat
Sliding closet doors	Silicone	In channels	Semiannually	Light covering coat
Hinges	Light household oil or general-purpose white lubricant	On hinge pins	Semiannually	One drop. Remove pin, clean, apply oil and work back and forth in hinge
Double-hung windows; combination storms and screens	Silicone	Along channels on both sides	Semiannually	Light covering coat
Sash locks	Light household oil or general-purpose white lubricant	At joint	Semiannually	One drop

Lumber basics for the craftsman

When you go to your lumber yard to buy material for a project or for home repair, knowing what and how to select can save you time and money

By W. CLYDE LAMMEY

■ LUMBER IN YOUR local yard comes in many classified forms, sectional sizes and lengths. Before you buy you should know these classifications and the various grades and their adaptability to the work you intend to do.

Also, you should know how to make a simple estimate of the amount of material and the various kinds, sizes and grades you will need for a project or for home repair. A few careful measurements—perhaps a simple rough sketch and a few jottings—can mean appreciable savings in time and money.

There are only two basic classifications of *softwood lumber,* but these in turn are broken down into gradings ranging from that commonly referred to as *select* to the *lowest board grading,* suitable only for limited uses.

select grade

The select grade, *No. 1 clear,* or *A grade* as it is sometimes called, is top quality and is intended for use where appearance, strength and finishing qualities are of first importance.

common grade

No. 2 grade, or common, has some minor defects with one side clear, and is suitable for gen-

SEE ALSO

Abrasives . . . Additions, house . . . Adhesives . . . Angles, compound . . . Attic dormers . . . Basement remodeling . . . Bearing walls, removing . . . Birdhouses . . . Book shelves . . . Cabanas . . . Calipers . . . Ceilings . . . Circle scribers . . . Clamps . . . Claw hammers . . . Concrete blocks . . . Contractors . . . Decks . . . Dovetail joints . . . Drawers . . . Energy, saving . . . Finishes, wood . . . Floors . . . Firewood . . . Frames, picture . . . Garage remodeling . . . Garages, storage . . . Garden shelters . . . Gazebos . . . Handsaws . . . Hardboard . . . House additions . . . House painting . . . Joinery . . . Jointers . . . Kilns . . . Legs, furniture . . . Log cutting . . . Measurements . . . Molding cutters . . . Moldings . . . Nails . . . Patios . . . Plasterboard . . . Plywood . . . Room dividers . . . Routers . . . Sabre saws . . . Sanding . . . Sawhorses . . . Scaffolding . . . Scrapers . . . Screened summer rooms . . . Shapers . . . Sheathing . . . Shims . . . Shop techniques . . . Shop tools . . . Siding . . . Staining, wood . . . Stains, removing . . . Stairs . . . Summer houses . . . Veneering . . . Wood bending . . . Woods

STANDARD LUMBER SIZES

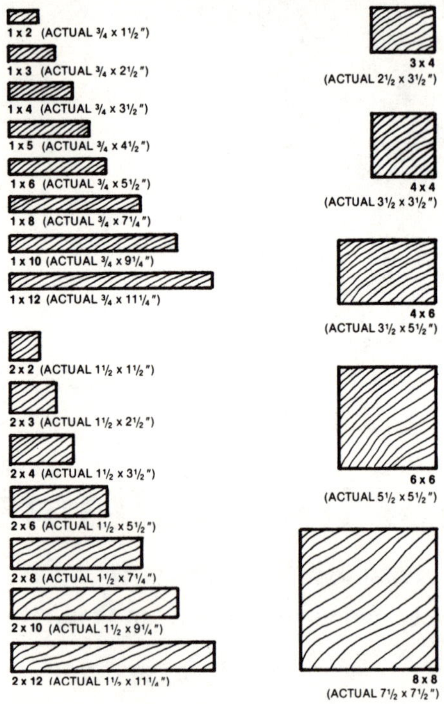

eral use where such slight defects can be concealed simply by exposing the good side or through the finishing process.

These grades of select stock are again broken down. *B-grade and better* is devoid of any but small, concealable blemishes such as slight off-color veins, usually on one face only. *C-grade* will perhaps have very small, tight knots and possibly sap streaks, and may include heart and sap wood in a single piece. Finally comes *D-grade* with imperfections that can be hidden only by painting.

There is often a further breakdown of common such as *No. 1 grade,* which may contain medium to small, tight knots in great profusion, and other quite minor blemishes. It is suitable for a natural knotty finish, such as that so often applied to knotty-pine walls.

No. 2 grading of common may contain more and larger but still sound knots; also more varied blemishes, yet still suitable for a knotty finish or paint. In addition this grade is suitable for rough flooring and paneling where appearance or maximum strength is secondary.

No. 3 grade has some loose knots. Also, there may be knots of irregular size ranging from large to small and there will likely be more evident flaws. However, the grade is still useful for rough shelving, sheathing, subflooring, and temporary outdoor applications where plain utility is the main requirement.

Nominal and Minimum Dressed Dry Sizes of Finish, Ceiling and Partition, at 19 Percent Maximum Moisture Content.

ITEM	THICKNESSES		FACE WIDTHS	
	NOMINAL	MINIMUM DRESSED	NOMINAL	MINIMUM DRESSED
	Inches	Inches	Inches	Inches
Finish (May have to be special ordered)	⅜	5/16	2	1½
	½	7/16	3	2½
	⅝	9/16	4	3½
	¾	⅝	5	4½
	1	¾	6	5½
	1¼	1	7	6½
	1½	1¼	8	7¼
	1¾	1⅜	9	8¼
	2	1½	10	9¼
	2½	2	11	10¼
	3	2 9/16	12	11¼
	3½	3 1/16	14	13¼
	4	3 9/16	16	15¼
Ceiling	⅜	5/16	3	2⅛
	½	7/16	4	3⅛
	⅝	9/16	5	4⅛
	¾	11/16	6	5⅛
Partition	1	23/32	3	2⅛
			4	3⅛
			5	4⅛
			6	5⅛

WOOD SIDING SELECTION CHART

Material	Nominal Size	Dressed	Face
Shiplap	1x6	5½	5⅛
	1x8	7¼	6⅞
	1x10	9¼	8⅞
	1x12	11¼	10⅞
T&G	1x4	3⅝	3⅛
	1x6	5⅜	5⅛
	1x8	7⅛	6⅞
	1x10	9⅛	8⅞
	1x12	11⅛	10⅞
S4S	1x4	3½	3½
	1x6	5½	5½
	1x8	7¼	7¼
	1x10	9¼	9¼
	1x12	11¼	11¼
Panel Pat terns	1x6	7/16	5 7/16
	1x8	7⅛	6¾
	1x10	9⅛	8¾
	1x12	11⅛	10¾
Bevel Siding	1x4	3½	3½
	1x6	5½	5½
	1x8	7¼	7¼
	1x10	9¼	9¼
	1x12	11¼	11¼

No. 4 grade is of still lower quality, adaptable to crating and some types of concrete forms. It also is usable in such applications as temporary structures.

No. 5 is the lowest grade and is only applicable where limited strength will serve the purpose and where other requirements, such as appearance, are not a factor.

special gradings

There are also special gradings for some species of pine, such as that of Idaho origin. The select grades are designated *supreme, choice* and *quality,* and the common gradings *colonial, sterling, standard utility* and *industrial.*

Individual pieces of lumber less than 2 in. thick and 8 in. or more in width are generally referred to as *boards,* while pieces less than 2 in. thick and less than 8 in. wide are usually designated as *strips.* "Strips" as defined where you buy lumber may specifically denote *furring* strips, ie., 1x2s and 1x3s. Actual sizes of furring may be slightly less than ¾ x 1½ and ¾ x 2½ inches. The thickness (¾-inch) may be about 1/32-inch off; the width may be 1/32- to ⅛-inch off. If your measurements are critical, be sure to check the sizes before you buy.

dimension lumber

Pieces more than 2 in. and less than 5 in. in thickness and widths up to 12 in. are usually designated as *dimension lumber,* which is commonly used in heavy framing. Pieces 4 in. or more in the smallest sectional dimension are called *timbers.* The accompanying chart gives the sectional sizes of those in common use.

Notice especially that sizes given in the chart are the finished sizes you get at the lumber yard. Older sizes have been reduced in the interest of wood conservation. For example, what was formerly supplied as a 2x4 measured 1⅝ x 3⅝ in. These older dimensions have been reduced to 1½ x 3½ in., and similar fractional reductions have been made in the finished sectional sizes of other classifications. The new dimensions must be taken into account when you order, especially if you are replacing old work with new. It should be noted also that dimensions given in the chart may vary slightly due to swelling or shrinkage, and that these "specs" apply generally to lumber cut

LUMBER SELECTION CHART

Nominal Size	Seasoned Or Dry	Green Or Unseasoned	Size Before Standard Change
1x4	¾x3½	25/32x3 9/16	25/32x3⅝
1x6	¾x5½	25/32x5⅝	25/23x5½
1x8	¾x7¼	25/32x7½	25/32x7½
1x10	¾x9¼	25/32x9½	25/32x9½
1x12	¾x11¼	25/32x11½	25/32x11½
2x4	1½x3½	1 9/16x3 9/16	1⅝x3⅝
2x6	1½x5½	1 9/16x5⅝	1⅝x5½
2x8	1½x7¼	1 9/16x7½	1⅝x7½
2x10	1½x9¼	1 9/16x9½	1⅝x9½
2x12	1½x11¼	1 9/16x11½	1⅝x11½
4x4	3½x3½	3 9/16x3 9/16	3⅝x3⅝
4x6	3½x5½	3 9/16x5⅝	3⅝x5½
4x8	3½x7¼	3 9/16x7½	3⅝x7½
4x10	3½x9¼	3 9/16x9½	3⅝x9½
4x12	3½x11¼	3 9/16x11½	3⅝x11½
6x6	5½x5½	5 9/16x5 9/16	5¾x5¾

NOTE: Seasoned or Dry lumber has a 19% or less moisture content.
Green or Unseasoned lumber has more than 19% moisture content.

HARDWOOD FLOORING

Type	Size In Inches	Spacing	Nailing
T&G Blind- nailed	25/32x3¼ 25/32x2¼ 25/32x2 25/32x1½	10-12 in. Same Same Same	7d or 8d screw or cut nail Same Same Same
T&G Blind- nailed over subflooring	½x2 ½x1½ ⅜x2 ⅜x1½	10 in. Same 8 in. Same	5d screw, cut, or casing nail Same 4d casing nail Same
Square- edge nailed through top face	5/16x2 5/16x1½ 5/16x1⅓	2 nails in 7 in. Same 1 nail in 5 in. on alternate sides	1-in., 15 ga. barbed floor brad, cement-coated Same Same

Note: If ½-inch-thick subflooring used, nail into joists with additional nailing between the joists.

from conifers, the trees that yield most of the softwood lumber.

allowance for waste

When you buy lower grades of lumber the cutaway waste often tends to increase more or less proportionally to the price. In some instances you may have to allow as much as 20 to 30% for waste; in other instances this percentage may be extreme even for the lower grades. To save money, consider the need carefully before you buy. If both appearance and strength are factors then you may gain by grading up rather than down. If the need is purely utility then you can often grade down with a savings in cost more than offsetting the loss in waste.

As an example, you need a number of 1x6x8s for edge-to-edge placement, where two-edge nailing, medium strength, and *not* appearance are the main requirements. Here medium-sized and even large tight knots, common surface flaws, and minor twist are permissible.

However, in this order you would have to reject pieces having between-ends slivering, long splits at ends, large loose knots located at edges, any small holes, and excessive twist. The nature of the job may permit cutting out defects and butt-joining ends of shorter lengths. In this case you might buy several extra pieces and still save a little money with a lower grade of lumber, achieving the desired result by judicious cutting.

Hardwood lumber, cut from deciduous (broad-leaved) trees, is generally graded according to quality but is also furnished in a variety of thicknesses ranging from ⅛ in. to ¾ in. and in random

FACTORY AND SHOP LUMBER CHART

Material	Nominal Thickness	Nominal Width	Dressed Thickness	Dressed Width
Material is S2S; thickness also applies to T&G	1 (4/4) 1¼ (5/4) 1½ (6/4) 1¾ (7/4) 2 (8/4) 2½ (10/4) 3 (12/4) 4 (16/4)	5 in. and wider 4 in. and wider in 4/4 No. 1 Shop And 4/4 No. 2 Shop	25/32 (4/4) 1 5/32 (5/4) 1 13/32 (6/4) 1 19/32 (7/4) 1 13/16 (8/4) 2⅜ (10/4) 2¾ (12/4) 3¾ (16/4)	All In Rough Size See below.

Rough size: 80% of shipment is ⅛-in. thicker than the standard surface size; 20% is 3/32-inch. thicker than surfaced size.
Widths are ⅛-inch wider than standard surfaced widths.
Lengths of factory and shop lumber are 6 ft., and longer in multiples of 1 foot.

widths and lengths surfaced two sides (S2S) and four sides (S4S). This is usually classified as cabinet-grade lumber in which small defects are permissible, generally on one face only.

In another classification most of these common cabinet woods (hardwoods) are furnished in a range of thicknesses from ¼ in. to 1¾ in. and in varying widths and lengths up to 48 in., with longer lengths available on order. In this grading the woods are specially selected, rated "triple A" (AAA), in which no defects except the most minor are permissible. All are cut to specified lengths and surfaced S3S—that is, surfaced smooth both sides and one edge—or S4S.

some softwoods are hardwoods

When you buy hardwoods, either from a yard or by mail order, keep in mind that some softwoods are classed as hardwoods because these are cut from broad-leaved (deciduous) trees. An example is basswood, a softwood very similar to white pine in texture and workability. But the basswood tree is broad-leaved and thus the lumber is classed as hardwood.

Some dealers stock both domestic and imported woods, and catalog these by the square foot and in random lengths and widths, surfaced two sides (S2S). You will also find imported woods cut to given widths and lengths ranging from ⅛ in. to ¾ in. in thickness, and in lengths from 18 to 48 in. in length. These are especially selected for color and grain, and are clear with only minor defects permissible on one side.

special widths

Also there will be special widths in some woods, such as the mahoganies, ranging up to 20 in. Nearly all such woods, both domestic and imported, are also supplied as turning squares and square blocks in various sizes and lengths, both roughsawed and finished on four sides to a given dimension.

Processed lumber such as cedar-closet lining, hardwood flooring and shiplap, are usually sold in bundles containing a given number of square feet; the individual boards are the same width and, in the case of the first two items, each piece is tongued and grooved. Usually the flooring and closet lining come in random lengths and the boards are matched closely for color and quality. In closet lining, they also are matched for knot pattern. The shiplap comes with both edges rabbeted so that adjoining boards can be fitted flush and level.

select each piece

No two boards cut from the same tree are ever the same in knot pattern, grain or even in color. The grain, knots if any, surface details and color will only be characteristic of that particular cut at the mill. If your dealer permits you to select for a special project, look for boards similar in color and grain pattern. If you take time to study each piece, you can produce a satisfactory match, but never a precise one. In fact, some variation may even enhance the final appearance of your finished work.

When you buy framing stock, such as 2x4s, for repair of a wall where you have to fit the new studs into an old opening, it will be necessary to "widen" the new 2x4s to avoid a noticeable dip or depression. One way to do this is to build out the new 2x4 to the width of the old with strips cut from ⅛-in. hardboard, tacked to one edge of the new studs.

Make your own fishing spoons

An expert fisherman tells you how to make these sure-fire bass and steelhead lures. All you need is a kitchen spoon, tin snips, a drill, some paint and your imagination. The design can be one of your own choosing and the price is as reasonable as an ordinary five-and-dime spoon

By C. L. HOWARD

■ MOST FISHERMEN have a sizable investment in fishing lures. Many of these lures are of the spoon variety costing a dollar or more apiece. When a lure is lost—especially if it's a favorite—a rather pained expression crosses the angler's face.

But now you can have all the "spoons" you want for less than 10 cents each. No need to fret if some are lost in the weeds or high branches of trees.

Fishing spoons are easy to make and exceptionally cheap.

The raw material is spoons—the kind you eat with. To keep harmony in your family, it's best not to raid your wife's silver drawer. It's true that silver fishing lures can be a prestige item with your buddies, but it's not worth the expense or furor on the home front.

So your best bet is cheap metal spoons. You can get a bagful at your local five-and-dime or discount store. Better yet, check junk yards, surplus stores or rummage sales.

Select a variety of shapes and sizes. Different shapes can be made into lures that have different actions in the water. Different sizes affect the overall cost of each lure. You can get two lures from most spoons—one lure from the bowl, another from the handle. But you can make three lures just from the handles of other spoons, such as ice-tea spoons or soup spoons.

SEE ALSO
Casting, fly . . . Fishing tackle . . . Fly fishing . . . Ice fishing

STEP 1. Mark the center line and hole locations with a pencil or crayon. Dent hole location with a center punch so the drilling will be accurate.

STEP 2. Drill two holes in each spoon with a 7/64-inch bit. In thicker spoons, countersink with 1/4-inch bit to make it easier to attach clip and hook.

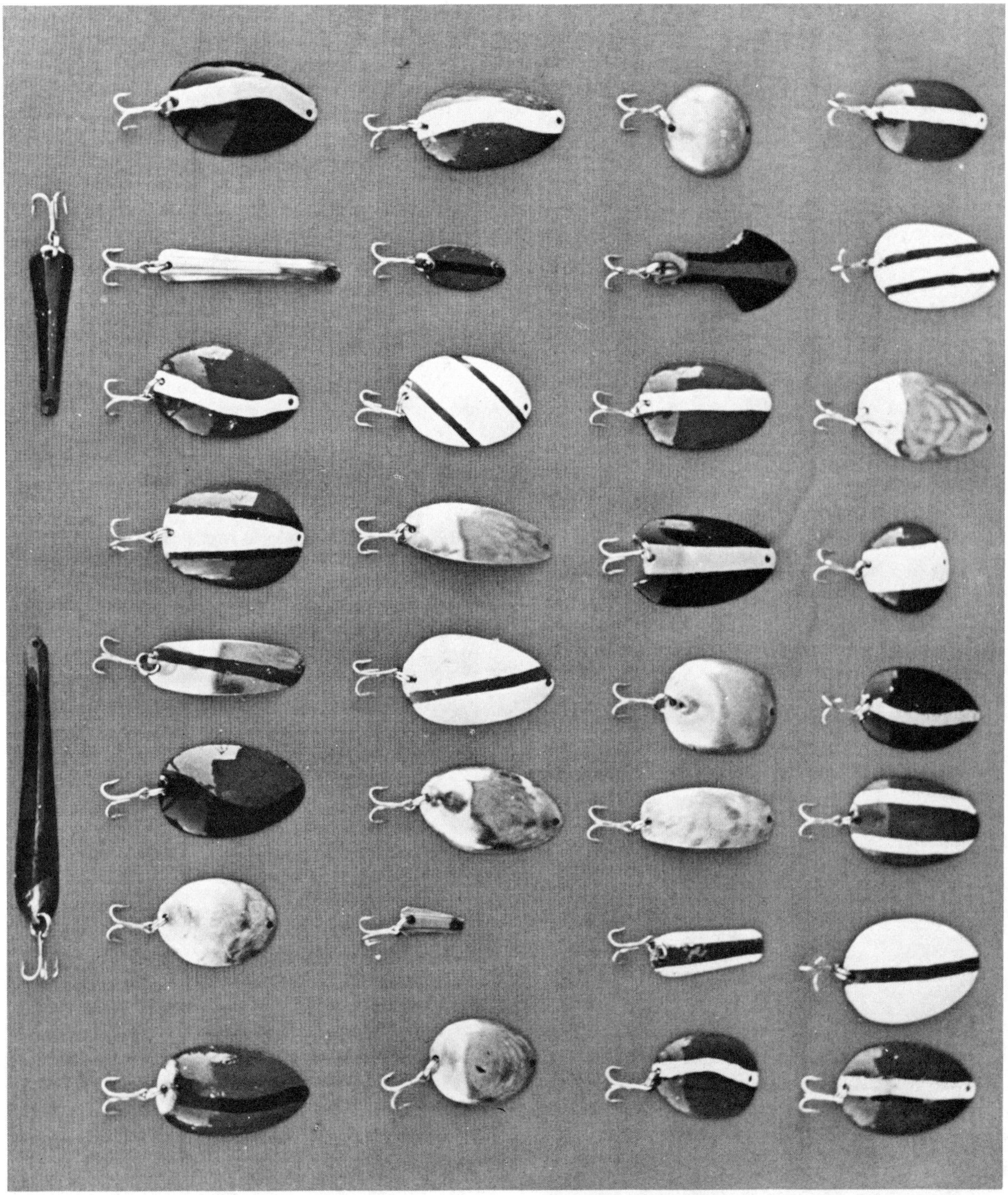

FINISHED PRODUCTS can be painted with any designs you think will entice fish. Try new ideas not only in designs, but in spoon configurations. Several can be right for you.

From whatever spoons you select, you can make four different types of lures. There's the oval lure, the arrow-shaped lure, the bent-tail lure and the handle lure.

The oval lure, made from the spoon itself, is great for casting. This is the best design for slow-speed, bottom-bouncing retrieves. The slightest jerk on the line will send this lure into erratic gyrations. The arrow design and the

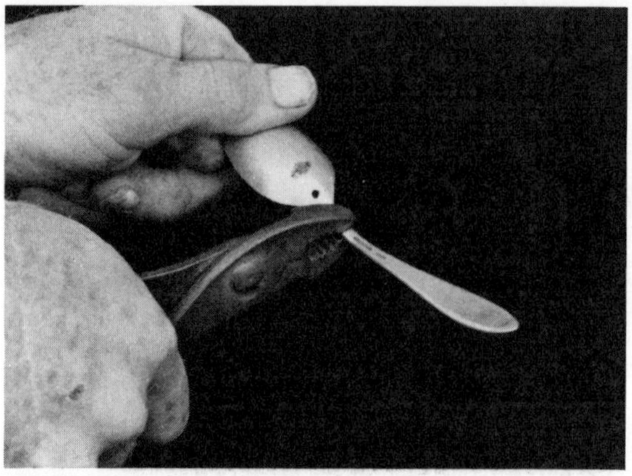

STEP 3. Use pliers or vise to break handle away from spoon. Make sure rear hole is so located that the handle breaking point is not right at the hole.

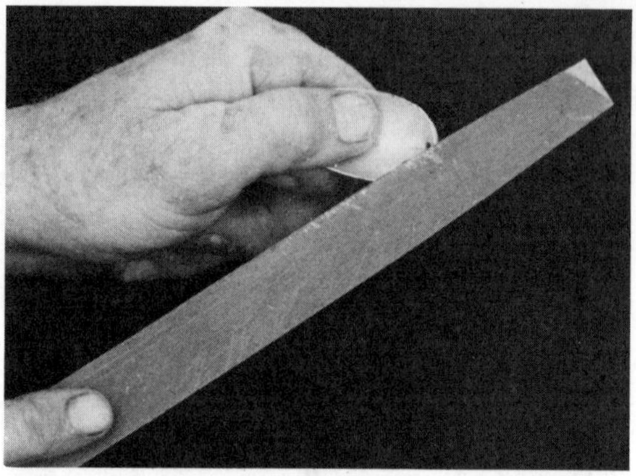

STEP 4. Smooth ragged edges with a file or an electric grinder. At this point, you can also file spoon so configuration of the lure is any width desired.

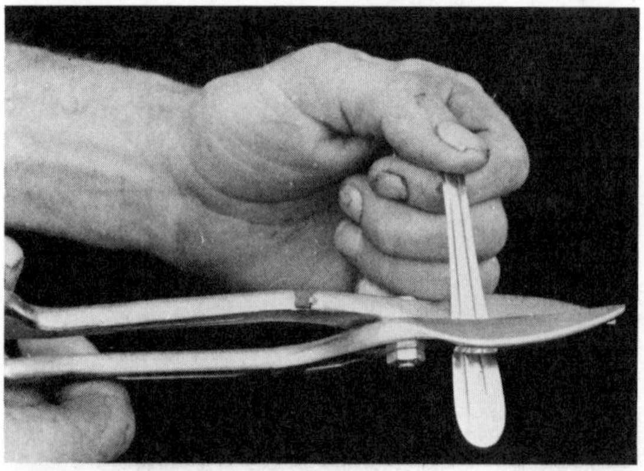

STEP 5. Cut handle to any length. Using 10-inch snips, round off the ends. Then file edges smooth. Mark and dent spots for holes. Use 7/64-inch drill bit.

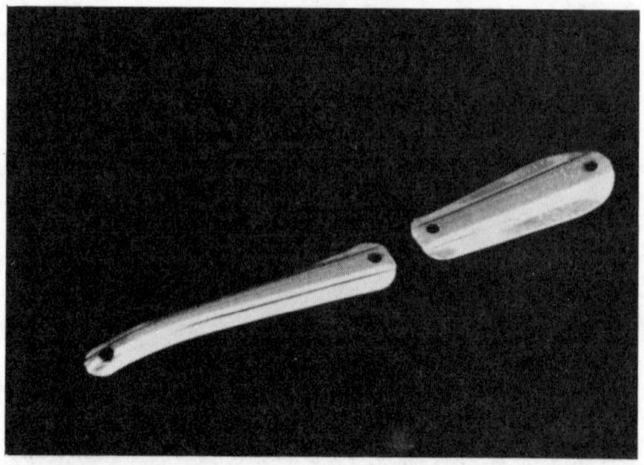

STEP 6. Only two lures were cut from this handle, but it's large enough to cut three small lures. Note handle shape. Some bend is needed for lure action.

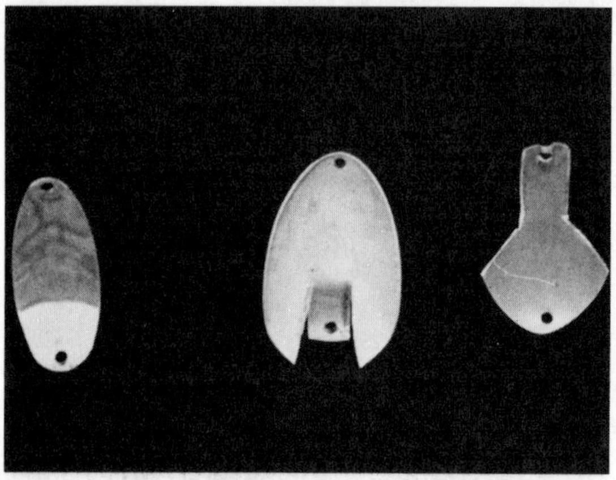

STEP 7. Here are three possible shapes. The center lure is of the bent-tail variety which wobbles when trolled. So does the arrow-shaped lure.

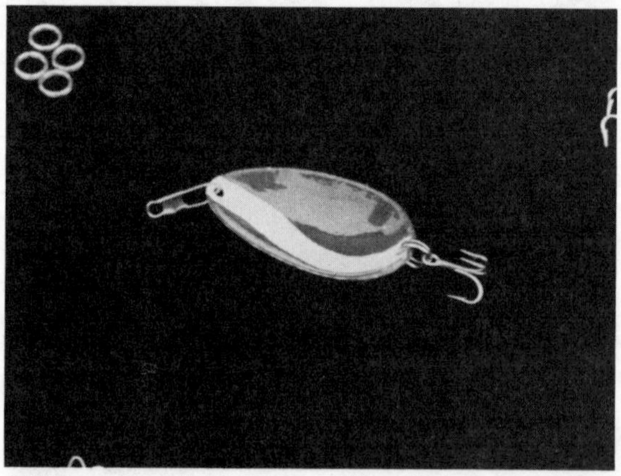

STEP 8. Attach hook to lure with split ring. Add snap or swivel snap. When painting lures, use a metal touch-up enamel found in auto-parts shops.

bent-tail design, both made from the spoon section, are good trolling lures. These two types will wobble instead of making complete revolutions that hopelessly twist your line.

Lures made from spoon handles can be used for either casting or trolling.

You can make all the spoon lures you want by following the simple instructions below the how-to pictures on this and the preceding pages. The designs shown here have been tried and proven. But don't hesitate to experiment with other designs.

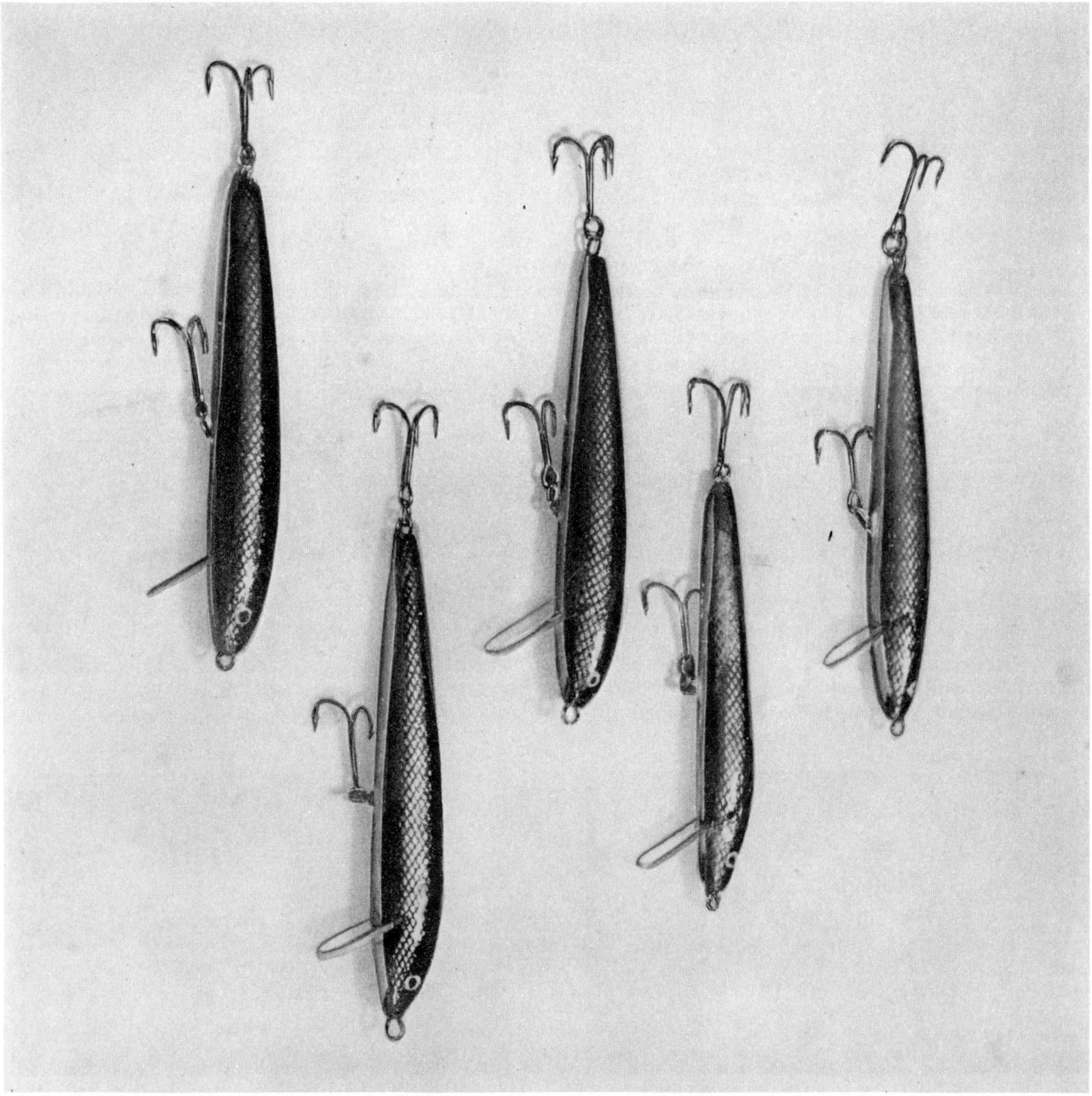

How to make a wobbler minnow lure

By PETER CAMPANER

You can produce your own quality version of one of the most successful lures in recent angling history for a fraction of the cost of a store-bought model

■ THIS LURE not only looks like a baitfish, it imitates the wobbling, darting action of one that's injured. And nothing turns on hungry pike or largemouth bass like the sight of crippled bait! It's sure to help you land that big one you've been hankering for.

Yet these lures are among the most expensive on the market. A good deal of hand labor still goes into the manufacture of some versions of the wobbler, and the loss of two or three of them can really sour the memory of an otherwise

SEE ALSO
Casting, fly . . . Fishing tackle . . . Fly fishing . . . Ice fishing

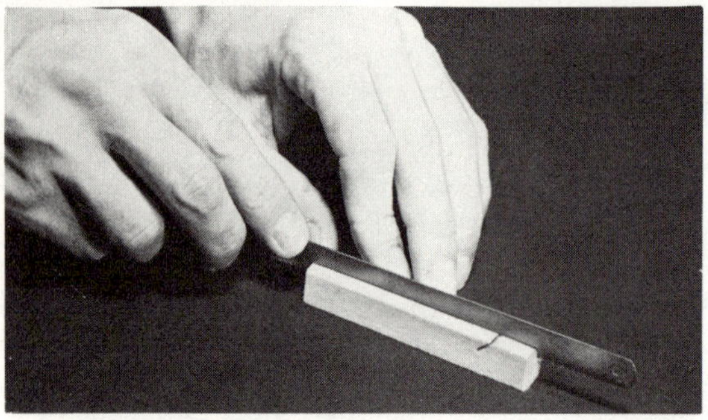

1. MAKE DIAGONAL CUT ¼-inch deep ¾ inch from the end. Make another ¼-inch cut down center of the block.

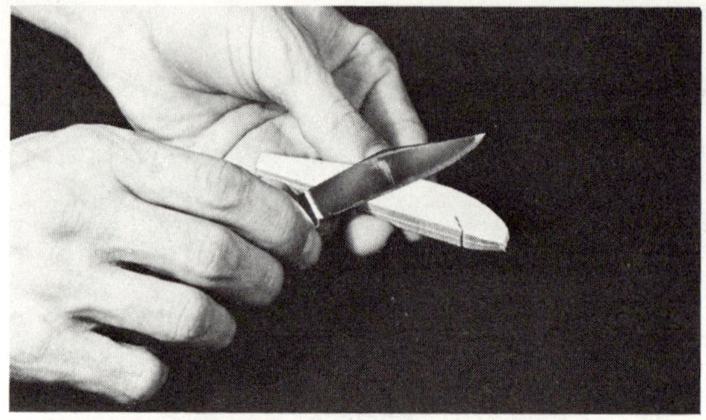

2. CUT BALSAWOOD to basic minnow shape, removing an even amount of the material from each side.

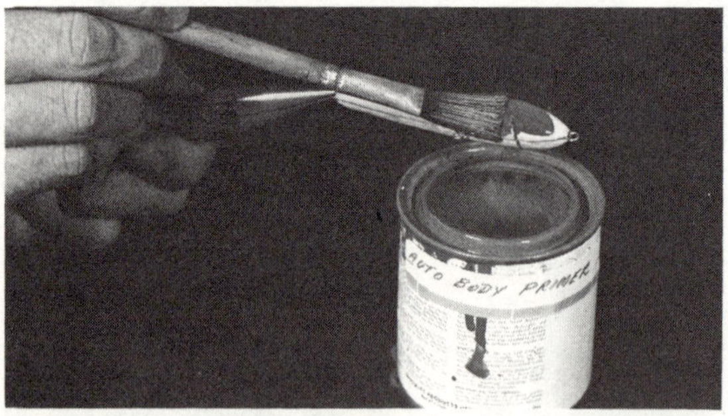

5. COAT ALL SURFACES and crevices with red oxide primer. When dry, smooth with No. 400 wet paper.

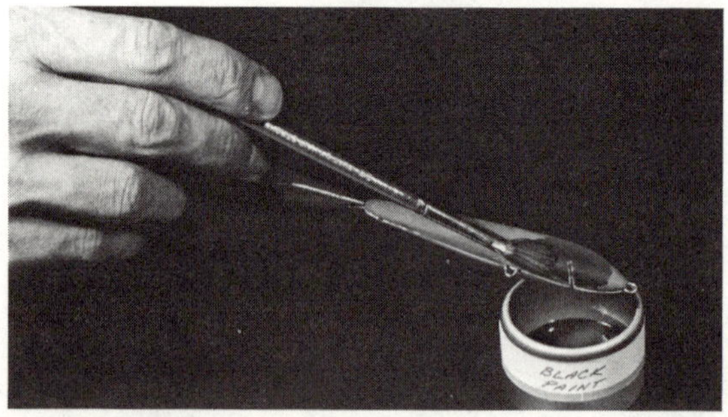

6. ANY COLOR may be used, but glossy black enamel offers the best contrast. Paint the entire lure.

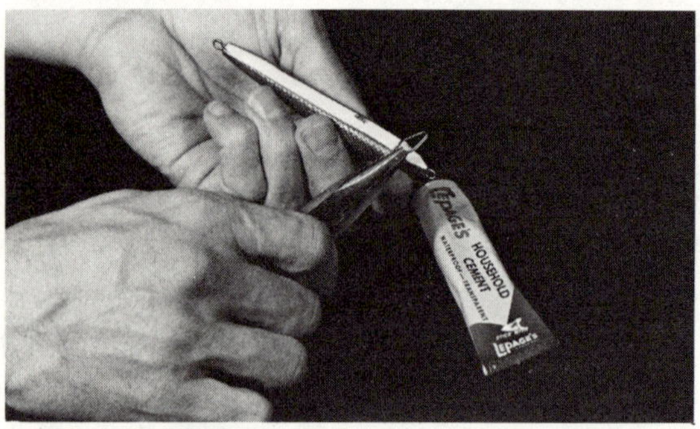

9. PLASTIC MAY be cut with soldering gun attachment or by scoring with a sharp knife and breaking along the score line. Set it in slot with waterproof glue.

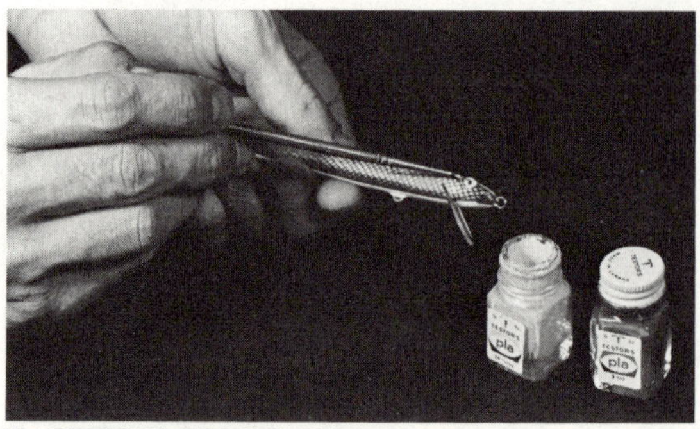

10. OPTIONS FOR COLOR contrast are as varied as the rainbow, but a combination of painted yellow eyes and red mouth has worked best for the author.

pleasant outing.

Since so much of the cost is in manual labor, why not do the work yourself? You can make a dozen or more lures in different sizes and colors at a fraction of the retail cost. Besides the work will give you a chance to use up those nearly empty cans of spray paint you've been saving!

In addition to the satisfaction of turning a dull balsa plug into a bright baitfish replica, you'll experience a kind of pride that can never be bought when you land your first fish on a lure you made in your own workshop.

Basically the lure consists of a balsa wood body in the shape of a minnow with a wire insert

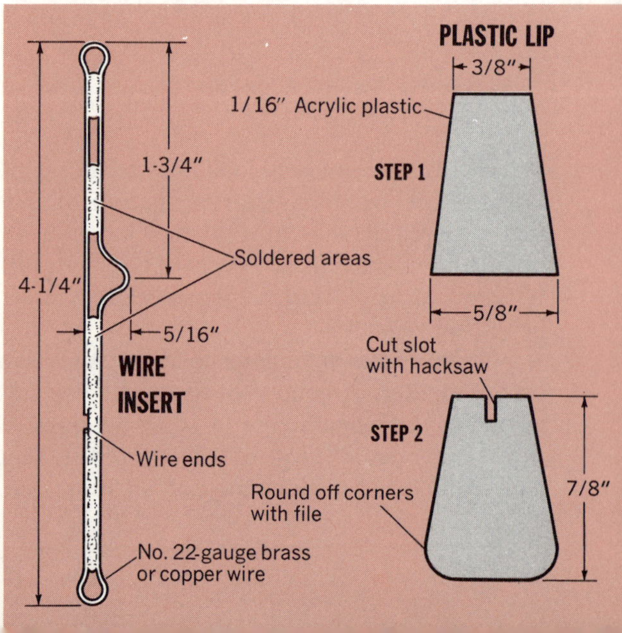

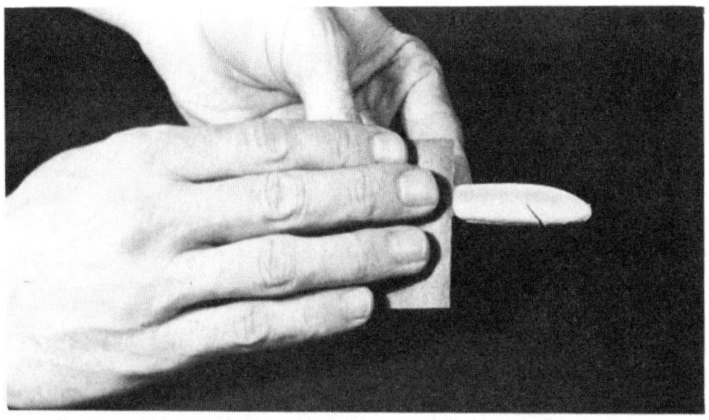

3. TRIM AND SAND smooth—¼-inch lengthwise cut is to hold the wire prepared as in diagram (bottom p. 1892).

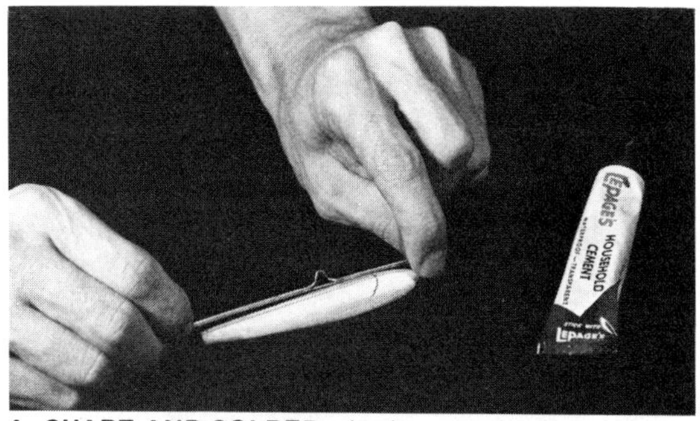

4. SHAPE AND SOLDER wire insert; with waterproof glue, fix it in the slot. Diagonal cut is for plastic lip.

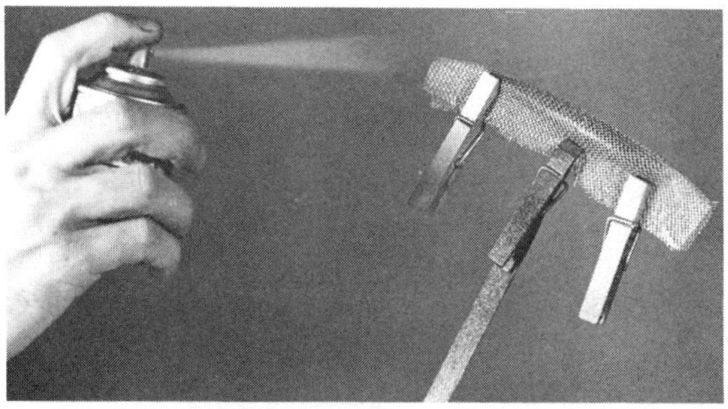

7. FOR SCALE EFFECT, wrap the lure in fiberglass window screen. Hold it diagonally with spring-type clothespin and spray it with gold or silver paint.

8. CUT WATERPROOF tape 4 inches long and ¼ inch wide and then make a slit where the wire insert protrudes. Fasten to lure bottom and cut slot for plastic lip.

11. FOR SHEEN and a permanent bond to protect paint from knocks and fish's teeth, coat the entire lure with polyurethane liquid plastic synthetic varnish.

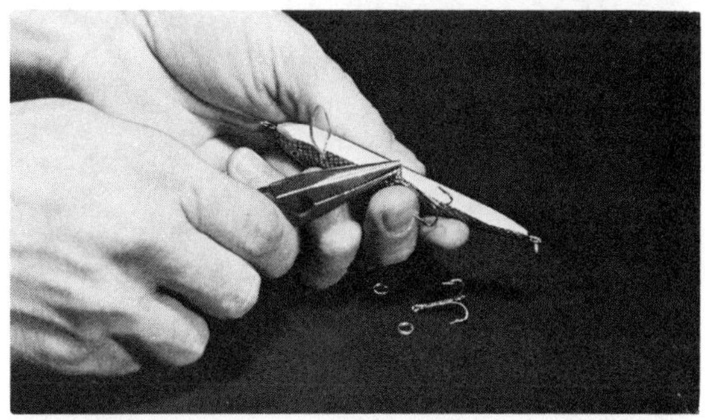

12. FASTEN HOOKS with split rings to wire insert. No. 3 or No. 4 split ring and No. 4 or No. 5 treble hooks seem to offer the best balance for this size lure.

to hold the hooks and a plastic lip to supply the swimming action. Materials available at most hobby shops are: balsawood (stock piece ½ by 3 by 36 inches), 22-gauge (or a substitute approximately this size) brass or copper wire, red oxide primer, spray paint (black, silver or gold), acrylic plastic sheet $^1/_{16}$ or $^3/_{32}$-inch, white waterproof plastic tape (type used to repair wading pools), split rings and treble hooks.

You'll need a sharp knife, hacksaw blade, soldering gun, fine sandpaper, and No. 400 wet or dry oxide paper.

Instructions are for a 4-inch minnow lure made from a balsa plug ½ by ⅝ by 4 inches. Alter dimensions *and* hook size for larger plugs.

After Step 7, the top of the lure can be resprayed with black enamel if gold or silver scaling overlaps too much. The plastic lip is made from acrylic plastic or scrap pieces salvaged from plastic lids. Action of the lure can be changed by bending the front end of the wire insert. Bend down to increase the wobble; up for less action. If the lure tends to turn over, bend wire in the opposite direction until it runs true.

Best results are obtained with a small snap swivel on a light line. Split shot or a small trolling sinker can be used 18 inches in front of the lure to increase depth. Good luck fishing!

A tree for magazines and newspapers

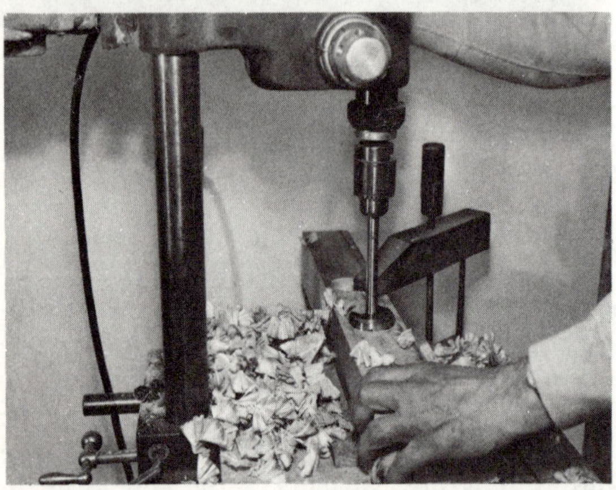

BYPASSING HOLES through the post are made with a 2-in. multi-spur bit chucked in the drill press.

SEE ALSO

Drill press techniques . . . Plexiglass projects . . . Wood lathes . . . Wood lathe techniques

■ HERE'S SOMETHING DIFFERENT in a newspaper and magazine holder. Standing 26½ in. high it will hold up to seven rolled magazines and papers.

The post is a piece 2⅞ in. sq. which is cross-bored on adjacent faces with a 2-in. power bit and fitted with a half-lapped "hall tree" base at the bottom and a lathe-turned finial at the top. If you don't have a lathe, you can forget the finial and simply point the end of the member like a fence post.

When boring the holes, clamp a scrap board to the underside of the work so you'll have clean-cut holes when the bit emerges. The boring should be done on a drill press. The cross base is fastened to the end of the post with 2-in. flathead wood screws and glue.

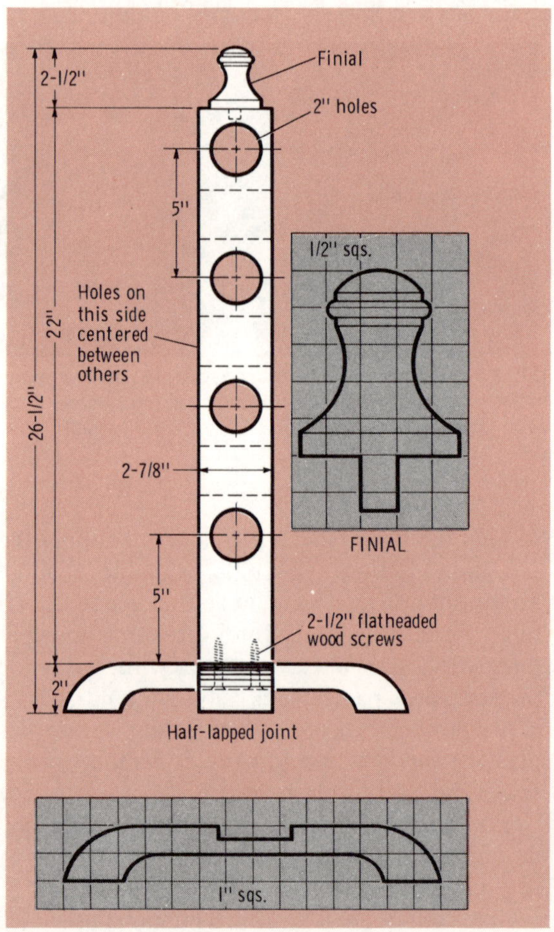

Magazine bucket

By DON SHINER

WITH TOP RIM removed and discarded, the keg is sawed on a line 7 in. up from the bottom to cut away the staves on each side. Two full staves remain.

A CIRCULAR SHELF, 11 in. in diameter, is next nailed between the two upright staves that are left after cutting the keg. This is placed 4 in. from top.

■ THERE'S HARDLY A THING that can't be put to new use once it's tossed out, and that goes for nail kegs. By retaining their rustic look and cutting away part of their sides, you can come up with real conversation pieces in the form of magazine buckets, knitting holders, smoking stands—you name it.

Chances are your hardware store will give you an empty. Remove the top band and select the two best staves opposite each other to support a circular shelf and a dowel handle. Draw a line 7 in. up from the bottom and saw off the other staves.

As a sewing basket, the keg can be fitted with a lift-out lid resting on three small blocks glued to the inside. A spool serves as a knob.

Finally, the keg is sanded a bit, inside and out, and given a painted, dry-brush treatment that leaves the wood bare in spots. Two coats of varnish complete it. This charming homespun item will be right at home with hooked rugs and spinning wheels.

PAINTED GREEN or tan with a dry brush so the wood shows through here and there, the keg takes on a worn antique look which adds to its rustic charm.

A DOWEL HANDLE is added last. Place it between the staves at the very top. A nail in each end holds it. Lift-out lid can be added to the bucket bottom.

SEE ALSO
Gifts, Christmas . . . Sewing cabinets . . . Sewing centers . . . Storage ideas

White stains on block walls

In 1952 my house foundation was treated with oil-base paint. Periodically (every five or six years), I've repainted it. Ten years ago I buffed it, filled in the more porous areas and holes with nonshrinking filler and repainted, using a latex paint. Shortly after this I noticed an area having alkali stains. This area wouldn't accept any paints. Whatever I put on lasted three months, then fell off.

The area, about 12 ft. long and near the top of the wall, gets weather only when it rains. No one else in the neighborhood has this problem. What can be the trouble? How can I correct it?—Burl Miner, Havre, Mont.

Your wall is suffering from a severe case of efflorescence—the effect of moisture on the water-soluble salts in the concrete and masonry. It usually shows up as white, but green or brown stains are not uncommon. This chemical reaction will not take place unless moisture is present. Stop it and you cure the problem.

My neighbor's basement suddenly developed efflorescence after 15 years. We tracked the cause to a moved splash block under his shrubs, allowing water from the downspout to run down and wet the foundation wall. The salt stains will brush off, but the source of moisture *must* be removed to keep them from reappearing.

To vent or not to vent

The guy who installed my 30-gallon gas-fired water heater said I didn't have to vent the gas to the exterior, and that if I put tin over my floor joists above to keep them from drying out, I'd have a much more energy-efficient burner, because I'd be warming my basement from the burned gases.—J.C., Fall River, Mass.

In this order, I:

1. Received your letter.
2. Tried calling you immediately, but information couldn't locate "J.C."
3. Hope that by the time you receive this you only have an enormous headache.
4. Can't believe you'd joke about anything so serious. By all means, get that heater vented *immediately*—your life may depend on it.

Walls come crumbling down

The stone walls of the basement where I teach ceramic classes are posing an annoying problem and potential danger. The mortar keeps falling from the joints. What can I do to retain it?—Lucille E. Rohler, Brookston, Ind.

Your solution lies in regrouting the stone walls. This involves scraping out some of the existing mortar and repointing with new mortar. The depth of scraping depends on the size of the stones, but the more mortar you can remove without causing the stone to loosen, the stronger the wall will be.

I suggest that you purchase the small-size bags of mortar mix. Although you'll be paying a premium price for sand, the convenience of carrying sand and cement downstairs in one bag is well worth the extra cost.

Thoroughly remix the dry mix in a wheelbarrow or mortar pan; then add water. Add only enough water to make the mix pliable. Too much water or water pressure while mixing will wash the cement coating off the tiny granules of sand and weaken their bond.

Brush a little water on the stones and joints with a whitewash brush. Then push the mortar into the joints with a small pointing trowel. Finish off by pressing with a length of dowel to give the joints a finished look. Wear heavy rubber gloves and goggles when you work with cement products.

Sweating basement walls

Sweat is forming on the inside surfaces of three basement walls in my brother's new home. There's even a puddle of water forming in the middle of the floor. The fourth wall is exposed entirely on the outside, with no landfill against it. This is a new house, and we would like to have a dry basement. The building inspector says this is common in homes built in this area, as the warm basement walls and cold earth cause sweating. What do you say?—Joseph Feneck, Brentwood, N.Y.

Without seeing the actual condition, it sounds more like moisture seeping through block and joints than sweating. The fact that one wall is exposed indicates that the home is on sloping ground. In this situation there's always the possibility that water is running downhill and hitting the foundation walls.

You might try regrading around the base to divert water away from the wall and adding splash blocks to your downspouts. If this doesn't help, adding a membrane water-proofing and drain tile is, perhaps, the one certain cure. As your brother's home is already built, it may be best to employ a reliable contractor with a small backhoe to do the digging.

I cannot stress enough the importance of this work to anyone contemplating building a new house. At that point, the cost is relatively low.

METRIC CONVERSION

Conversion factors can be carried so far they become impractical. In cases below where an entry is exact it is followed by an asterisk (*). Where considerable rounding off has taken place, the entry is followed by a + or a - sign.

CUSTOMARY TO METRIC

Linear Measure

inches	millimeters
1/16	1.5875*
1/8	3.2
3/16	4.8
1/4	6.35*
5/16	7.9
3/8	9.5
7/16	11.1
1/2	12.7*
9/16	14.3
5/8	15.9
11/16	17.5
3/4	19.05*
13/16	20.6
7/8	22.2
15/16	23.8
1	25.4*

inches	centimeters
1	2.54*
2	5.1
3	7.6
4	10.2
5	12.7*
6	15.2
7	17.8
8	20.3
9	22.9
10	25.4*
11	27.9
12	30.5

feet	centimeters	meters
1	30.48*	.3048*
2	61	.61
3	91	.91
4	122	1.22
5	152	1.52
6	183	1.83
7	213	2.13
8	244	2.44
9	274	2.74
10	305	3.05
50	1524*	15.24*
100	3048*	30.48*

1 yard =
.9144* meters
1 rod =
5.0292* meters
1 mile =
1.6 kilometers
1 nautical mile =
1.852* kilometers

Fluid Measure

(Milliliters [ml] and cubic centimeters [cc or cu cm] are equivalent, but it is customary to use milliliters for liquids.)

1 cu in = 16.39 ml
1 fl oz = 29.6 ml
1 cup = 237 ml
1 pint = 473 ml
1 quart = 946 ml
= .946 liters
1 gallon = 3785 ml
= 3.785 liters
Formula (exact):
fluid ounces × 29.573 529 562 5*
= milliliters

Weights

ounces	grams
1	28.3
2	56.7
3	85
4	113
5	142
6	170
7	198
8	227
9	255
10	283
11	312
12	340
13	369
14	397
15	425
16	454

Formula (exact):
ounces × 28.349 523 125* =
grams

pounds	kilograms
1	.45
2	.9
3	1.4
4	1.8
5	2.3
6	2.7
7	3.2
8	3.6
9	4.1
10	4.5

1 short ton (2000 lbs) =
907 kilograms (kg)
Formula (exact):
pounds × .453 592 37* =
kilograms

Volume

1 cu in = 16.39 cubic centimeters (cc)
1 cu ft = 28 316.7 cc
1 bushel = 35 239.1 cc
1 peck = 8 809.8 cc

Area

1 sq in = 6.45 sq cm
1 sq ft = 929 sq cm
= .093 sq meters
1 sq yd = .84 sq meters
1 acre = 4 046.9 sq meters
= .404 7 hectares
1 sq mile = 2 589 988 sq meters
= 259 hectares
= 2.589 9 sq kilometers

Kitchen Measure

1 teaspoon = 4.93 milliliters (ml)
1 Tablespoon = 14.79 milliliters (ml)

Miscellaneous

1 British thermal unit (Btu) (mean)
= 1 055.9 joules
1 calorie (mean) = 4.19 joules
1 horsepower = 745.7 watts
= .75 kilowatts
caliber (diameter of a firearm's bore in hundredths of an inch)
= .254 millimeters (mm)
1 atmosphere pressure = 101 325* pascals (newtons per sq meter)
1 pound per square inch (psi) = 6 895 pascals
1 pound per square foot = 47.9 pascals
1 knot = 1.85 kilometers per hour
25 miles per hour = 40.2 kilometers per hour
50 miles per hour = 80.5 kilometers per hour
75 miles per hour = 120.7 kilometers per hour